CAPITAL BUDGETING AND INVESTMENT ANALYSIS

CAPITAL BUDGETING AND INVESTMENT ANALYSIS

Alan C. Shapiro

PEARSON
Prentice
Hall

Upper Saddle River, New Jersey

Library of Congress Cataloging-in-Publication Data

Shapiro, Alan C.
  Capital budgeting and investment analysis / Alan C. Shapiro.—1st ed.
    p. cm.
  Includes index.
  ISBN 0-13-066090-6
  1. Capital budget. 2. Capital investments—Evaluation. 3.
Corporations—Growth. 4. Investment analysis. I. Title.

  HG4028.C4S48 2004
  658.15'4—dc22

                       2004021114

Executive Editor: David Alexander
Editor-in-Chief: Jeff Shelstad
Project Manager: Francesca Calogero
Executive Marketing Manager: Sharon Koch
Managing Editor: John Roberts
Permissions Supervisor: Charles Morris
Manufacturing Buyer: Michelle Klein
Cover Design: Bruce Kenselaar
Cover Illustration/Photo: Will Crocker / Image Bank / Getty Images, Inc.
Composition: Laserwords
Full-Service Project Management: nSight

Credits and acknowledgments borrowed from other sources and reproduced, with permission, in this textbook appear on appropriate page within text.

Pearson Education LTD.
Pearson Education Singapore, Pte. Ltd
Pearson Education, Canada, Ltd
Pearson Education–Japan

Pearson Education Australia PTY, Limited
Pearson Education North Asia Ltd
Pearson Educación de Mexico, S.A. de C.V.
Pearson Education Malaysia, Pte. Ltd

ISBN 0-13-066090-6

To my children
Tom and Kathryn
who have given me so much happiness

Brief Contents

Contents

Preface

Capital Budgeting and Investment Analysis is concerned with the most important problem facing management—finding or creating investment projects that are worth more than they cost. This function, also known as the *investment decision*, involves allocating funds over time in such a way that shareholder wealth is increased. Of the many decisions top management must make, none is likely to have more impact than the decision to invest capital, since this often involves large, extended commitments of money and management time.

The basic philosophy of this book is that deciding what assets to invest in has a far greater bearing on the value created by most companies than does the decision of how to sell claims against those assets (also known as the *financing decision*). Its purpose is to help develop in students the critical analytical skills required to assess potential investments.

Topics covered include the basics of capital budgeting, the estimation of project cash flows and the project cost of capital, risk analysis in capital budgeting, and corporate strategy and its relationship to the capital-budgeting decision. Throughout, the book emphasizes how management creates value for its shareholders.

TOPIC COVERAGE

This is a short book, containing only seven chapters and several appendices. As such, it is suitable for a mini-course in capital budgeting or for a course that covers capital budgeting as a key but not exclusive topic. These chapters and the topics they cover are as follows:

Chapter 1 examines the basics of capital budgeting, including the criteria by which projects must be evaluated, the capital-budgeting process, and the different types of investment projects that one is likely to encounter. As part of this chapter, we review the basic drivers of shareholder value—cash flow, time, and risk—and see how these drivers affect the basic criteria by which to evaluate capital-budgeting projects.

Chapter 2 presents and compares five alternative methods that companies can use to evaluate prospective investments. These methods include net present value, internal rate of return, profitability index, accounting rate of return, and payback period. It also surveys the capital-budgeting techniques most commonly used by leading U.S. companies. Appendix 2A examines two complex problems that sometimes arise in capital budgeting and shows how to deal with them. These include the existence of capital rationing and mutually exclusive projects with significantly different lives.

Chapter 3 discusses the estimation of project cash flows. It distinguishes between total and incremental cash flows, shows how to calculate the initial investment required, and deals with the estimation of operating cash flows. The chapter also discusses how to incorporate the terminal value and points out some potential sources of bias in the estimation of cash flows. Appendix 3A discusses the general rules for depreciating property, while the effects of inflation on project cash flows are examined in Appendix 3B. Appendix 3C shows how the basic principles of capital budgeting can be modified to deal with the unique aspects of foreign investments, such as differences between project and parent company cash flows, expropriation, blocked funds, and exchange rate changes.

Chapter 4 discusses the analysis of projects whose cash flows are contingent on how management responds to future, unknown events. The contingent nature of these cash flows arises because of the flexibility that companies often have in changing their decisions in response to new information and changing circumstances. This flexibility gives companies what has come to be termed real, or growth, options. Failure to account for the options available to managers to adjust the scope or scale of a project will lead to a downward bias in estimating project cash flows.

Chapter 5 presents and evaluates the techniques that firms use to incorporate risk in the capital-budgeting process. These techniques include adjusting the discount rate, adjusting project cash flows, and using certainty-equivalent cash flows. Other methods of risk analysis are presented as well, including sensitivity analysis, decision-tree analysis, and simulation analysis.

Chapter 6 introduces the issue of cost of capital, the determination of how much projects must yield to make it worthwhile to invest in them. It discusses the relationship between a project's riskiness and its cost of capital and shows how to calculate a firm's overall cost of capital as well as the divisional cost of capital. Appendix 6A discusses some international dimensions to cost of capital estimation.

Chapter 7 discusses corporate strategy and its relationship to the capital-budgeting decision, focusing on those factors that have contributed to success in the past. Topics covered include the concept of economic rents and what happens to opportunities for positive NPV projects in a competitive industry over time, the nature of market imperfections that give rise to economic rents and how one can design investments to exploit these imperfections, and the evolution of domestic firms into multinational corporations (MNCs). The latter topic incorporates a discussion of the rationale and means whereby MNCs transfer abroad their competitive strengths.

DISTINCTIVE FEATURES

Capital Budgeting and Investment Analysis shows how companies go about creating value by undertaking activities and purchasing or creating assets that are worth more than they cost. Some of the features that distinguish it from its competitors are as follows:

Practical Approach.   There is nothing quite so practical as a theory that works. I have tried to reinforce this belief by taking a common sense approach to finance. This involves showing students *why* the various theories discussed make sense and *how* to use these theories to solve problems. The book relates the subject matter to material that students are already familiar with or have learned in previous chapters, making it less intimidating and more interesting. Basic intuition is emphasized throughout.

Numerous Applications of Finance Principles.   In keeping with its down-to-earth approach, the book contains numerous real-world examples and vignettes that help illustrate the application of financial theories and demonstrate the use of financial analysis and reasoning to address various issues in capital budgeting. No other text has as many or as interesting examples of finance in practice. These examples promote understanding of basic investment principles and add interest to finance.

Appeal to Nonfinance Majors.   Since so many of the issues dealt with by nonfinancial executives have financial implications from determining advertising budgets and credit policies to investing in management training programs, it is clear that capital-budgeting theory has broad application to general management as well. Persuading readers who are not interested in pursuing a career in finance of this fact is a different matter. I have attempted to motivate these doubting Thomases by using numerous illustrations, scattered throughout the text, of the application of capital-budgeting principles to nonfinancial problems.

Emphasis on Value Creation.   The text emphasizes two related issues: how companies create value and how capital budgeting can facilitate the process of value creation. The focus is on how the financial manager can add value to the firm by smart investment decision making. Its guiding principle is that financial management is subordinate to the "real" business of the firm, which is to produce and sell goods and services. These latter activities all entail decisions regarding investment in real or intangible assets.

Coverage of International Topics.   On a more personal note, I believe that managers must view business from a global perspective; international is not just another section of the domestic economy, like office machines or autos, which can be ignored at no cost. Instead, an international orientation has become a business necessity, not a luxury. Those American television manufacturers determined to limit themselves to purely domestic operations learned this lesson the hard way; their greatest competitive threat came from companies located 8,000 miles away, across the Pacific, not from other American producers. To facilitate the development of a global perspective on capital budgeting, I have tried to integrate domestic and international financial topics–such as cost of capital, cash flow estimation when foreign currencies are involved, and corporate strategy and capital budgeting–throughout the book. To the extent I have succeeded, this is one of the distinctive features of the text.

Numerous Questions and Problems.   Another distinctive feature of *Capital Budgeting and Investment Analysis* is the large number of end-of-chapter questions and problems and their close relationship to the material in the chapters. Good conceptual questions are as important as computational problems in promoting understanding and the ones in the book are consistently challenging, interesting, and extremely useful. They provide practical insights into the types of decisions faced by financial executives and offer practice in applying financial concepts and theories.

Additional Features.   The book also includes a number of other distinguishing features that relate to the subject matter covered:

- It features a detailed discussion of estimating project cash flows, including incremental versus total cash flows, the effects of inflation on cash flows, and the valuation of growth options. It gives students hands-on experience in estimating project cash flows and helps them gain an appreciation for the real-world difficulties in valuing projects. (Chapters 3 and 4).
- It integrates international issues that arise in capital budgeting throughout the text, including estimating foreign project cash flows, determining the appropriate cost of capital for foreign projects, and designing a foreign expansion strategy. (Chapters 4, 6, and 7).

- It provides a discussion of risk that points out the many ways in which total risk can affect expected future cash flows, even if it does not affect the discount rate (Chapter 5).
- It features a separate chapter on corporate strategy that helps readers understand the origins and characteristics of positive net present value projects (Chapter 7).

AUDIENCE

Capital Budgeting and Investment Analysis is designed for use in masters-level courses and advanced undergraduate courses in capital budgeting and corporate financial management. It can also be used in bank management courses and executive development programs.

ACKNOWLEDGMENTS

I have been greatly aided in developing *Capital Budgeting and Investment Analysis* by the helpful suggestions of the following reviewers:

Omar Benkato, Ball State University
Gil Charney, Webster University
Shannon M. Donovan, Bridgewater State College
Arnell D. Johnson, University of Central Oklahoma
Aboubaker S. Meziani, Montclair State University
Thomas H. Thompson, University of Texas at Arlington

About the Author

Alan C. Shapiro is the Ivadelle and Theodore Johnson Professor of Banking and Finance and past chairman of the Department of Finance and Business Economics, Marshall School of Business, University of Southern California. Prior to joining USC in 1978, he was an Assistant Professor at the Wharton School of the University of Pennsylvania (1971–1978). He has also been a Visiting Professor at Yale University, UCLA, the Stockholm School of Economics, University of British Columbia, and the U.S. Naval Academy. Professor Shapiro received a B.A. in Mathematics from Rice University (1967) and a Ph.D. in Economics from Carnegie Mellon University (1971).

His specialties are corporate and international financial management. His bestselling textbook *Multinational Financial Management* (Seventh Edition, 2003) is in use in most of the leading MBA programs around the world. He has also written *Modern Corporate Finance* (1990), cited by the *Journal of Finance* as potentially the "standard reference volume in corporate finance," *Foundations of Multinational Financial Management* (Fifth Edition, 2004), *International Corporate Finance* (1989), and, with Sheldon Balbirer, *Modern Corporate Finance: An Interdisciplinary Approach to Value Creation* (Prentice Hall, 2000).

Dr. Shapiro is currently researching the links between corporate finance and corporate strategy. One outcome of this research is the article "Corporate Stakeholders and Corporate Finance," for which he and co-author Brad Cornell received the 1987 Distinguished Applied Research Award from the Financial Management Association and which is the most frequently cited article published in *Financial Management* since 1985.

Dr. Shapiro has consulted with the FBI, the Federal Home Loan Bank, RTC, the American Law Institute, the Department of Justice, SEC, the Department of Energy, the Internal Revenue Service, FDIC, and numerous firms and banks, including Dow Chemical, Abbott Laboratories, Aetna, Anheuser-Busch, IBM, Caltex, Texas Instruments, Arco Chemical, NCR, GTE, SBC Communications, Scott Paper, Time Warner, Pacific Enterprises, Northrop Grumman, OKC, Computer Sciences Corporation, General Foods, Vulcan Materials, Flying Tiger Line, Wells Fargo, Pepsico, North Broken Hill, BankAmerica, and Citicorp. He frequently serves as an expert witness in cases involving valuation, economic damages, S&Ls, international finance, takeovers, and transfer pricing. In addition, he is a director of Remington Oil and Gas Corp., a government-appointed director of Lincoln S&L, and a past director of OKC Corp.

He has won several teaching awards and has taught in numerous executive education programs, including programs sponsored by Yale University, the Wharton School of Business, University of Southern California, UCLA, UC Berkeley, Columbia

University, University of Hawaii, University of Washington, University of Melbourne, Stockholm School of Economics, and the American Management Association. Dr. Shapiro also conducts numerous in-house training and executive programs for banks, corporations, government agencies, consulting firms, and law firms in the areas of corporate finance and international finance and economics. He has lectured on problems of international finance and economics in Munich, Tokyo, Frankfurt, Seoul, Hong Kong, Singapore, Guangzhou, Shanghai, London, Oxford, Sydney, Melbourne, Mexico City, Monterey, Santiago, Rome, Budapest, Vienna, Buenos Aires, and Paris. In October 1993, *Business Week* recognized him as one of the ten most in-demand business school professors in the United States for teaching in in-house corporate executive education programs.

Dr. Shapiro has published more than 50 articles in such leading academic and professional journals as the *Journal of Finance, Harvard Business Review, Columbia Journal of World Business, Journal of Financial and Quantitative Analysis, Review of Financial Studies, Journal of Business, Journal of International Money and Finance, Financial Management, Management Science,* and *Journal of Applied Corporate Finance.* In 1988, he was cited as one of the "100 Most Prolific Authors in Finance." Another study published in 1991 ranked him as one of the most prolific contributors to international business literature. He has also published two monographs, *International Corporate Finance: Survey and Synthesis* and *Foreign Exchange Risk Management.*

CAPITAL BUDGETING AND INVESTMENT ANALYSIS

Introduction to Capital Budgeting

> *There is a tide in the affairs of men*
> *Which, taken at the flood, leads on to fortune:*
> *Omitted, all the voyage of their life*
> *Is bound in shallows and in miseries.*
>
> — SHAKESPEARE,
> *Julius Caesar*

This book deals with what is perhaps the most important topic in corporate finance: the analysis of capital expenditures—investments expected to generate cash flows beyond the first year. Of the many decisions that top management must make, none is likely to have more impact than the decision to invest capital, since this often involves large, extended commitments of money and management time. The *Survey of Current Business*, published by the U.S. Department of Commerce, underscores this point by revealing that in 2002, the total capital expenditures of all firms in the United States exceeded $1.1 trillion. Intel alone spent $7.5 billion in 2001 on new manufacturing facilities. More important, the sum of these decisions determines a firm's future course and hence its market value. For example, the choice for an electric utility between going nuclear or remaining with coal is of utmost importance to both its owners and its customers. Similarly, General Electric's decision back in 1970—to exit the mainframe computer business rather than make the massive investments necessary to remain competitive with IBM—and Honeywell's decision to buy, and then sell, that business have had enormous implications for these firms and their shareholders over the past three decades. More recently, AT&T's decision to invest $120 billion in the cable TV business in the late 1990s and then sell off that business for $52 billion in 2001 has dramatically affected the company and its shareholders.

Simply put, the **capital-budgeting decision**, which is the allocation of funds among alternative investment opportunities, is crucial to corporate success. It is not surprising, therefore, that firms devote so much effort to planning capital expenditures. It should also be evident that the nature and consequences of the capital-budgeting process mandate that top-level executives in marketing and production, as well as in other vital areas, participate; investment decisions are too important to be left to financial executives alone.

This recommendation is in line with current corporate thinking. Well-managed companies insist that investment projects flow from a sound strategic business plan that explicitly considers the competition and charts a course to build and maintain competitive advantage. For example, General Motors' decision to hook up with Toyota to build small cars in California reflects GM's thinking about its ability to compete with Japanese auto companies in this segment of the car market as well as the likely behavior of its other competitors. Ford, whose small, sporty entry—the Mustang—had been floundering in the face of competition from domestic and foreign auto makers, responded with a plan to invest $500 million to build a small car in Mexico designed by Japan's Toyo Kogyo Co. (producer of the Mazda), mainly for sale in the United States. We will study the link between corporate strategy and capital budgeting in Chapter 7. This chapter and the next one are primarily concerned with determining the appropriate level and allocation over time of capital resources and how one goes about achieving this objective.

In this chapter, we shall examine some basics of capital budgeting. Section 1.1 presents the criteria by which projects must be evaluated. These criteria lay the foundation for the capital-budgeting techniques presented in Chapter 2. Section 1.2 discusses the capital-budgeting process and Section 1.3 classifies the different types of investment projects that one is likely to encounter.

1.1 The Capital-Budgeting Decision

As mentioned above, a **capital expenditure** is any cash outlay expected to generate cash flows lasting longer than a year. This definition brings within the scope of the capital-budgeting framework, many decisions that bear little resemblance to the massive projects typically associated with this process. One such decision is PepsiCo's gamble in 1991 of over $120 million on a new ad campaign that featured Ray Charles and the Raylettes promoting its "You got the right one, baby" campaign ("Uh-huh"). This decision reflects the use of advertising—on which U.S. companies spent over $230 billion in 2000—to build brand names, a critical intangible asset in many businesses. Another such decision is Motorola's expenditure of $120 million annually to upgrade the skills of its workforce. Some other nontraditional capital-budgeting decisions include refunding debt, launching a price war, determining the level and direction of research and development activities (which accounted for almost $200 billion in spending by corporate America in 2001 alone), enrolling managers in executive education programs, establishing an in-house drug or alcohol abuse control program, acquiring a new firm or liquidating an existing company, and deciding whether to lease or buy a new piece of equipment.

In recent years, managers have become more sophisticated in allocating capital resources and more concerned about return on investment. In large part, this is a response to a combination of high capital costs and the poor returns many companies have been earning on their assets. In part, too, it reflects the availability of more analytical tools to perform these analyses and an increased supply of technically qualified managers capable of applying them.

THE OBJECTIVE OF CAPITAL BUDGETING

The ultimate aim of capital budgeting is to maximize the market value of the company's common stock and, thereby, the wealth of its shareholders. The rationale for focusing on shareholder value begins with the simple economic notion that people try to maximize their well-being. Part of this well-being stems from the consumption of goods and services. All else being equal, this means that people generally prefer more wealth to less, where wealth represents the ability to consume. One way that people acquire more wealth is to defer consumption and invest the freed-up money in a company. Those who are relatively risk averse become bondholders, lending money to the company in return for a promised interest rate and repayment of the loan at an agreed-upon future date. Those who are willing to bear more risk will become shareholders, providing equity capital to the company in return for partial ownership of it. As partial owners of the firm, stockholders receive a proportional share of the firm's profits and losses. However, stockholders have only a *residual* interest in the company's earnings; bondholders and other creditors must be paid off before stockholders can claim any of the firm's earnings.

The Importance of Shareholder Value

The relevance of the foregoing discussion to financial management is that the shareholders are the legal owners of the firm and management has a fiduciary obligation to act in the shareholders' best interests. Other stakeholders in the company do have rights, but these are not coequal with the rights of shareholders. Shareholders provide the risk capital that acts as a shock absorber to cushion the claims of other stakeholders. The value of the firm could drop by as much as the value of equity capital and the company would still have enough assets to honor the claims of bondholders and noninvestor stakeholders. Allowing alternative stakeholders coequal control over capital supplied by others is equivalent to allowing one group to risk someone else's capital. This would undoubtedly impair future equity formation and produce numerous other inefficiencies. Without shareholders and their equity capital, for example, companies would be all-debt financed and would continually face the prospect of financial distress or bankruptcy.

A more compelling reason for focusing on creating shareholder wealth is that those companies that do not are likely to wind up with a **value gap**—the difference between the value of the company if it were optimally managed and the actual value of the company. Companies with large value gaps are prime takeover targets and candidates for a forced corporate restructuring. Conversely, maximizing shareholder value provides the best defense against a hostile takeover: a high stock price. In 1984, for example, Walt Disney Co. was a takeover target when its stock price was at $55. By 1998, when new management had lifted its stock to over $1,600 (adjusting for stock splits), Walt Disney was no longer a target. No one could afford to pay a higher price for Disney and still expect to earn a competitive return.

Boards of directors are also becoming more active in looking out for shareholders' interests and are demanding that chief executive officers (CEOs) do the same and be held more accountable for their companies' performance. Over the past decade, activist boards of companies with large value gaps forced out the heads of IBM, General Motors, Apple, Digital Equipment, Goodyear, Borden, Allied-Signal, American Express, Westinghouse, Compaq, Kodak, and Tenneco, and forced major restructurings at all these firms as well as at Sears.

At the same time, historical evidence tells us that the longer that restructuring to close a value gap is delayed, the greater the cost, the trauma, and extent of the restructuring that must ultimately occur (e.g., the more employees that must eventually be let go), and the less the certainty of success (e.g., IBM).

Simply put, this is not a zero-sum game—where gains to shareholders come at the expense of other stakeholders; there is no inherent economic conflict between the two. Indeed, maximizing shareholder value is not merely the best way, it is the *only* way to maximize the economic interests of *all* stakeholders over time. For example, companies with the best record of value creation—Coca-Cola, Southwest Airlines, Disney, GE, and Wal-Mart—are also among the best at human resource management and taking care of their customers.

Companies that build shareholder value also find it easier to attract equity capital. Equity capital is especially critical for companies that operate in a riskier environment and for companies that are seeking to grow. Both these characteristics describe most companies today.

The import of this discussion is that the primary objective of financial management is to maximize the shareholders' well-being. Because shareholders have invested their money in the expectation of being made better off financially, this objective translates into maximizing shareholder wealth. Maximizing shareholder wealth, in turn, is tantamount to maximizing the firm's share price.

Although it is recognized that an institution as complex as the modern corporation does not have a single, unambiguous will, the principle of shareholder wealth maximization provides a rational guide to financial decision making.

Basic Drivers of Shareholder Value

In order to benefit shareholders, we need to know what affects stock prices. Here, we can call on an enormous body of research. According to this research, shareholder value depends on cash flow, time, and risk. The more cash that shareholders receive and the sooner they expect to receive that cash, the better off they are. Alternatively, the riskier the expected future cash flows, the less value shareholders place on them.

In most economies of the world, including our own, people consume by spending money to buy goods and services. The more money one has, the more one can consume. Firms benefit their shareholders, therefore, by providing them with cash, either by paying current dividends or by reinvesting the money to pay future dividends. This statement, simple as it sounds, has a profound and controversial implication: Accounting profits not associated with cash flows are of no value to investors. It means, for example, that switching depreciation methods for reporting—but not tax—purposes—so as to boost reported profits does not benefit shareholders because it does not affect cash flow.

By forcing managers to evaluate business strategies on the basis of prospective cash flows, the shareholder value approach favors strategies that enhance a company's cash flow generating ability—which is good for everyone, not just shareholders. It is well for politicians and other commentators to reflect on the fact that you have to first create wealth before you can distribute it; that is, shareholders are not the only beneficiaries of corporate success. Companies with lots of cash have more money to distribute to all of their stakeholders, not just shareholders. They also create more opportunities for employee advancement.

The other two dimensions to shareholder value are time and risk. Investors discount cash to be received in the future, reducing its value today. The interest rate at which this discounting of future cash flows takes place is always positive; that is, the rate of interest that people expect to receive on their investments is always positive. There are two basic reasons for this expectation. First, people generally prefer present consumption over consumption in the future. This *positive time preference* means that people value the current use of resources (goods) more highly than they do their future use. Those who have strong preferences for immediate consumption will borrow from those who are less impatient and willing to delay satisfying their wants. Because the second group also has positive time preference, the first group must pay it a positive rate of interest to gain its acquiescence in the transaction.

Even without positive time preference, however, we would still see a positive real rate, because resources can be used productively over time. Some goods, like trees and cattle, physically grow over time, whereas other goods, like wine and cheese, may improve in quality with age. Most important, resources can be converted into capital goods — goods like machinery and trucks — that produce more goods and services. Because in our world more is preferred to less, the present use of resources must have a positive price; competition among potential users will ensure that this is so.

The existence of a positive rate of interest results in what is known as the **time value of money**, the notion that a dollar today is worth more than a dollar in the future. The difference in the values of current and future dollars is determined by the rate of interest. Thus, if the interest rate is 10% per annum, the **present value**, or value in terms of today's dollars, of one dollar a year from now is $0.91. This is because $0.91 invested today at 10% will be worth $0.91 × 1.10 = $1 one year from now. Alternatively, the **future value** of one dollar today is $1.10 a year from now.

The interest rate at which future cash flows are discounted increases with risk. In other words, investors demand to be compensated for the risks they expect to bear. Compensation is required because investors are generally risk averse; that is, all other things being equal, investors prefer less risk to more risk. Of course, all other things are usually not equal, and so managers and investors must constantly select among choices entailing different amounts of risk and promised returns. To ensure comparability among the various alternatives, it is necessary to convert the uncertain future cash flows associated with each of the alternatives into their present values. This requires discounting the future cash flows for both the time value of money and the degree of risk involved.

CAPITAL-BUDGETING PRINCIPLES AND CRITERIA

The objective of maximizing shareholder wealth translates into the following capital-budgeting principles:

- Select the same projects investors would select if they had the same information.
- Take all projects that would increase shareholder wealth.
- Reject all projects that would decrease shareholder wealth.

From our discussion up to now, we know that for an investment analysis to be consistent with the goal of shareholder wealth maximization, it must meet the following three criteria:

1. It should place higher weight on earlier cash flows than on more distant cash flows. It should not weight cash flows arising in different time periods the same.
2. It should value all cash inflows and outflows associated with the project. It should ignore those elements of reported earnings that do not reflect cash flows and factor in any cash inflows and outflows that do not show up in reported earnings.
3. It should penalize more heavily the expected cash flows of riskier projects. Other things being equal, it should rank riskier projects as being less desirable.

As we will see in the next chapter, these evaluation criteria are satisfied by the net present value decision rule. Now, however, we review the capital-budgeting process and the classification of investment projects.

1.2 The Capital-Budgeting Process

Unlike stock and bond investments, the investment proposals that enter the corporate capital-budgeting process are not just sitting around waiting to be selected. *People must think them up.* Sometimes a project arises naturally, as when a machine tool wears out and must be replaced or a new and more efficient production process appears on the market and must be evaluated against the existing way of doing things. Other investment opportunities appear out of the blue. A salesperson may propose the development of a more efficient blood analysis unit using microelectro-mechanical systems (MEMS) technology based on lab technicians' complaints that existing units are too slow and error prone, or an engineer in research and development may design a novel combination cellphone/handheld computer.

All four situations require a capital-budgeting decision. As a general rule, and certainly for each project outlined here, a company will want to gather additional information before making its decision. In the case of the worn-out machine tool, the company must first decide whether demand is sufficient to justify replacement. Assuming that replacement is justified, the firm must then consider the alternative machine tools available as well as their relative costs and productivity. Similarly, the up-front cost of the new production process must be evaluated in terms of its savings in operating costs relative to those of the current process.

With regard to the latter two projects—the development of a more efficient blood analysis unit and the introduction of a new cellphone/handheld computer—the firm must decide whether the products involved are commercially viable. Commercial viability of new products is a function of development, production, and distribution costs, as well as the likely size of the market. Market size, in turn, depends on the final sales price: The lower the price is, the larger the sales volume will be. In the case of the enhanced blood analysis unit, the R&D people must first decide whether such a product is technically feasible. If it is, marketing research must then estimate the unit's future sales. The judgment of market size will depend in part on the expected costs of manufacturing and distributing such a unit. This requires consultation with people in engineering and production as well as in transportation and marketing.

The new cellphone/computer must undergo a similar analysis, except that technical feasibility is already established. However, it is rare that a product emerges from the lab ready to be marketed as is. Usually, marketing research will suggest that the addition of several other features, provided they are not too costly, such as a larger color screen can expand the product's market share. Ascertaining the cost of providing these features will require further research and development work and more discussions with engineering and production.

Most firms have a formal process for creating and evaluating capital projects. This usually includes preparing short-run capital budgets on the basis of anticipated equipment replacement and expansion requirements for the next year or so. Many firms now develop five-year and ten-year capital budgets as well on the basis of longer-range sales forecasts and the plant and equipment necessary to meet the resulting demand.

Most capital budgets are driven by sales forecasts. The budgeting process typically begins with forecasts of future sales by the company economist and the sales department, using data on macroeconomic trends (e.g., the level of interest rates, domestic and foreign GNP growth rates, money supply changes, the value of the dollar) and specific market developments (e.g., competitor actions, customer requirements, government regulations). These sales forecasts are then converted into production forecasts and reviewed with the production department, which estimates the necessary additions to plant and equipment to meet the planned output. There may be several alternative methods for achieving the production targets, and they must be compared and evaluated. The resulting investment proposals will be sent upstairs where top management will review them, taking into account the cost of obtaining capital to fund these projects, and will determine the level and allocation of capital expenditures.

Although many investment opportunities that arise cannot be predicted, most well-run firms systematically gather the marketing and technical information that forms the basis for these potential projects. This requires major investments in the production and assessment of information, usually in the form of an active R&D program and a well-funded market research effort.

Because the economic environment is so unpredictable, capital budgets cannot remain static. As the sales forecasts, cost estimates, and technical assumptions on which they are premised change, investment plans must also change. The appropriate response to changed economic circumstances is not always readily apparent, but well-managed companies constantly scan the environment to pick up clues as to how to modify their capital budgets. For example, the huge increase in energy costs following the quadrupling of oil prices in late 1973 and the tripling of oil prices in 1979 made economical a number of energy conservation projects and oil- and gas-drilling programs that were previously unprofitable. On the other hand, the subsequent drop in energy prices in 1981 and beyond led oil companies such as Exxon and Occidental Petroleum to cancel their synthetic fuel extraction projects and to cut back on drilling activities.

Exhibit 1.1 illustrates how shifting oil prices change the economics—for better and for worse—of oil well investments. In general, drilling activity (as measured by the oil rig count—the number of drilling rigs in operation) rises and falls with oil prices. The steep decline in energy prices in late 1985 had particularly adverse effects on oil well drilling. This, in turn, led to the bankruptcy of numerous drilling companies and their clients. The oil rig count picked up in 2000 with the jump in oil prices.

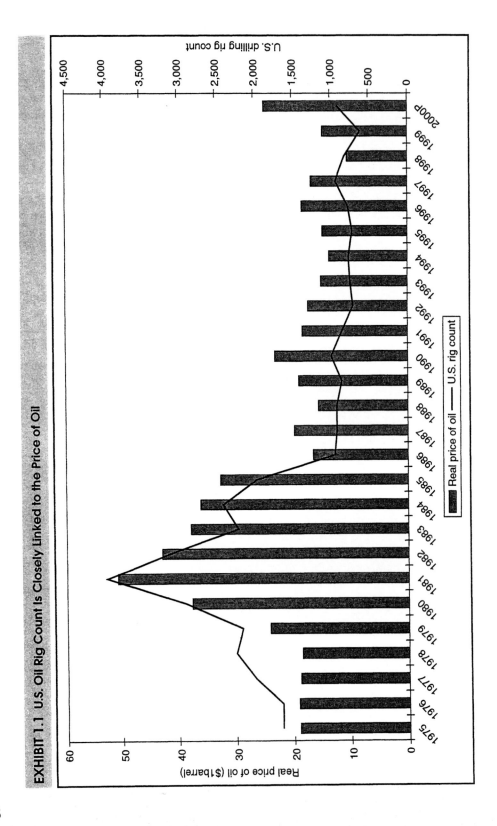

EXHIBIT 1.1 U.S. Oil Rig Count Is Closely Linked to the Price of Oil

Similarly, rising labor costs—like a new union contract that boosts wages—will lead companies to begin searching for lower-cost production alternatives. Possibilities that might be considered range from purchasing labor-substituting equipment to shutting down some operations and contracting out work to nonunion plants to building a plant overseas in a country such as Mexico or China, where labor costs are lower.

Many firms have a policy of decentralizing decisions when possible, and capital budgeting is no exception. Division managers are usually able to short-circuit the centralized process described above and initiate their own projects when the proposed investment is below a minimum sum, say, $50,000 or less. Projects requiring more than that amount must go through the full review process. In this way, scarce management time is allocated to those decisions likely to be the most consequential for the firm.

1.3 Classifying Capital-Budgeting Projects

Carefully evaluating investment proposals is often costly, as it requires substantial amounts of money and time for information gathering and assessment. For some projects, experience has shown that a detailed evaluation is not warranted considering the costs involved; for others, a thorough analysis makes sense.

INVESTMENT CATEGORIES

The following four investment categories, several of which were introduced informally in Section 1.2, have proved to be of value in classifying projects according to the thoroughness of the analysis required.

Equipment Replacement

Over time, plant and equipment become obsolete and must be replaced. Obsolescence could be due to the higher cost of maintaining older equipment, new technological developments that result in more efficient equipment, or a shift in factor input costs that changes the benefit–cost equation for existing equipment. An example of the latter situation is the increase in energy costs that led many airlines to replace the older gas-guzzling engines on their jet fleets with more energy-efficient ones. Similarly, a labor cost increase has often provided the impetus for replacing a labor-intensive production process with a more capital-intensive process.

Expansion to Meet Growth in Existing Products

This includes expenditures to meet projected increases in demand for a firm's existing products. Demand increases can be due to either growth in existing markets or a decision to expand sales into new domestic and foreign markets. Firms in the extractive industries (e.g., oil, coal, copper, aluminum) must constantly invest in the exploration and development of new sources of raw materials as existing wells and mines are depleted.

Expansion Generated by New Products

Companies such as Sony (Japan), Philips (Netherlands), and 3M (United States), not coincidentally all of which are multinational corporations (for reasons discussed in Chapter 7), thrive by continually introducing new products and phasing out older products facing strong competition. This requires large expenditures on market research, R&D, and advertising and promotion. It may also lead to investments in new facilities in locations around the world.

Projects Mandated by Law

This category would include investments in pollution control equipment to comply with various emission standards, investments required to comply with safety standards, and any other non-revenue-producing expenditures. These investments are usually contingent on another investment's being made. For example, if Pacific Gas & Electric puts up another coal-fired generator, it will have to install special scrubbers to remove particles from the effluent smoke. The decision whether to build the new plant must be based on the total cost of the plant, including the scrubbers as well as the generating equipment.

Sometimes, however, environmental regulations are retroactive. For example, U.S. Steel may be required to install pollution control devices on an existing steel mill. In such a case, U.S. Steel would have to weigh the cost of complying with the regulation against the cost of shutting down the facility.

Investments in these four categories differ in the amounts of information available and the risks involved. The trade-off is between a more comprehensive analysis and higher evaluation costs. Routine replacement decisions and mandated investments in profitable plants are typically made without much supporting documentation. As risk increases—from cost reduction projects to expansion in existing product lines to projects involving new products—the analysis becomes more detailed, and the amount of information collected increases. Similarly, within each investment category, the larger is the dollar amount involved, the more scrutiny of the investment there will be. For example, a $100 million sewage treatment plant will be examined more carefully than will an investment of $5,000 in safety railings.

PROJECT INTERACTIONS

Pairs of projects fall into one of three categories; they can be independent, mutually exclusive, or contingent. The specific category determines how the projects must be evaluated.

Independent Projects

Independent projects are projects whose acceptance or rejection are independent of one another. For example, a firm may want to purchase new cars for its salespeople at the same time that it is considering putting up a new headquarters building. The firm could accept one, both, or none of these projects because they bear no relation to one another.

Mutually Exclusive Projects

If projects are mutually exclusive, the acceptance of one will preclude the selection of any alternative projects. For example, several years ago, United Airlines was faced with the choice of buying Boeing 747s, Lockheed L-1011s, or McDonnell Douglas DC-10s. It decided to buy the DC-10s, foreclosing the possibility of buying the 747s or L-1011s. Mutually exclusive investment opportunities often appear in other forms as well. For instance, when expanding overseas, a firm may have several mutually exclusive business alternatives, including exporting from domestic plants, licensing a foreign manufacturer, or building foreign production facilities.

Contingent Projects

As we saw previously, Pacific Gas & Electric's investment in scrubbers to control pollution was contingent on building a new coal-fired generator: no new generator, no scrubber. In general, a contingent project is one whose acceptance depends on the adoption of another project. When several projects are mutually dependent—that is, you cannot take one without the others (e.g., a new plant and a new parking lot for the new employees)—they should be lumped together and treated as one project.

Often, contingent investments are more subtle. Here is an example of a contingent investment decision that is linked to the overall corporate strategy.

BOX 1.1

APPLICATION: INVESTING IN MEMORY CHIP PRODUCTION

Since 1984, most U.S. semiconductor manufacturers have been losing money in the memory chip business. The only profitable part of the chip business for them is in making microprocessors and other specialized chips. Why do they continue investing in facilities to produce memory chips despite their losses in this business?

U.S. companies care so much about memory chips because many see them as the key to the entire semiconductor industry. Memory chips are manufactured in huge quantities and are fairly simple to test for defects, which make them ideal vehicles for refining new production processes. Having worked out the bugs by making memories, chip companies apply an improved process to hundreds of more complex products. Until recently, without manufacturing some sort of memory chip, it was very difficult to keep production technology competitive. Thus, making profitable investments elsewhere in the chip business was contingent on producing memory chips. As manufacturing technology has changed, diminishing the importance of memory chips as process technology drivers, U.S. chipmakers such as Intel have stopped producing DRAMs.

1.4 Summary and Conclusions

This chapter introduced the topic of capital budgeting. We saw that the ultimate aim of capital budgeting is to maximize the market value of the company's common stock and, thereby, the wealth of its shareholders. This goal translates into evaluating projects on the basis of their cash flows. To account for the effects of time and risk, future project cash flows must be discounted, with more distant and riskier cash flows being discounted more heavily than nearer and more secure cash flows.

Four investment categories have proved to be of value in classifying projects according to the thoroughness of the analysis required. These categories include equipment replacement, expansion to meet growth in existing products, expansion generated by new products, and projects mandated by law. As risk increases—from cost reduction projects to expansion in existing product lines to projects involving new products—the analysis becomes more detailed, and the amount of information collected increases. Similarly, within each investment category, the larger is the dollar amount involved, the more scrutiny of the investment there will be. We also saw that pairs of projects can be categorized as independent, mutually exclusive, or contingent.

Capital-Budgeting Principles and Techniques

I dipt into the future far as human eye could see,
Saw the vision of the world and all the wonder that would be.
—TENNYSON,
Locksley Hall

Once a firm has compiled a list of prospective investments, it must then select from among them that combination of projects that maximizes the company's value to its shareholders. This requires that the company be able to place a value on each project — the same value that shareholders themselves would estimate if they had the same information that is available to corporate management. To achieve this objective, we must translate the basic principles of capital budgeting into evaluation techniques capable of applying these principles.

Sections 2.1 and 2.2 present and compare the alternative methods that companies can use to evaluate prospective investments. These methods include net present value (NPV), internal rate of return (IRR), profitability index (PI), accounting rate of return, and payback period. Section 2.3 surveys the capital-budgeting techniques most commonly used by leading U.S. companies. Appendix 2A examines two complex problems that sometimes arise in capital budgeting and shows how to deal with them.

2.1 Net Present Value

As we saw in Chapter 1, to be consistent with the goal of shareholder wealth maximization, the value placed on a prospective investment project must satisfy three criteria:

- It must focus on cash and only cash.
- It must account for the time value of money.
- It must account for risk.

The only value that is consistent with these criteria is the project's **net present value**—the present value of the project's future cash flows minus the cost of the project.

NET PRESENT VALUE DECISION RULE

Investments with positive NPVs add to shareholder wealth; those with negative NPVs reduce shareholder wealth. Companies, therefore, should invest in positive NPV projects and reject negative NPV projects. This is the net present value investment decision rule.

The NPV rule is implemented as follows: *Calculate the present value of the expected net cash flows generated by the investment, using an appropriate discount rate, and subtract from this present value the initial net cash outlay for the project. If the resulting NPV is positive, accept the project; if it is negative, reject it. If two projects are mutually exclusive, accept the one with the higher net present value.*

In other words, if an investment is worth more than it costs, accept it; if it costs more than it is worth, reject it. By taking into account all cash flows, only cash flows, and the time value of money, NPV evaluates projects in the same way that investors do. Therefore, it is consistent with the objective of shareholder wealth maximization.

The discount rate used in calculating an investment's NPV, also called the **cost of capital** or the required return, is the minimum acceptable rate of return on projects of similar risk. It is determined by the required return in the market for investments of comparable risk. As a corollary, investments undertaken by the same company that have different risks will have different required returns. For now, we take the cost of capital as given. In Chapter 6, we shall study its derivation in detail.

In mathematical terms, the formula for NPV is expressed in Equation 2.1:

$$\text{Net present value} = -\text{Initial cash investment} + \text{Present value of future cash flows}$$

$$NPV = -I_0 + \frac{CF_1}{1+k} + \frac{CF_2}{(1+k)^2} + \cdots + \frac{CF_n}{(1+k)^n} \qquad (2.1)$$

$$= -I_0 + \sum_{t=1}^{n} \frac{CF_t}{(1+k)^t}$$

where I_0 is the initial cash investment, CF_t is the net cash flow in period t, k is the cost of capital for the project, and n is the economic life of the investment.

The initial investment includes any working capital requirements. **Working capital** refers to the money the firm must invest in accounts receivable, inventory, and cash to support the sales and production of its products or services.

Net cash flow is usually calculated as profit after tax plus depreciation and other noncash charges such as deferred income taxes less any additions to working capital during the period. This measure includes all project cash inflows and outflows and ignores noncash items. Depreciation is added back to income because it is a noncash charge. A **noncash charge** is one that shows up as a cost of doing business but that entails no cash outlay. For example, the depreciation charge is supposed to reflect the diminished economic value of the plant and equipment. However, the company does not incur a cash cost associated with this charge. Additions to working capital are subtracted from earnings because they consume cash, even though they do not affect reported earnings. For example, whether a company is paid today or paid next year for a sale of merchandise today, its reported earnings will be the same. In both cases, they will rise upon completion of a profitable sale. The timing of the cash flow from the sale will differ, however, depending on the payment terms. With payment in one year, the company will receive no cash this year. In the next year, when the account receivable is paid off, the company's cash flow will rise but earnings will be unaffected. Because it is cash, and only cash, that matters to shareholders, we shall focus exclusively on an investment's cash flows.

The next chapter shows in more detail how to go about estimating the cash flows associated with a project. Here is an illustration, however, of how one might proceed.

BOX 2.1

APPLICATION: SPECTRA'S DYE PLANT

Suppose Spectra Inc., a profitable firm, is considering an investment of $6 million in plant and equipment to produce dye under a five-year contract for sale at $10 per pound. The terms of the contract call for the delivery of 800,000 pounds of dye in the first year and 1,600,000 pounds per year in each of the next four years. At the end of year 5, the plant is expected to be scrapped and sold for its book value of $1 million.

The investment is expected to have the following characteristics:

Variable cost	$6.50 per pound
Fixed cost, excluding depreciation	$1,700,000 per year
Depreciation	$1,000,000 per year
Tax rate	40%
Working capital requirement	$1,200,000 (freed at the end of year 5)

Including working capital, the initial investment for this project is $7.2 million. Spectra's projected annual net income and net cash flows are shown in the following table:

	Year 1	Years 2, 3, 4, and 5
Revenue	$10 × 800,000 = $8,000,000	$10 × 1,600,000 = $16,000,000
Variable cost	$6.50 × 800,000 = $5,200,000	$6.50 × 1,600,000 = $10,400,000
Fixed cost	1,700,000	1,700,000
Depreciation	1,000,000	1,000,000
Income before tax	$100,000	$2,900,000
Tax (@ 40%)	40,000	1,160,000
Net income	$60,000	$1,740,000
Depreciation	1,000,000	1,000,000
Net cash flow	$1,060,000	$2,740,000
Recovery of working capital		1,200,000
Proceeds of plant sale		1,000,000
Year 5 only		$4,940,000

If the required return on Spectra's investment is 10%, we can calculate the present value of the investment's year-by-year cash flows. The $4.94 million cash flow in year 5 equals the $2.74 million net cash flow for the year plus the recovery of $1.2 million in working capital plus the proceeds of $1 million from the plant sale. Because the plant was sold for its book value, there was no gain or loss and hence the sale entailed no tax consequences.

According to these calculations, which appear in Exhibit 2.1 on page 18, the present value of the cash flows from Spectra's investment in the dye plant is $10,225,510. Subtracting off the initial $7.2 million investment yields a *net* present value for the project of $3,025,510. If 10% is the correct discount rate, the project should be undertaken.

CONTINGENT PROJECTS

When one project is contingent on undertaking another project, they should be treated as one. We saw this in Chapter 1 in the case of Pacific Gas & Electric's investment in scrubbers, which was contingent on purchasing a coal-fired generator. Here is another example and the manner in which the NPV rule deals with it.

BOX 2.2

APPLICATION: PUFFIN STEEL'S IRON ORE PROJECT

In a previously unexplored region in the remote Northwest Territories of Canada, Puffin Steel, Ltd., has discovered reserves of iron ore. It will cost $90 million to purchase and transport mining equipment to the site. The cost of extracting ore is estimated to be $50 per ton, and it can be sold for $150 a ton at Great Lakes ports. The mine can produce 200,000 tons a year and will be exhausted in 20 years.

To transport the ore south, Puffin will need to construct a rail line at a cost of $30 million. The cost of transporting a ton of ore is $10 by rail. Given a required rate of return of 15%, what are the NPVs for the mine and the railway? Which project(s) should Puffin undertake?

SOLUTION

$$NPV_{mine} = \sum_{t=1}^{20} (\$150 - 50) \times \frac{200,000}{(1.15)^t} - 90,000,000$$

$$= \$100 \times 200,000 \times PVIFA_{15,20} - 90,000,000$$

$$= \$20,000,000 \times 6.2593 - 90,000,000$$

$$= \$125,186,000 - 90,000,000$$

$$= \$35,186,000$$

$$NPV_{railway} = \sum_{t=1}^{20} -\$10 \times \frac{200,000}{(1.15)^t} - 30,000,000$$

$$= -\$2,000,000 \times PVIFA_{15,20} - 30,000,000$$

$$= -2,000,000 \times 6.2593 - 30,000,000$$

$$= -\$12,518,600 - 30,000,000$$

$$= -\$42,518,600$$

Although the mine is a positive NPV project, whereas the railroad is a negative NPV project, the mine is *contingent* on the existence of the railroad, and so they cannot be considered separately. They must either be jointly accepted or rejected. Because their combined NPV of –$7,332,600 is less than zero, they both should be rejected.

STRENGTHS AND WEAKNESS

The most desirable property of the NPV criterion is that it evaluates investments in the same way that shareholders do. Thus, it is consistent with shareholder wealth maximization. The NPV criterion also has the desirable property that it obeys the **value additivity principle**. This means that the NPV of a set of independent projects is just the sum of the NPVs of the individual projects. With value additivity, managers can consider each project on its own. The value additivity principle implies that the value of a firm equals the sum of the values of its component parts. Consequently, when a firm undertakes a series of investments, its value increases by an amount equal to the sum of the NPVs of the accepted projects. Thus, if Spectra invests in the dye plant, its value should increase by $3,025,510, the NPV of the project.

Another implication of value additivity is that when confronted with mutually exclusive projects, a firm should accept the one with the highest NPV because it will make the largest contribution to shareholder wealth. For example, if a firm has the choice of buying one of two machine tools, one with an NPV of $5,000 and the other with an NPV of $7,000, it should buy the latter. Shareholders will benefit by investing in either machine tool, but they will be $2,000 better off with the second machine than with the first one.

The basic weakness of NPV is that many corporate executives and nontechnical people have a tough time understanding the concept. The opportunity cost of money and present values of future sums of money are not intuitively obvious to most people; and misunderstood concepts are often misused or not used at all. Applying the NPV also entails the problem of computing the proper discount rate.

2.2 Alternative Investment Evaluation Criteria

Although NPV is the theoretically correct technique for evaluating investments, other capital-budgeting methods are also popular. This section will examine four of these "incorrect" methods because you should be familiar with what is done in practice. These techniques can be divided into two broad categories: nondiscounted cash flow (non-DCF) methods and **discounted cash flows** (DCF) methods. The critiques of these methods will rely on their consistency with the criterion of shareholder wealth maximization.

NONDISCOUNTED CASH FLOW CRITERIA

Nondiscounted cash flow criteria include those methods that do not rely on discounted cash flows. Two such methods, both widely used, are the payback period and the accounting rate of return.

Payback Period

The **payback period** is defined as the length of time necessary to recoup the initial investment from net cash flows. Its application can be illustrated by referring to the example of Spectra's dye plant.

The total initial investment for this project, including plant and equipment and working capital, is $7,200,000. The data from Exhibit 2.1 indicate that by the end of the third year, the cumulative cash flow will be $1,060,000 + $2,740,000 + $2,740,000 = $6,540,000. This leaves another $7,200,000 – $6,540,000 = $660,000 until payback. If the cash flow is spread evenly throughout the year, the payback will occur in another 660,000/2,740,000 = 0.24 years. So the payback period is 3.24 years.

Decision Rule

The application of the payback method to investment analysis is straightforward: *Projects with a payback less than a specified cutoff period are accepted, whereas those with a payback beyond this figure are rejected.* So if Spectra had a three-year payback requirement, the investment would be rejected. With a cutoff period of four years, it would be accepted. The maximum acceptable payback period typically varies for different projects according to their perceived risk: The riskier the project is, the shorter the required payback will be.

EXHIBIT 2.1 Illustration of How to Calculate the Net Present Value of Spectra's Proposed Dye Plant

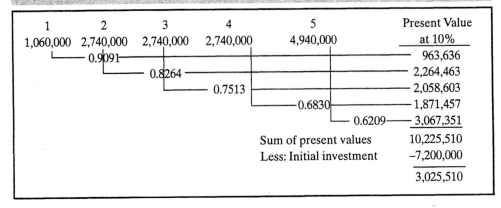

1	2	3	4	5	Present Value at 10%
1,060,000	2,740,000	2,740,000	2,740,000	4,940,000	
	0.9091				963,636
		0.8264			2,264,463
			0.7513		2,058,603
				0.6830	1,871,457
				0.6209	3,067,351
			Sum of present values		10,225,510
			Less: Initial investment		–7,200,000
					3,025,510

Strengths and Weakness

Payback was once the most commonly used method for choosing among alternative investment proposals. It is still widely used, and the reasons are evident: It is simple to understand and easy to apply. Despite its ease of application, however, payback has two major weaknesses:

1. *It ignores the time value of money.* The timing of cash flows is of critical importance because of the opportunity cost of money. Yet, payback assigns the same value to a dollar received at the end of the payback period as it does to one received at the beginning.

2. *It ignores cash flows beyond the payback period.* Spectra's project is expected to generate $2.74 million in year 4 and $4.94 million in year 5. With a cutoff period of three years, though, the $7.68 million generated in the last two years ($2.74 million + $4.94 million) is ignored in evaluating the project. The payback method is clearly biased against longer-term projects; if a quick payoff is not forthcoming, the project will be rejected.

One variant of the payback method is to look at the present value or **discounted payback period**. This is the length of time it takes for the present value of the cash inflows to equal the cost of the initial investment. We can see from the last column of Exhibit 2.2, which duplicates the calculations in Exhibit 2.1, that the cumulative present value for Spectra's investment at the end of year 4 is $7,158,159. This contrasts with an initial investment of $7.2 million. Thus, the discounted payback period is slightly over four years. Again, however, the $4.94 million cash flow in year 5 is ignored; that is, it does not affect Spectra's assessment of the value of investing in this project. For example, if Spectra's discounted payback period were four years, this investment would not pass muster even though investors value it highly.

Accounting Rate of Return

The **accounting rate of return**, also known as the **average rate of return** or **average return on book value**, is defined as the ratio of average after-tax profit to average book investment—the initial investment less accumulated depreciation; it is an average return on investment (ROI). Specifically, the accounting rate of return for an

EXHIBIT 2.2 Present Values of Cash Flows for Spectra's Dye Plant

Year	Cash Flow	×	Present Value Factor (10%)	=	Present Value	Cumulative Present Value
1	1,060,000		0.9091		963,636	963,636
2	2,740,000		0.8264		2,264,463	3,228,099
3	2,740,000		0.7513		2,058,603	5,286,702
4	2,740,000		0.6830		1,871,457	7,158,159
5	4,940,000		0.6209		3,067,351	10,225,510

investment with an expected life of *n* years is as follows:

$$\text{Accounting rate of return} = \frac{\sum_{t=1}^{n} (\text{After}-\text{tax profit in year } t)/n}{(\text{Initial outlay } + \text{ Ending book value})/2} \qquad (2.2)$$

In the case of Spectra's proposed investment, its average net income and net book value can be calculated from the data in Exhibit 2.3.

The average net income is $1,404,000 ($7,020,000/5) and the average book value of investment is $4,700,000 [($7,200,000 + $2,200,000)/2]. Therefore, according to Equation 2.2, the accounting rate of return on Spectra's investment is 1,404,000/4,700,000 = 29.9%.

Decision Rule

To apply this method, the firm must specify its target rate of return. *Investments yielding a return greater than this standard are accepted, whereas those falling below it would be rejected.* According to this criterion, Spectra would undertake the dye plant project as long as its target return on book value is less than 29.4%.

Strengths and Weakness

Like payback period, accounting rate of return is simple to apply. Similarly, it has glaring weaknesses:

1. *It ignores the time value of money.*   By using average income, the accounting rate of return gives too much weight to future flows. It treats income derived in year 5 the same way as it treats income received in year 1, ignoring the fact that early income is more valuable than is later income. It also takes no account of the investment's timing, even though an investment at the start of the project is costlier in present value terms than is one required in a future period.

2. *It is based on accounting income instead of cash flow.*   As pointed out earlier in this chapter, cash flow and reported income often differ. Income is measured according to accounting conventions that treat some cash outflows as operating expenses and others as capital expenses. Operating expenses are deducted immediately from income, whereas capital expenses are depreciated. Only the current

EXHIBIT 2.3 Net Income and Net Investment Figures for Spectra's Dye Plant

Year	Net Income	Initial Investment	Cumulative Investment	Net Investment (book value)
0	—	7,200,000	—	7,200,000
1	60,000	7,200,000	1,000,000	6,200,000
2	1,740,000	7,200,000	2,000,000	5,200,000
3	1,740,000	7,200,000	3,000,000	4,200,000
4	1,740,000	7,200,000	4,000,000	3,200,000
5	1,740,000	7,200,000	5,000,000	2,200,000
Total	7,020,000			

period's depreciation charge will affect current income and this depreciation charge is arbitrary, depending on the depreciation method used. (The next chapter presents some of the acceptable methods of depreciating assets.) Thus, the book value of assets and earnings — and therefore the average return on book value — depends on which items are treated as capital expenditures and how quickly these assets are depreciated. Because shareholders judge their well-being according to their ability to consume, they value only the cash provided by companies; earnings not associated with cash flows cannot be spent and therefore are of no value to investors. Despite the logic of focusing on investment cash flows, the accounting rate of return takes only income into account.

Consider, for example, the trio of projects A, B, and C depicted in Exhibit 2.4. The investment in each case is $6,000, depreciated at a constant rate of $2,000 per year down to an ending value of 0. With an initial investment of $6,000 and a final investment value of 0, the average book value over the three-year life of each investment is $3,000 [($6,000 + 0)/2]. The average annual income for each project is $1,000. The average return on book, therefore, is 1,000/3,000 = 33% for all three projects. Hence, they all are equally desirable or undesirable from the standpoint of the accounting rate of return. Yet A is clearly more desirable than B or C because more of its cash flows are received in the early years, thereby giving it the highest present value of the three. Similarly, C is more desirable than B when the time value of money is taken into account.

DISCOUNTED CASH FLOW CRITERIA

The DCF criteria include two widely used discounted cash flow techniques other than net present value: internal rate of return and the PI or benefit–cost ratio.

Internal Rate of Return

The **internal rate of return** (IRR) is the discount rate that sets the present value of the project cash flows equal to the initial investment outlay. In other words, the IRR is the discount rate that equates the project NPV to zero. The IRR of a project, therefore, determines the maximum interest rate at which you would be willing to borrow to

EXHIBIT 2.4 Cash Flow and Income

	Year 1	Year 2	Year 3
Project A			
Cash flow	$4,000*	$3,000	$2,000
Income	2,000	1,000	0
Project B			
Cash flow	2,000	3,000	4,000
Income	0	1,000	2,000
Project C			
Cash flow	3,000	3,000	3,000
Income	1,000	1,000	1,000

*Annual cash flow equals income plus $2,000 in depreciation.

finance the project. It is calculated as the rate of return r for which

$$NPV = \sum_{t=1}^{n} \frac{CF_t}{(1 + r)^t} - I_0 = 0 \qquad (2.3)$$

Applying Equation 2.3 to the Spectra Company example above and taking the cash flows from Exhibit 2.1, we find the IRR as the solution r to

$$\frac{1,060,000}{(1 + r)} + \frac{2,740,000}{(1 + r)^2} + \frac{2,740,000}{(1 + r)^3}$$

$$+ \frac{2,740,000}{(1 + r)^4} + \frac{4,940,000}{(1 + r)^5} - 7,200,000 = 0$$

Using an Excel spreadsheet with the IRR function, we find an exact value for the IRR of 22.44%. An alternative, and more difficult, approach is to approximate the IRR by trial and error, by calculating the project NPV for several different values of r to home in on the point at which the NPV turns from positive to negative.

The relationship between the NPV of a project and the discount rate used to calculate the NPV is known as the project's **net present value profile**. The NPV profile for Spectra's prospective dye investment is shown in Exhibit 2.5. As the discount rate increases, the NPV of the project decreases. The point that the NPV profile crosses the horizontal axis yields the IRR. In the case of Spectra's project, NPV = 0 at r = 22.44%, corroborating the spreadsheet's result.

Decision Rule

The rule for using IRR in investment analysis is as follows: *If the IRR exceeds the cost of capital for the project, the firm should undertake the project; otherwise, the project should be rejected.* The rationale for this rule is that any project yielding more than its cost of capital will have a positive net present value.

According to this criterion, Spectra should invest in the dye facility if, and only if, the project's cost of capital is less than 22.44%. For independent projects, the IRR rule leads to the same investment decisions as does the NPV rule as long as the project NPV behaves as depicted in Exhibit 2.5, that is, whenever project cash flows are such that an increase in the discount rate causes a decrease in the project's NPV. This will be the case, for example, if all cash flows subsequent to the initial investment are positive.

Strengths and Weaknesses

As we will see in a moment, the IRR method has some serious shortcomings when cash flows change sign more than once or when mutually exclusive projects are involved. However, although NPV is a more practical approach, many firms prefer IRR because managers seem to visualize and understand more easily the concept of a rate of return than they do the concept of a sum of discounted dollars. Because of the attractiveness and widespread use of the IRR method, it is worthwhile pointing out the problems with IRR.

EXHIBIT 2.5 NPV Profile for Spectra's Investment

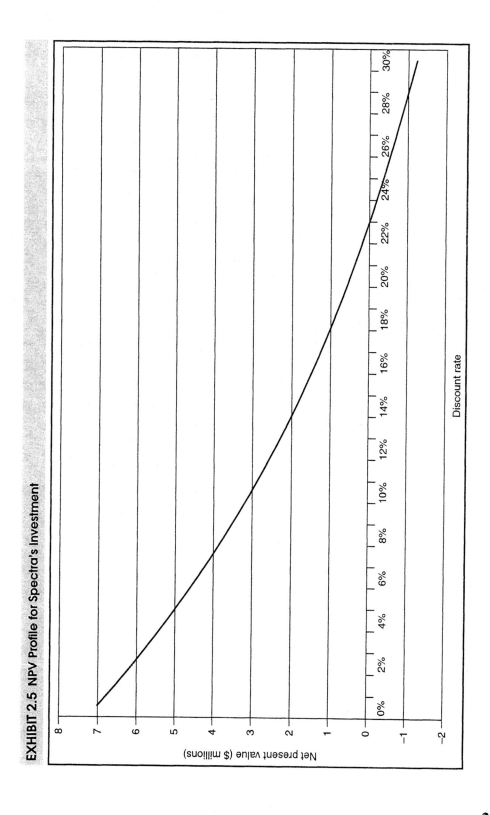

Net present value ($ millions)

Discount rate

1. *Multiple rates of return.* When an investment has an initial cash outflow, a series of positive cash inflows, and then at least one additional cash outflow, there may be more than one IRR; that is, more than one discount rate will produce a zero NPV. Theoretically, the number of solutions may be as great as the number of sign reversals in the stream of cash flows (i.e., a shift from a cash outflow to a cash inflow or vice versa). This would be the case, for example, with a nuclear reactor, a coal mine, a logging operation, or any other project that has shutdown and cleanup costs following termination of the project. In practice, however, unless the abandonment costs are very large relative to the scale of the investment, the problem of multiple IRRs seldom arises.

BOX 2.3

APPLICATION: ESTIMATING MULTIPLE IRRs

Demonstrate that the following project has internal rates of return of 0%, 100%, and 200%.

Year	0	1	2	3
Cash flow	−$200	+$1,200	−$2,2000	+$1,2000

SOLUTION

To show that the project has multiple internal rates of return, it is necessary to show that the present value of future cash flows at each IRR just equals the initial investment of $200.

$$200 = \frac{1,200}{1} - \frac{2,200}{1} + \frac{1,200}{1}$$

$$= 200 \Rightarrow IRR = 0$$

$$200 = \frac{1,200}{2} - \frac{2,200}{(2)^2} + \frac{1,200}{(2)^3}$$

$$= 600 - 550 + 150$$

$$= 200 \Rightarrow IRR = 100\,\%$$

$$200 = \frac{1,200}{3} - \frac{2,200}{(3)^2} + \frac{1,200}{(3)^3}$$

$$= 400 - 244.44 + 44.44$$

$$= 200 \Rightarrow IRR = 200\,\%$$

These multiple IRRs show up in the project's NPV profile depicted in Exhibit 2.6 on page 25.

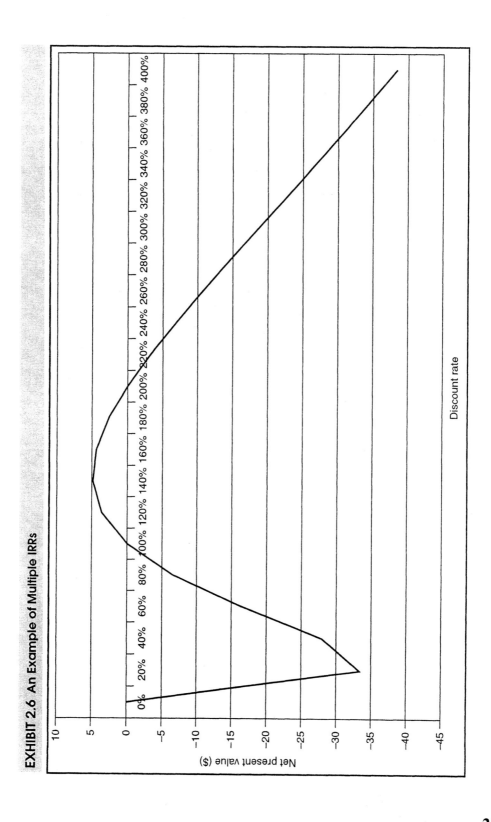

EXHIBIT 2.6 An Example of Multiple IRRs

25

2. *Mutually exclusive projects.* Firms sometimes have to select one of several alternatives to do the same thing. For example, Ford could have built its new small car plant in Alabama instead of in Mexico. In the case of such mutually exclusive choices, NPV and IRR can favor conflicting projects. Consider, for example, projects A and B in Exhibit 2.7. Project A has the higher IRR, but project B has the higher NPV when the discount rate is 17%. Therefore, A is preferred under IRR, whereas B is preferred under the NPV rule.

NPV and IRR are most likely to give conflicting signals when the mutually exclusive projects are substantially different in the *timing of cash flows* or in *scale*.

Timing of Cash Flows

The conflict in the IRR and NPV rankings of projects A and B arises because of differences in the timing of their cash flows, with most of A's cash flows coming in the early years and most of B's cash flows coming in the later years. The reason that these different cash flow patterns lead to different project rank orderings is that IRR implicitly assumes that intermediate cash flows occurring during the life of the project can be reinvested at a rate equal to the IRR, whereas NPV implicitly assumes a reinvestment rate equal to the project's cost of capital. Forced to choose between two mutually exclusive investments, the NPV method will always provide the correct answer because it more realistically represents the opportunity cost of funds for the firm's shareholders.

Scale Differences

To see how scale differences, or differences in the amount of the initial investment, could lead to different project rankings, consider the following two projects, one of which requires an initial investment of $100,000 and the other an initial investment of $1,000,000:

	Cash Flow for Project		
Year	X	Y	Y–X
0	−$100,000	−$1,000,000	−$900,000
1	$140,000	$1,250,000	$1,110,000
NPV ($k = 15\%$)	$21,739	$86,957	—
IRR	40%	25%	—

At a 15% discount rate, Y has a much larger NPV than X, which favors Y over X. On the basis of IRR, however, X is the better project. The conflicting messages occur because NPV takes account of size differences in the initial investment, whereas IRR does not. The NPV criterion in this case is correct, assuming there is no capital rationing. If the company's capital budget is restricted for some reason, you must take into account the incremental outlay of $900,000 for project Y relative to project X (column Y–X).

EXHIBIT 2.7 Differences Between Rankings by NPV and IRR

| Year | Cash Flow for Project | |
	A	B
0	−1,000,000	−1,000,000
1	800,000	100,000
2	300,000	400,000
3	200,000	500,000
4	100,000	800,000
NPV (k = 17%)	$81,154	$116,781
IRR	22.99%	21.46%

One advantage of using IRR is that it permits an investment analysis without requiring advance specification of the discount rate. The calculated IRR can then be used as a benchmark against which to judge the likely cost of capital or required return for the project. If the IRR is greater than any reasonable estimate of the cost of capital, the project should be accepted; if the IRR turns out to be less than the cost of capital is likely to be, the project should be rejected. If the IRR falls between the minimum and maximum likely values of the cost of capital, however, the firm will have to devote additional effort to estimating the project's required return. For example, a firm may decide that the required return for a project is definitely less than 18% but more than 12%. If the IRR turns out to be 21%, the project should be accepted without further ado. Similarly, if the IRR is 9%, it should be rejected. An IRR of 14%, however, will force the firm to calculate more carefully its cost of capital.

Profitability Index

The **profitability index** (PI), also called the **benefit–cost ratio**, of a project equals the present value of future cash flows divided by the initial cash investment:

$$PI = \frac{\sum_{t=1}^{n} \dfrac{CF_t}{(1 + k)^t}}{I_0} = \frac{(NPV + I_0)}{I_0} \qquad (2.4)$$

For Spectra's project, applying Equation 2.4 yields a profitability index of 1.42:

$$PI = \frac{\$10,225,510}{\$7,200,000} = 1.42$$

In other words, the project returns a present value of $1.42 for every $1.00 of the initial investment.

Decision Rule

As long as the profitability index exceeds 1.00, the project should be accepted. For a given project, NPV and PI give the same accept–reject signal. It is easy to see why. As shown, $PI = (NPV + I_0)/I_0$. Therefore, $PI > 1$ implies that $NPV + I_0 > I_0$ or $NPV > 0$. Similarly, $PI < 1$ implies that $NPV < 0$.

Strengths and Weaknesses

Although these two criteria always yield the same accept–reject decision, NPV and PI sometimes disagree in the rank ordering of acceptable projects. This conflict in project ranking is important when there are mutually exclusive projects and when there is capital rationing. We shall discuss the problem of capital rationing in Appendix 2A.

Mutually Exclusive Projects

In the section on IRR, we saw that when scale differences exist, there can be a conflict with NPV over project rankings. The same is true for PI. We can see this using the same example as the one presented in that section:

	Project X	Project Y
Initial investment	–$100,000	–$1,000,000
NPV ($k = 15\%$)	$21,739	$86,957
PI	1.22	1.09

Both projects are acceptable because they have $NPV > 0$ and $PI > 1$. If the projects are mutually exclusive, however, X will be more attractive when ranked by PI, whereas Y will be better when ranked by NPV.

In this case, as in all cases in which there is a conflict in rankings (unless there is capital rationing), the firm should select the project with the higher NPV. The reason is the same as before: The best project is the one that adds the most value to the firm and that has the highest net present value.

2.3 Surveys of Capital-Budgeting Techniques Used in Practice

A recent survey by John Graham and Campbell Harvey sheds some light on the capital-budgeting techniques most commonly used by leading U.S. companies.[1] Exhibit 2.8 summarizes the 392 responses they received from their survey, which was sent to the chief financial officers of all (1998) Fortune 500 companies along with 4,440 firms with officers who are members of the Financial Executives Institute (FEI) (313 of the Fortune 500 CFOs are also FEI members). Because the total number of responses to the questions on primary and secondary techniques in use exceeds the number of respondents, it is evident that some companies use several quantitative capital-budgeting techniques.

---

[1]Graham, J., and Harvey, C. "How Do CFOs Make Capital Budgeting and Capital Structure Decisions?" *Journal of Applied Corporate Finance*, Spring 2002, pp. 8–23.

EXHIBIT 2.8 Survey Evidence on the Popularity of Different Capital-Budgeting Methods*

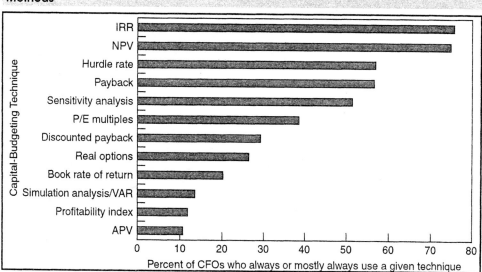

*These figures equal the percentage of CFOs who always or almost always use a particular techinique. IRR represents Internal Rate of Return, NPV is Net Present Value, P/E is the Price to Earnings ratio, VAR is Value At Risk, and APV is Adjusted Present Value. The survey is based on the responses of 392 CFOs, as are the rest of the figures in this paper.
Source: John Graham and Camphell Harvey, "How Do CFOs Make Capital Budgeting and Capital Structure Decisions?" *Journal of Applied Corporate Finance*, Spring 2002, p. 11.

The results indicate a strong preference for techniques that explicitly consider the time value of money, with 74.9% of CFOs always or almost always using NPV and 75.7% always or almost always using IRR. According to these data, NPV is a much more widely used capital-budgeting technique today than it was just 10 or 20 years ago. However, large companies were significantly more likely to use NPV than were small firms. Moreover, highly leveraged firms and dividend-paying firms were significantly more likely (across all size categories) to use NPV and IRR than firms with low debt ratios and non-dividend payers. Graham and Campbell also report that companies whose CEOs had MBAs were more likely to use NPV than firms whose CEOs did not. Finally, public companies were significantly more likely to use NPV and IRR than were private corporations.

These data also reveal that the most popular secondary or supplemental method of evaluation is the payback period (56.7% always or almost always used it), with small firms using payback almost as frequently as they used NPV or IRR. The authors explain the persistence of the payback method, in part, to its simplicity along with top management's lack of familiarity with more sophisticated techniques. However, they also note that payback period may provide useful information for severely capital-constrained firms. Such firms may not survive if an investment project does not pay positive cash flows early on, even if expected cash flows longer term are positive. Moreover, even if the firm survives, having its money tied up in a project with large negative cash flows early on may preclude it from pursuing other promising investments during the next few years. This explanation is consistent with the fact that only about 20% of the companies said they used accounting rate of return.

2.4 Summary and Conclusions

One of the most important tasks of top management is to decide on the investments that their firms should make. In this chapter, we examined several different evaluation procedures that managers use to analyze potential projects. These included three DCF techniques—net present value, internal rate of return, and profitability index—and two nondiscounted cash flow techniques—payback period and accounting rate of return.

Net Present Value

Net present value (NPV) is defined as the present value of future cash flows, discounted at the appropriate cost of capital, minus the initial net cash outlay for the project. Projects with a positive NPV should be accepted; negative NPV projects should be rejected. If two projects are mutually exclusive, the one with the higher NPV should be accepted. This method takes into account all cash flows, only cash flows, and the time value of money.

Internal Rate of Return

The IRR is the discount rate that sets the present value of the project cash flows equal to the initial investment. In other words, the IRR is the discount rate that equates the project NPV to zero. The NPV and IRR methods yield similar accept–reject decisions except when projects are mutually exclusive. When a conflict arises, the NPV method should always be used.

Profitability Index

The PI or benefit–cost ratio, of a project equals the present value of future cash flows divided by the initial cash investment. Like the IRR method, it leads to accept–reject decisions that are the same as those provided by the NPV method. For mutually exclusive projects, conflicts between PI and NPV should always be resolved in favor of the NPV method except when capital rationing occurs. In that case, when the firm cannot or will not raise sufficient funds to undertake all positive NPV projects, PI can sometimes provide superior investment decisions.

Payback Period

Payback is defined as the length of time necessary to recoup the initial investment from net cash flows. The firm specifies a maximum payback period for its investments. If a proposed investment has a payback less than the maximum, it is acceptable; otherwise, it should be rejected. Although widely used, payback has serious weaknesses because it ignores (1) the time value of money and (2) cash flows beyond the payback period.

Accounting Rate of Return

The accounting rate of return equals the ratio of average after-tax profit to average book investment; it is an average return on investment (ROI). Projects with a return that exceeds the minimum return set by the firm are accepted; those that do not make this cutoff are rejected. This method is seriously flawed because it (1) focuses on earnings instead of cash flows and (2) ignores the time value of money.

We concluded that, in general, the NPV method is the most appropriate method to use in evaluating potential investments because it is the one most consistent with the way in which shareholders would themselves evaluate the investments. The NPV method properly focuses on cash, rather than accounting profits, and emphasizes the opportunity cost of the money invested. It recognizes that the cash that a firm gets out of a project should be greater than the cash put in *plus* the interest that could have been earned by investing the money elsewhere. Thus, the NPV approach discounts future cash flows to current dollars, recognizing the alternative return that shareholders could realize if they had the cash now rather than in the future.

REFERENCES

Bierman, Jr., H., and Smidt, S. *The Capital Budgeting Decision.* 6th ed. Macmillan: New York, 1984.

Lorie, J.H., and Savage, L.J. "Three Problems in Capital Rationing." *Journal of Business,* October 1955, pp. 229–239.

Solomon, E. "The Arithmetic of Capital Budgeting Decisions." *Journal of Business,* April 1956, pp. 124–129.

Weingartner, H.M. *Mathematical Programming and the Analysis of Capital Budgeting Problems.* Prentice-Hall: Englewood Cliffs, N.J., 1963.

SAMPLE PROBLEMS

1. Charter Manufacturing, a steel maker, has invested $1.5 million in a more energy efficient melting system. This new system will cut its energy costs by $10 a ton.

   a. If Charter produces 25,000 tons of steel annually, what is its payback period? Assume these savings will continue indefinitely.
   Answer: The new system will save Charter $250,000 ($10 × 25,000) in energy costs annually. With a $1.5 million investment, the payback period is six years (1,500,000/ 250,000).

   b. What is the IRR on this investment?
   Answer: The NPV for this investment, using a discount rate of r, is –$1.5 million + $250,000/$r$. The IRR for this investment is r = 250,000/1,500,000 = 16.67%.

   c. What is the NPV of the new system using an 8% discount rate?
   Answer: The NPV for this investment is –$1.5 million + $250,000/0.08 = $1,625,000.

2. Polaroid recently installed new equipment that recycles the solvent, CFC-113, through a closed-loop system. By recycling the CFC-113, which has been implicated in stratospheric ozone depletion, Polaroid realizes a net savings of $90,000 annually from lower disposal costs and reduced purchases of new solvents.

   a. If the equipment costs $500,000 and will be depreciated straight-line over its eight-year life, what is Polaroid's NPV on this investment? Assume a 40% corporate tax rate and a 9% discount rate.
   Answer: Since Polaroid will take an annual depreciation charge on this investment of $62,500 ($500,000/8), its projected net annual cash flow from this new equipment equals

   $$\text{Net cash flow} = (\text{Cost savings} - \text{depreciation})(1 - 0.4) + \text{depreciation}$$

   $$= (\$90,000 - 62,500) \times 0.6 + \$62,500 = \$79,000$$

   The present value of this eight-year annuity is $79,000 × 5.5348, or $437,249. Subtracting off the original investment of $500,000 yields an NPV of –$62,751. On the basis of this negative NPV, the investment appears to be destroying value for Polaroid.

b. Are there any other factors that might influence this investment decision?

Answer: This analysis assumes that both the cost of using CFC-113 and the cost of its disposal will remain constant over time. Given the increasingly stringent environmental regulations, such an assumption is unwarranted. Just a small increase in these costs will change this analysis around. For example, an increase in annual after-tax cost savings of $62,751/5.5348 = $11,337 will just turn this project into a breakeven proposition. This translates into before-tax annual cost savings of $11,337/.6 = $18,895.

QUESTIONS

1. a. What is the relationship between accounting income and economic profit?
   b. What is the relationship between accounting rate of return and economic rate of return?

2. In 1991, AT&T laid a transatlantic fiber optic cable costing $400 million that could handle 80,000 calls simultaneously. What is the payback on this investment if AT&T uses just half its capacity while netting one cent per minute on calls?

3. The satisfied owner of a new $15,000 car can be expected to buy another ten cars from the same company over the next 30 years (an average of one every three years) at an average price of $15,000 (ignore the effects of inflation). If the net profit margin on these cars is 20%, how much should an auto manufacturer be willing to spend to keep its customers satisfied? Assume a 9% discount rate.

4. Demonstrate that the following project has internal rates of return of 0%, 100%, and 200%.

Year	1	2	3	4
Cash flow	-$1,200	+7,200	-13,200	+7,200

5. During 1990, Dow Chemical generated the following returns on investment in its different business units:

Business Unit	Return on Investment (%)
Plastics	16.6
Chemicals/Performance Products	16.7
Consumer Specialties	12.7
Hydrocarbons/Energy	5.2
Other	1.6
Dow Chemical overall	11.8

a. Given these returns, which of the business units should Dow invest additional capital in?
b. What additional information would you need in order to make that decision?

PROBLEMS

1. A firm is considering investing in a project with the following cash flows:

Year	1	2	3	4	5	6	7	8
Net cash flow ($)	2,000	3,000	4,000	3,500	3,000	2,000	1,000	1,000

The project requires an initial investment of $12,500, and the firm has a required rate of return of 10%. Compute the payback, discounted payback, and net present value, and determine whether the project should be accepted.

2. The Pennco Oil Co. must decide whether it is financially feasible to open an oil well off the coast of China. The drilling and rigging cost for the well is $5,000,000. The well is expected to yield 585,000 barrels of oil a year at a net profit to Pennco of $5 a barrel for four years. The well will then be effectively depleted but must be capped and secured at a cost of $4,000,000. Pennco requires an annual rate of return of 14% on its investment projects. Should Pennco open the well? (Assume all of a year's production occurs at the end of the year.)

3. Jack Nicklaus, the golfing pro and real estate developer, is thinking of acquiring an 800-acre property outside Atlanta, which he intends to turn into an exclusive community for 600 families. The cost of this property and the necessary improvements is $30 million. After setting aside a mandatory 25% of the property as green space, he figures he can sell the remaining lots for an average of $90,000 an acre. By putting in a golf course on the 200 acres of green space, Nicklaus believes he can instead sell the lots for an average of $140,000 an acre. The golf course, including clubhouse, has a projected price tag of $6 million. In either event, the project is expected to take eight years to sell out at a rate of 75 lots per year. Jack Nicklaus faces a marginal tax rate of 40% and can write off his land and development costs by prorating these costs against each lot sold.

   a. If his required return is 14%, should Jack Nicklaus go ahead with the initial project (i.e., a community with no golf course)?
   b. Should he put in the golf course?

4. The Coin Coalition is trying to get the U.S. government to replace the dollar bill with a gold-colored dollar coin. One argument is cost savings. A dollar bill costs 2.6 cents to produce and lasts only about 17 months. A dollar coin, on the other hand, while costing 6 cents to produce, lasts for 30 years. About 1.8 billion dollar bills must be replaced each year. The start-up costs of switching to a dollar coin are likely to be quite high, however. These costs have not been estimated.

   a. What are the projected average annual cost savings associated with switching from the dollar bill to a dollar coin?
   b. Taking into account only the cost savings estimated in part a, how high can the start-up costs for this replacement project be and still yield a positive NPV for the U.S. government? Use an 8% discount rate.

5. Recent Census Bureau data show that the average income of a college-educated person was $34,391 versus $24,701 for those who have not attended college. At the same time, the annual tuition at public universities was $1,566 versus $7,693 for private colleges. In the following questions, assume there is no difference in income between public and private university graduates.

   a. On the basis of these figures, what is the payback period for a college education, taking into account the four years of lost earnings while being in college? Do these calculations for both public and private colleges.
   b. Assuming college graduation at age 22 and retirement at age 65, what is the IRR on a college degree from a public university? A private university?
   c. Assuming a 7% discount rate, and the same working life as in part b, what is the net present value of a college degree from a public university? A private university?

6. The Fun Foods Corporation must decide on what new product lines to introduce next year. After-tax cash flows are listed below along with initial investments. The firm's cost of capital

is 12% and its target accounting rate of return is 20%. Assume straight-line depreciation and an asset life of five years. The corporate tax rate is 35%. All projects are independent.

Project	Investment	Year 1	2	3	4	5
A	$5,000	$800	$1,000	$350	$1,250	$3,000
B	$7,500	$1,250	$3,000	$2,500	$5,000	$5,000
C	$4,000	$600	$1,200	$1,200	$2,400	$3,000

a. Calculate the accounting rate of return on the project. Which projects are acceptable according to this criterion? (*Note*: Assume net income is equal to after-tax cash flow less depreciation.)
b. Calculate the payback period. All projects with a payback of fewer than four years are acceptable. Which are acceptable according to this criterion?
c. Calculate the projects' NPVs. Which are acceptable according to this criterion?
d. Calculate the projects' IRRs. Which are acceptable according to this criterion?
e. Which projects should be chosen?

7. Aptec, Inc., is negotiating with the U.S. Department of Housing and Urban Development (HUD) to open a manufacturing plant in South Central L.A., the scene of much of the rioting in April 1992. The proposed plant will cost $3.5 million and is projected to generate annual after-tax profits of $550,000 million over its estimated four-year life. Depreciation is straight-line over the four-year period and Aptec's tax rate is 35%. However, given the risks involed, Aptec is looking for a tax-exempt government subsidy. According to Aptec, the subsidy must be able to achieve any of the following four objectives:

(1) Provide a two-year payback.
(2) Provide an accounting rate of return of 35%.
(3) Raise the plant's IRR to 22%.
(4) Provide an NPV of $1 million when cash flows are discounted at 18%.

a. For each alternative suggested by Aptec, develop a subsidy plan that minimizes the costs to HUD of achieving Aptec's objective. You can schedule the subsidy payments at any time over the four-year period.
b. Which of the four subsidy plans would you recommend to HUD if it uses a 15% discount rate?

8. The Fast Food chain is trying to introduce its new Hot and Spicy line of hamburgers. One plan (S) will include a big media campaign but less in-house production capability. The other plan (L) will concentrate on a more gradual roll out of the project but will involve more investment in personnel training and so forth. The cost of capital is 15%. The cash flows ($000) are listed below. The initial investment for each is $400,000.

Plan	Year 1	2	3	4	5
S	$250	$250	$150	$100	$50
L	$100	$125	$200	$250	$125

a. Construct the NPV profiles for plans (S) and (L). Which has the higher IRR?
b. Which plan should Fast Food choose using the NPV method?
c. Which plan (S or L) should Fast Food choose? Why?
d. At what cost of capital will the NPV and the IRR rankings conflict?

9. The Roost Corp. is considering a multiple-use dockside complex in a major lakeside city. Roost uses accounting rate of return as its sole capital-budgeting criterion. The sales and expenses (excluding depreciation) are as follows ($000):

Year	1	2	3	4	5
Sales	$800	$5,000	$15,000	$25,000	$25,000
Expenses	$700	$3,500	$10,500	$17,500	$18,500

Investment in the project is $40 million today and the accelerated depreciation schedule applicable to this project is:

Year	1	2	3	4	5
(%)	15	22	21	21	21

a. Should Roost accept the project using straight-line depreciation? Assume a target rate of return of 15%. Its tax rate is 40%.
b. Would your answer to (a) change if Roost used accelerated depreciation?
c. With a cost of capital of 10%, would the project have a positive NPV under straight-line depreciation? Under accelerated depreciation?

10. Sweet Delights Co. is considering a marketing policy for its brand of chocolates. Two *mutually exclusive* advertising strategy changes are under consideration. The cash flows associated with each are as follows. The cost of capital for Sweet Delights is 10%.

Strategy	Year 0	1	2	3	4	5
A	–80	+40	+40	+40	–	–
B	–40	+20	+20	+20	+20	+20

a. Which of the two strategies would you prefer if *neither* decision can be repeated (i.e., all future strategies/ decisions are expected to have zero NPVs)?
b. Which of the two strategies would you prefer if each strategy can be repeated as often as possible?

Appendix 2A

Special Problems in Capital Budgeting

Although the net present value rule typically suffices to select the best combination of investment projects, some additional techniques are necessary in certain situations. These include the existence of capital rationing and mutually exclusive projects with significantly different lives. This appendix shows how to deal with these special problems in capital budgeting.

APPENDIX 2A.1

CAPITAL RATIONING AND CAPITAL BUDGETING

In evaluating the different investment criteria so far, we have implicitly assumed there were no limits on the availability of capital to fund the projects with positive NPVs. This is not always the case. Rather than accept all profitable investment opportunities, some firms constrain the size of their capital budgets. Whenever such a constraint exists, we have the situation known as **capital rationing**. Capital rationing may be self-imposed or externally imposed.

A conservatively managed firm may be unwilling to incur additional debt or to issue new shares, which will thus limit capital expenditures to internally generated cash flow. Alternatively, a firm may limit the number of attractive projects it undertakes because management time is scarce and the firm fears that it will be unable to adequately supervise all of them at one time. The size of the capital budget would serve as a surrogate for the demands on management time.

External constraints may also lead to capital rationing. For example, a firm's current lenders may restrict the amount of future borrowing it can do. If the firm refuses to raise additional equity—for example,

because management or a large shareholder fears losing control of the company—the firm's capital budget will be constrained by the amount of funds generated internally.

In one survey, Lawrence Gitman and John Forrester found that about half of all respondents practice capital rationing.[2] The most often cited reason for restricting the capital budget was management's desire to limit borrowing. Other major causes of capital rationing are described in Exhibit 2A.1.

When constraints prevent the firm from undertaking all acceptable projects, it must select from among them the subset of projects that gives the highest net present value. This may necessitate accepting several smaller and less profitable projects that fully utilize the budget constraint rather than one large project that results in an unutilized portion of the budget.

Capital budgeting with rationing can get quite complicated when the initial outlays occur in more than one period and the capital budget is also constrained over several periods. Under these circumstances, the firm can apply various mathematical programming techniques such as linear or integer programming to solve for

---

[2]Gitman, L.J., and Forrester, Jr., J.R. "A Survey of Capital Budgeting Techniques Used by Major U.S. Firms." *Financial Management*, Fall 1977, pp. 66–71.

EXHIBIT 2A.1 Major Causes of Capital Rationing

	Responses	
Cause	Number	Percent
Debt limit imposed by outside agreement	10	10.7
Debt limit placed by management external to the organization	3	3.2
Limit placed on borrowing by internal management	65	69.1
Restrictive policy imposed upon retained earnings for dividend payment	2	2.1
Maintenance of a target earnings per share or price-earnings ratio	14	14.9
Total responses	94	100.0

Source: Lawrence J. Gitman and John R. Forrester, Jr., "A Survey of Capital Budgeting Techniques Used by Major U.S. Firms," *Financial Management*, Fall 1977, p. 69.

the optimal combination of projects.[3] When all the initial outlays occur in the first period, a simpler, heuristic approach using the PI is available:

1. Calculate the PI for each project.
2. Rank all projects in terms of their PIs, from the highest to the lowest.
3. Starting with the project having the highest PI, go down the list and select all projects having $PI > 1$ until the capital budget is exhausted.

Exhibit 2A.2 lists six potential projects along with their initial investments, NPVs, and PIs. The underscores on the project rankings indicate where the capital budget of

$5 million is fully spent. The projects selected under the NPV method are D and C, with a combined NPV of $780,000. Alternatively, the PI method selects projects F, A, E, and D with a group NPV of $875,000.

This example shows that the NPV method does not necessarily select the best combination of projects under capital rationing. The PI approach will select the optimal combination of projects, provided that (1) the budget constraint is for one period only and (2) the entire budget can be consumed by accepting projects in descending order of PI. The first condition rules out multiperiod budget constraints that can be dealt with only through mathematical

EXHIBIT 2A.2 Capital-Budgeting Example with Capital Rationing ($5 million budget constraint)

Project	Initial Investment	NPV	PI	Ranking NPV	Ranking PI
A	500,000	100,000	1.20	1. D	F
B	500,000	70,000	1.14	2. C	A
C	2,000,000	300,000	1.15	3. E	E
D	3,000,000	480,000	1.16	4. F	D
E	1,000,000	170,000	1.17	5. A	C
F	500,000	125,000	1.25	6. B	B

[3]The seminal work in applying linear and integer programming to the capital-rationing problem is H. Martin Weingartner, *Mathematical Programming and the Analysis of Capital Budgeting Problems*. Prentice-Hall: Englewood Cliffs, N.J., 1963.

programming techniques. The second condition avoids problems that might arise when projects are indivisible; that is, fractional projects are not feasible (e.g., you do not build just 90% of a bridge). When projects are indivisible, applying the PI approach may lead to an underutilized budget because the next available project might be too large. If this happens, the PI method cannot be used. It will be necessary to check various combinations of projects that fit within the budget constraint to see which one has the highest NPV. For example, suppose that project E's cost is actually $1,005,000. If the capital budget constraint is firm, then the PI method would require dropping project D (because it has the next-lowest PI), and the NPV method would have selected the best group of projects.

Many financial economists argue that sufficient funds are available from capital markets to finance any positive NPV projects. Hence, capital rationing must be a self-imposed phenomenon. Furthermore, they argue, because capital rationing results in firms passing up projects with positive NPVs, it is an unwise policy to follow. In the preceding example, by imposing a $5 million budget constraint, the firm had to turn down projects B and C, thereby losing the chance to add $370,000 to the shareholders' wealth.

As mentioned earlier, however, the availability of capital may not be the limiting factor that leads to capital rationing. Management time could well be the scarce resource that must be allocated among a limited number of projects. Noneconomic motives may also play a role in capital rationing. For example, many owners are reluctant to share control of their firm to gain additional financing. Thus, capital rationing is not a mirage but is a real phenomenon that must be dealt with at times.

APPENDIX 2A.2

MUTUALLY EXCLUSIVE PROJECTS WITH DIFFERENT ECONOMIC LIVES

Suppose a company is considering replacing its old Dole truck with either another new Dole or a new Daihatsu. Both trucks have the same capacity, but the Dole truck is sturdier than the Daihatsu. As a result, the Dole's life expectancy is five years as opposed to four years for the Daihatsu. In addition, the Dole's annual operating costs of $3,000 are $1,000 less than the Daihatsu's annual operating costs of $4,000. However, the Daihatsu costs only $7,500, whereas the Dole costs $12,000. These data are summarized as follows:

	Dole truck	Daihatsu truck
Initial cost	$12,000	$7,500
Salvage value	0	0
Life	5 years	4 years
Operating cost	$3,000/year	$4,000/year

One way to choose between these mutually exclusive investments is to compare the present values of their costs. Assuming a discount rate of 8%, the PVs for each truck are as follows:

Year	Dole	Daihatsu
0	$12,000	$7,500
1	$3,000	$4,000
2	$3,000	$4,000
3	$3,000	$4,000
4	$3,000	$4,000
5	$3,000	—
Present value of cost at 8%	$23,978.10	$20,740.40

Is the Daihatsu truck preferable because it has the lower present value of cost? Not necessarily. Because the Daihatsu will wear out in four years, it must be replaced one year earlier than the Dole. Hence, the two investments are not directly comparable.

One solution technique is to assume a cash salvage value for the Dole after four years of service. An alternative approach to handling mutually exclusive investments with unequal lives is to assume that at the expiration of the economic life of each asset, the firm will invest in new assets with identical characteristics. This means that if the company decides to buy a Daihatsu today, it will buy a new one every four years. Similarly, if the firm buys a Dole, it will replace it with a new Dole every five years. Thus, the firm will buy replacement chains of Daihatsus or Doles.

Given the asset replacement assumption, we can calculate the equivalent annual cost of using mutually exclusive assets. The **equivalent annual cost** of an asset is an annuity that has the same life as the asset whose present value equals the cost of the asset. In the case of the truck purchase decision, in which the discount rate is 8%, if the firm buys a Daihatsu, it is a toss-up between paying out $7,500 every four years to buy a new Daihatsu or paying a four-year annuity of $7,500/$PVIFA_{8,4}$ = $7,500/3.3121 = $2,264.42. The equivalent annual cash cost of a Daihatsu, therefore, is $4,000 + 2,264.42 = $6,264.42. Similarly, if it buys a Dole, the firm

is indifferent to either paying out $12,000 every five years or paying a five-year annuity of $12,000/$PVIFA_{8,5}$ = $12,000/3.9927 = $3,005.49. This yields an equivalent annual cost of operation for a Dole of $3,000 + 3,005.49 = $6,005.49.

We see from the analysis that buying a chain of Doles is equivalent to paying out $6,005.49 annually, whereas a chain of Daihatsus is equivalent to an annual cash outflow of $6,264.42. Because the Dole's equivalent annual cost is $258.93 less than the Daihatsu's cost, the Dole is the preferable purchase.

This suggests the following rule for comparing mutually exclusive assets with unequal economic lives: *Compute the equivalent annual cost of each asset. Select the asset with the lowest equivalent annual cost.* For a revenue-generating project, this rule becomes: *Select the project with the highest equivalent annual net cash flow.*

The validity of this rule depends crucially on the assumption that each asset will be replaced with an identical asset. If we know that in reality the Dole will be replaced with a Roadhog, then the equivalent annual cost rule will be suboptimal relative to the following rule: *Calculate the NPV of each mutually exclusive investment on the basis of specific assumptions about the reinvestment opportunities that will become available in the future; select the investment having the highest NPV (or lowest present value of costs).*

PROBLEM

1. Owen Corporation plans to purchase a new machine that costs $120,000, has six years of economic life, and generates a net annual cash flow of $40,000 at the end of years 1–6 (all cash flows have taken into account depreciation and taxes). The firm also has the option to sell the machine at the end of years 1–6. The following are the net cash flows Owen will receive from the sale of the machine at the end of each year.

End of Year	Net Cash Flow From Sale ($)
1	100,000
2	85,000
3	75,000
4	60,000
5	30,000
6	0

The manager wants to determine an optimal replacement policy for the machine. Once a policy has been adopted, it will be implemented perpetually because it is assumed that the cost of the machine, the cash inflows, and the net cash flow from selling the old machines will be the same over time. Determine the optimal policy, assuming a 12% discount rate.

Estimating Project Cash Flows

If you can look into the seeds of time,
And say which grain will grow and which will not,
Speak.

　　　　　　　　　—SHAKESPEARE (MACBETH)

This chapter describes the estimation of the necessary cash flow input data for the project evaluation techniques developed in Chapter 2. Estimating the cash flows associated with a project—the cost of undertaking the project, the cash inflows during the life of the project, and the terminal or ending value of the project—is the most important and also the most difficult part of an investment analysis. Part of this difficulty stems from interactions between the project and the firm.

Shareholders are interested in how many additional dollars they will receive in the future for the dollars they lay out today. Hence, what matters to them is not the project's total cash flow per period but the **incremental cash flows** generated by the project, relative to the additional dollars they must invest today. To the extent that the project affects other aspects of the firm, as often happens, total and incremental project cash flows will differ. The distinction between total and incremental cash flows is a crucial one, therefore, and is discussed in Section 3.1. Section 3.2 discusses the replacement problem, where the firm is looking at replacing an existing piece of equipment with a new piece of equipment. It shows how to calculate the initial investment required, estimate the operating cash flows, and incorporate the terminal value in the analysis. Section 3.3 discusses the estimation of project cash flows associated with a new product introduction. Section 3.4 points out some potential sources of bias in the estimation of cash flows. Throughout this chapter, the effects of taxes on these cash flows are analyzed where relevant. The distinction between before-tax and after-tax cash flows is an important one because investors value only their share of a project's cash inflows and outflows; they derive no benefit from the government's share of project cash flows.

Appendix 3A discusses the general rules for depreciating property, while the effects of inflation on project cash flows are examined in Appendix 3B. Finally, Appendix 3C shows how the basic principles of capital budgeting can be modified to deal with the unique aspects of foreign investments, including differences between project and parent company cash flows, foreign tax regulations, expropriation, blocked funds, exchange rate changes and inflation, project-specific financing, and differences between the basic business risks of foreign and domestic projects.

3.1 Incremental versus Total Cash Flow

Incremental cash flow can differ from total cash flow for a variety of reasons. The following are some of them.

Cannibalization

When Coca-Cola introduced Diet Coke, it quickly became the best-selling diet drink in the United States. The success was not total, however, because Diet Coke caused the sales of Tab, Coke's other diet cola, to drop an estimated 25%. Similarly, a substantial number of Maxwell House Instant coffee drinkers switched to Maxim after Maxwell House introduced its new freeze-dried coffee.

These examples illustrate the phenomenon known as **cannibalization**, a new product taking sales away from the firm's existing products. Cannibalization also occurs when a firm builds a plant overseas and winds up substituting foreign production for parent company exports. To the extent that sales of a new product or plant just replace other corporate sales, the new project's estimated profits must be reduced by the earnings on the lost sales.

Exhibit 3.1 shows the profit consequences of product cannibalism for a firm that introduces a new product. This firm has a product, A, expected to generate sales of 800,000 units annually. Marketing and administrative costs are projected at $700,000. At a $5.00 per unit price and a $3.00 per unit variable cost, forecasted sales of A are $4 million with a profit of $900,000 (assuming there are no other costs).

The firm introduces a new product, B, that satisfies several, but not all, buyer requirements met by the existing product in addition to several other needs. Product B is priced at $4.00 per unit with a $2.50 per unit variable cost. Marketing and administrative expenses associated with B are projected to be $1 million. The lower price and modified product benefits are expected to result in annual sales for B of 1.2 million units. On the basis of these forecasts, B's profits are projected at $800,000. But the incremental profit associated with the launch of product B turns out to be much less. The reason is that product B cannibalizes 300,000 units of product A. The lost profits on these lost sales are $600,000 ($2.00 × 300,000). The incremental analysis appears in the final column. It reveals that the incremental profit from product B is only $200,000, 25% of what it appears to be without considering cannibalization's detrimental effects.

The previous examples notwithstanding, it is often difficult to assess the true magnitude of cannibalization because of the need to determine what would have happened to sales in the absence of the new product introduction. Consider the case of Maxim. At the same time that Maxwell House introduced Maxim, Nestle was readying its Taster's Choice line of freeze-dried coffee. If Maxwell House had not brought out Maxim, it might have lost Maxwell House Instant sales anyway. But instead of losing these sales to

EXHIBIT 3.1 An Example of Product Cannibalization

	Before Introduction of Product B	After Introduction of Product B			
	Product A Alone	Product A +	Product B =	Products A + B	Incremental Amount
Forecast unit sales	800,000	500,000	1,200,000	1,700,000	900,000
Source of volume					
New customers			700,000	700,000	700,000
Competitors' customers			200,000	200,000	200,000
Cannibalized customers			300,000	300,000	300,000
Repeat customers	800,000	500,000		500,000	–300,000
Total	800,000	500,000	1,200,000	1,700,000	900,000
Unit price	$5.00	$5.00	$4.00		
Total revenue	$4,000,000	$2,500,000	$4,800,000	$7,300,000	$3,300,000
Unit cost	$3.00	$3.00	$2.50		
Total variable cost	$2,400,000	$1,500,000	$3,000,000	$4,500,000	$2,100,000
Marketing and administrative expenses	700,000	700,000	1,000,000	1,700,000	1,000,000
Profit before tax	$900,000	$300,000	$800,000	$1,100,000	$200,000

Maxim, it would have lost them to Taster's Choice. Similarly, if the firm in the previous example had not introduced product B, one of its rivals might have done so and cost the firm sales of A. The *incremental* effect of cannibalization—which is the relevant measure for capital-budgeting purposes—equals the lost profit on lost sales *that would not otherwise have been lost* had the new product not been introduced. Those sales that would have been lost anyway should not be counted a casualty of cannibalization.

BOX 3.1

APPLICATION: GENERAL ELECTRIC CANNIBALIZES ITS CAT SCANNER

In the early 1980s, General Electric initially ignored the emerging magnetic resonance imaging (MRI) technology for medical diagnosis, largely because MRI would have cannibalized the market for GE's existing CAT scanners. Indeed, projected cannibalization was sufficiently extensive so that a DCF analysis showed a negative NPV for the introduction of MRI. However, senior management overruled the DCF analysis because it realized that if GE did not cannibalize its CAT scanners, someone else was going to.

Sales Creation

ICI, a British chemical company, significantly expanded its exports to Europe after investing in European production facilities that gave it a strong local market position in several product lines. Similarly, Ford's auto plants in England use parts made by its U.S. plants, parts that would not otherwise be sold if Ford's English plants were abandoned. On another note, Compaq Computer launched its low-priced Prolinea line of computers in the hope that its customers would later trade up to its higher-priced Deskpro machines.

In all three cases, an investment created or was expected to create additional sales for other products. This is the opposite of cannibalization. In calculating the project's cash flows, the additional sales and associated incremental cash flows should be attributed to the project.

Opportunity Cost

Suppose Texas Instruments (TI) decides to build a new plant outside Dallas on some land it bought 10 years ago. TI must include the cost of the land in calculating the value of undertaking the project. And this cost must be based on the current market value of the land, not the price TI paid 10 years ago. The reason is that if it were not used in this project, TI could sell the land and realize its current price.

Similarly, if ExxonMobil is calculating the profitability of building a new oil refinery, it must price the petroleum feedstock at the market price of oil, even if it is processing its own oil. Underpricing sales of its oil is equivalent to subsidizing the refinery by taxing oil production. This will make the refinery seem more profitable and oil operations less profitable than they really are. Although the profit effects of oil mispricing wash out for the company as a whole, the resulting profit distortions may lead ExxonMobil to invest in negative NPV refinery projects and pass up positive NPV oil production projects. This reasoning undercuts the argument by Du Pont at the time it acquired Conoco, a major oil firm, that its chemical operations would benefit from the acquisition by having access to lower-cost oil in the event that oil prices jumped again.

These examples demonstrate a more general rule. Project costs must include the true economic cost of any resource required for the project, regardless of whether the firm already owns the resource or has to go out and acquire it. This true cost is the **opportunity cost**, the cash the asset could generate for the firm should it be sold or put to some other productive use. It would be foolish for a jeweler who bought gold at $35 an ounce and made it into jewelry to sell that jewelry based on $35-an-ounce gold if the price of gold had risen to $400 an ounce. So too it would be foolish to value an asset used in a project at other than its opportunity cost, regardless of how much cash changes hands.

Sunk Costs

In 1976, the Army Corps of Engineers was trying to persuade the state of Florida that work should be resumed on a 110-mile barge canal across north central Florida. One of the arguments the corps used to justify spending an additional $300 million was that the $100 million already spent on the canal would be wasted if the project were to be abandoned. Similarly, when Lockheed was seeking federal loan guarantees to continue work on its ill-fated L-1011 Tri Star jet, its officials argued that if the project were abandoned, the $1 billion already spent on the plane would be lost.

These situations illustrate the **sunk cost fallacy**, the idea that past expenditures on a project should influence the decision whether to continue or terminate the project. Instead, that decision should be based on *future* costs and benefits alone. A bad project is a bad project, whether you have already sunk $1 or $1 billion into it. For example, the fact that you have already sunk $1 million into a dry hole searching for oil does not justify continued drilling in that spot if there's little probability of finding oil there. To think otherwise leads to a tendency to "throw good money after bad."

Despite the logic of looking only at future project benefits and costs, managers who commit themselves to a project often find it difficult to cut their losses, possibly because this public admission of failure would hurt their career possibilities. The market seems to be aware of the widespread tendency of managers to operate losing ventures in the hope that they will somehow become economically viable. Thus, when Lockheed finally announced its decision to terminate its Tri Star jet (in December 1981), the price of Lockheed stock jumped 18%. This was the investment community's way of expressing its relief that the cash hemorrhage was ending at last.

Transfer Pricing

By raising the price at which a proposed Navistar plant in Illinois will sell engines to its German subsidiary, Navistar can increase the apparent profitability of the new plant, but at the expense of its German affiliate. Similarly, if IBM lowers the price at which its computer divisions buy chips from its semiconductor division, IBM's new chip plant will show a decline in profitability, and the computer divisions' profits will rise.

It is evident from these examples that the prices at which goods and services are traded within a company, known as **transfer prices**, can significantly distort the profitability of a proposed investment. Where possible, the prices used to evaluate project inputs or outputs should be market prices, as in the ExxonMobil refinery example. If no market exists for the product, then the firm must evaluate the project on the basis of the cost savings or additional profits to it of going ahead with the project. For example, when Atari decided to switch most of its production to Asia, its decision was based solely on the cost savings provided by the new production facilities. This was the correct approach to use because the stated revenues generated by the project were meaningless, an artifact of the transfer prices used in selling its output back to Atari in the United States.

Transfer price adjustments are often made to reduce taxes. For example, while oil industry earnings suffered from declining energy prices in 1985, the pipeline subsidiaries of Exxon, Standard Oil, Atlantic Richfield, and British Petroleum gushed profits, earning an average return on sales of 30.5%, the highest for any industry on the Fortune Service 500 list. (Their average return on equity was 97.4%, the highest by far of any industry.) The four companies are the principal owners of the 800-mile Trans Alaska Pipeline System (TAPS), built in the 1970s to bring oil south from Prudhoe Bay to the ice-free port of Valdez for loading into tankers.

The pipeline subsidiaries charge their oil-producing parents around $6 a barrel to ship crude through TAPS, more than enough to pay interest on the bonds used to finance the pipeline, income taxes, and pipeline servicing costs. Even after allowing for the line's economic depreciation, it is estimated that TAPS turns a healthy profit of $1.85 per barrel.

Why does this line pump money? Alaskan officials suspect that the oil companies allow their pipeline subsidiaries to charge excessive shipping rates in order to avoid paying production royalties to the state. Royalties are calculated as a percent of the market value of the oil less transportation costs, and so a higher pipeline rate reduces the royalties the state can assess. If the oil companies really are manipulating transfer prices so as to reduce their taxes, then the profits of the pipeline alone will give a misleading picture of the value contributed by the pipeline to its parent companies.

Allocated Overhead

Often companies will charge projects for various overhead items like legal counsel, power, lighting, heat, rent, research and development, headquarters staff, management costs, and the like. From an economic standpoint, the project should be charged only for the additional expenditures that can be attributed to the project; those overhead expenses that are not affected by the project should not be included when estimating project cash flows.

Getting the Base Case Right

In general, a project's incremental cash flows can be found only by subtracting worldwide corporate cash flows without the investment—the **base case**—from postinvestment corporate cash flows. To come up with a realistic base case, and thus a reasonable estimate of incremental cash flows, the key question that managers must ask is, "What will happen if we *do not* make this investment?" Failure to heed this question led General Motors during the 1970s to slight investment in small cars despite the Japanese challenge; small cars looked less profitable than GM's then current mix of cars. As a result, Toyota, Nissan, and other Japanese automakers were able to expand and eventually threaten GM's base business. Similarly, many American companies—like Kodak and Zenith—that thought overseas expansion too risky or unattractive today find their domestic competitive positions eroding. They did not adequately consider the consequences of *not* building a strong global position.

The critical error made by these and other companies was to ignore competitor behavior and assume that the base case was the status quo. But in a competitive world economy, the least likely future scenario is the status quo. A company that opts not to come out with a new product because it is afraid that the product will cannibalize its existing product line is most likely leaving a profitable niche for some other company to exploit. Sales will be lost anyway, but now they will be lost to a competitor. Similarly, a company that chooses not to invest in a new process technology because it calculates that the higher quality is not worth the added cost may discover that it is losing sales to competitors who have made the investment. In a competitive market, the rule is simple: *If you must be the victim of a cannibal, make sure the cannibal is a member of your family.*

BOX 3.2

APPLICATION: IBM TRIES NOT TO CANNIBALIZE ITS MAINFRAMES

For many years, IBM was the king of computers, selling mainframes at huge profit margins. The advent of the microprocessor, and the powerful personal computers and workstations it helped create, changed all that, turning computer hardware into a low-margin commodity product. Instead of figuring out how to compete in this new world, however, IBM tried to protect its profitable mainframe business by slowing down or axing products that were even vaguely competitive with its mainframes. For example, in the mid-1970s, IBM researchers pioneered reduced instruction-set computing, or RISC, a revolutionary technology for designing faster computers. But the advance was not rushed into products, largely because it was seen as a menace to IBM's mainframe business. Competitors like Sun Microsystems, Dell Computers, Compaq, and Hewlett-Packard, with no mainframe business of their own to protect, took advantage of IBM's inertia by running rings around it in the personal computer and workstation markets (Sun harnessed RISC technology to now lead in RISC-based workstations), stealing sales from its mainframe business anyway. By trying so hard not to cannibalize its mainframes, IBM lost sales and profits to its competitors.

In contrast to IBM, Intel is a model cannibal. Once threatened by copycats cloning its popular 80386 chip, the semiconductor giant responded aggressively. Intel slashed prices, undercutting the cloners, then rolled out a better generation of chips that would eventually make its old lines obsolete. According to one analyst, "Intel said to competitors: 'You'd better run as fast as we are, because we're destroying the pavement behind us as we move along.' They plundered and burned the 386 market. Trashed it. Destroyed it."[1]

Accounting for Intangible Benefits

Related to the choice of an incorrect base case is the problem of incorporating intangible benefits in the capital-budgeting process. Intangibles like better quality, faster time to market, quicker and less error-prone order processing, and higher customer satisfaction can have a very tangible impact on corporate cash flows, even if they cannot be measured precisely. Similarly, many investments provide intangible benefits in the form of valuable learning experiences and a broader knowledge base. For example, investing in foreign markets can sharpen competitive skills: It exposes companies to tough foreign competition; it enables them to size up new products being developed overseas and figure out how to compete with them before these products show up in the home market; and it can aid in tracking emerging technologies that can be transferred back home. Adopting practices, products, and technologies discovered overseas can improve a company's competitive position worldwide.

---

[1]Quoted in Torres, C. "For Technology Winners, Seek Out the 'Cannibals'." *Wall Street Journal*, August 31, 1992, p. C1.

BOX 3.3

APPLICATION: INTANGIBLE BENEFITS FROM INVESTING IN JAPAN

The prospect of investing in Japan scares many foreign companies. Real estate is prohibitively expensive. Customers are extraordinarily demanding. The government bureaucracy can seem impenetrable at times. And Japanese competitors fiercely protect their home market.

But an investment in Japanese operations provides a variety of intangible benefits. More companies are realizing that to compete effectively elsewhere, they must first compete in the toughest market of all: Japan. What they learn in the process—from meeting the stringent standards of Japanese customers and battling a dozen relentless Japanese rivals—is invaluable and will possibly make the difference between survival and extinction. At the same time, operating in Japan helps a company like IBM keep up the pressure on some of its most potent global competitors in their home market. A position in the Japanese market also gives a company an early look at new products and technologies originating in Japan, enabling it to quickly pick up and transfer back to the United States, information on Japanese advances in manufacturing technology and product development, and monitoring changes in the Japanese market helps boost sales there as well.

Although the principle of incremental analysis is a simple one to state, its rigorous application is a tortuous undertaking. However, this rule at least points in the right direction those executives responsible for estimating cash flows. Moreover, when estimation shortcuts or simplifications are made, it provides those responsible with some idea of what they are doing and how far they are straying from a thorough analysis.

While some facets of capital budgeting require insight and judgment, others simply represent the execution of good technique. In the next two sections, we will apply the guidelines for identifying relevant project cash flows by looking at the two most frequently encountered issues in capital budgeting: the replacement problem and a new product introduction.

3.2 The Replacement Problem

As the name suggests, this class of investments represents a situation where the firm is looking at replacing an existing piece of equipment with a new piece of equipment. The motivation for these projects is typically either cost reduction or quality improvement (or both). To illustrate the cash flow patterns for an equipment replacement, consider the following example. Quantum Systems Co. is thinking about replacing an extrusion press purchased five years ago for $1,000,000. The press, which is used in the manufacture of semiconductors, is being depreciated on a straight-line basis over a 10-year life to a salvage value of zero. Annual depreciation is therefore $100,000, and the current book value of the old machine is $500,000.

The replacement extrusion press was developed by the company at a cost of $750,000. It would cost $2,000,000 to have it built and installed and would have a life of

EXHIBIT 3.2 Data on Quantum Systems' Investment in a New Extrusion Press

	Old Machine	New Machine
Cost of machine	$1,000,000	$2,000,000
Development cost		$750,000
Straight-line depreciation	10 years	5 years
Annual depreciation charge	$100,000	$300,000
Depreciated value	$500,000	–
Salvage value	?	$500,000
Marginal tax rate	35%	35%
Additional sales		$150,000
Net increase in working capital		$45,000

five years. The estimated salvage value at the end of five years is $500,000. For ease in calculation, we assume that depreciation will be straight-line over the five-year period with an estimated $500,000 salvage value. Thus, the annual depreciation charge would be ($2,000,000 – $500,000)/5 = $300,000.[2] Quantum Systems' marginal tax rate is 35%, equal to the top federal corporate tax rate. These data are summarized in Exhibit 3.2.

The new extrusion press is expected to be faster and more productive, boosting sales by about $150,000 annually. Quantum Systems estimates that its net working-capital-to-sales ratio is approximately 30%. This means the firm must invest an additional 0.30 × $150,000 = $45,000 in working capital if it decides to replace its old machine. The decision before management is whether to sell the existing extrusion press and purchase the new one.

ESTIMATING THE INITIAL INVESTMENT

The first order of business is to calculate the project's initial investment, which is the project's net cash outlay. This number, which includes any opportunity costs associated with undertaking the project, consists of four separate items:

1. *The cost of acquiring and placing into service the necessary assets.* The installed cost of the new press is given at $2,000,000. In practice, this figure is not "handed" to an analyst on a silver platter; instead, it may be necessary to pull together the machine's purchase price, estimated freight costs (if not included in the equipment's invoice price), and all estimated installation expenses. The sum of these items generally, net of the cost of land, serves as the basis for calculating depreciation and any investment tax credit (which is discussed later in this chapter).

2. *The necessary increase in working capital.* A project that boosts sales usually requires additional investments in accounts receivable, work-in-process and finished goods inventory, and cash on hand. These working capital items are offset to a certain extent by an automatic increase in accounts payable to the suppliers of labor, raw materials, components, and other inputs to the production process. The added investment in working capital is the difference between the additional working capital assets and additional noninterest-bearing working

---

[2]Later on, we shall adjust the depreciation charges to conform to current IRS regulations.

capital liabilities like accounts payable and taxes payable (also known as spontaneously generated liabilities) associated with the investment.

3. *The net proceeds from the sale of existing assets in the case of a replacement decision.* For example, when an airline decides to replace its current fleet of Boeing 747s with Boeing 777s, its net investment in the 777s will be reduced by the money it gets from the sale of its 747s.

4. *The tax effects associated with the sale of existing assets and their replacement with new assets.* This includes any tax write-offs, capital gains taxes, taxes on depreciation recapture, and investment tax credits.

On the basis of the data already presented, the net investment for Quantum in items 1 and 2 on the four-part list of initial investments is $2,045,000, the $2 million cost of the new press and the $45,000 in incremental working capital. The $750,000 investment in developing the machine is a sunk cost and not an incremental cash flow.

Estimating items 3 and 4 is more difficult. The net proceeds from the sale of the existing extrusion press depend on the tax treatment of these proceeds. Four possible situations can arise:

1. *The asset is sold for its book value.* If the firm sells the old extrusion press for its book value of $500,000, it will show neither a gain nor a loss on the sale, and so the proceeds will not be taxed. The net cash inflow on the sale of the machine in this case is $500,000.

2. *The asset is sold for less than its book value.* Suppose the old machine is sold for $400,000 – $100,000 less than its book value. In this case, the firm can write off the $100,000 loss. This reduces Quantum Systems' corporate taxes by an amount equal to the loss times its marginal tax rate, or $35,000 ($100,000 × 0.35). The reduction in taxes is treated as a cash inflow. The resulting net cash inflow from the sale is $435,000 ($400,000 + $35,000).

3. *The asset is sold for more than its book value but less than the initial purchase price.* Suppose the company sells the old machine for $700,000, $200,000 above its book value. Here, the excess over book value is considered to be a recapture of depreciation and so is taxed as ordinary income. This results in an increase in taxes equal to the amount of the gain times the marginal tax rate, or $70,000 ($200,000 × 0.35). The net cash inflow from the sale in this case is $630,000 ($700,000 – $70,000).

4. *The asset is sold for more than its original purchase price.* Suppose Quantum Systems manages to sell its old machine for $1,100,000. The amount by which the selling price exceeds the original purchase price, which is $100,000 in this case, is treated as a capital gain and is assumed to be taxed at a rate of 35%. The remaining gain over book value of $500,000 is considered a recapture of depreciation and is taxed at the firm's marginal income tax rate, also 35%. Thus, the total tax cost of this sale—assuming the capital gains rate is the same as the ordinary income rate, which it has not been historically—is $210,000 ($100,000 × 0.35 + $500,000 × 0.35). Net proceeds in this instance are $890,000 ($1,100,000 – $210,000).[3]

---

[3]Current federal tax law applies the same 35% tax rate to capital gains and ordinary income, but in the past, capital gains were ordinarily taxed at a substantially lower rate.

EXHIBIT 3.3 Initial Cost of New Extrusion Press: Four Scenarios

Case	1	2	3	4
Cost of new machine	$2,000,000	$2,000,000	$2,000,000	$2,000,000
+ Increase in working capital	45,000	45,000	45,000	45,000
− Sales price of old machine	500,000	400,000	700,000	1,100,000
= Pretax investment	$1,545,000	$1,645,000	$1,345,000	$945,000
+ Tax on proceeds of old machine	0	−35,000	70,000	210,000
= Initial cost of new machine	$1,545,000	$1,610,000	$1,415,000	$1,155,000

Exhibit 3.3 summarizes all the cost factors associated with replacing the old extrusion press with a new machine. The net investment cost — also called the initial or incremental cost — can vary from $1,155,000 to $1,610,000, depending on the net proceeds from the sale of the old machine.

Investment Tax Credit

An additional tax factor that will influence the size of the initial investment is the presence of an **investment tax credit** (ITC). The ITC allows a company to reduce its taxes by an amount equal to a specified percentage of the cost of qualifying new property placed into service. For example, under the Accelerated Cost Recovery System (ACRS) depreciation rules detailed in the Economic Recovery Tax Act of 1981, firms received a 10% tax credit for qualifying property having an ACRS recovery period of at least five years.

Although the ITC is gone for now, there is political pressure to resurrect it (between 1962 and 2002, the ITC slipped in and out of the tax code seven times). To demonstrate how to incorporate an ITC, Exhibit 3.4 assumes that there is a 10% ITC. This means that Quantum Systems will receive an ITC on its extrusion press equal to 10% of $2 million, or $200,000. This lowers the effective net investment in the new machine to between $955,000 and $1,410,000.

Multiyear Investments

Although we have been assuming that the initial investment occurs in the first year of the project, this is not necessarily the case. Consider the construction of a new factory. At time 0, the firm spends $18 million to acquire the land and buy building materials. In year 1, the plant is built at a cost of $7 million, and during the second year, the equipment

EXHIBIT 3.4 Initial Cost of New Extrusion Press with an ITC: Four Scenarios

Case	1	2	3	4
Initial cost of new machine with no ITC	$1,545,000	$1,610,000	$1,415,000	$1,155,000
− Investment tax credit	200,000	200,000	200,000	200,000
= Initial cost of new machine with ITC	$1,345,000	$1,410,000	$1,215,000	$955,000

for the plant is bought and installed at a total cost of $20 million. Assuming a cost of capital equal to 10%, the total initial outlay of $45 million will result in a present value cost of $40.9 million calculated as follows:

Year	Cost (millions)	×	Present Value Factor (10%)	=	Present Value (millions)
0	$18		1.000		$18.0
1	7		0.909		6.4
2	20		0.826		16.5
			Total		$40.9

Stretching out the investment reduces the present value of the initial cost; however, it also delays the receipt of project cash inflows. The net result is typically a reduction in the project NPV.

ESTIMATING OPERATING CASH FLOWS

Investors acquire the capital necessary to make the initial investment by reducing current consumption. They do this to consume more in the future. What matters to investors, therefore, are the incremental cash flows generated by the project. Apart from the terminal value of the project, the incremental after-tax cash flows result from the additional revenues, labor and/or material savings, energy cost reductions, and increased selling expenses associated with the project. These are the **operating cash flows** associated with the new investment, equal to the sum of the net income after tax plus any noncash costs such as depreciation and amortization of goodwill plus or minus any nonrevenue or nonexpense cash items such as a change in the level of working capital.[4] This leads to the following definition of the incremental operating cash flow OCF:

$$\begin{matrix} \text{Incremental} \\ \text{operating} \\ \text{cash flow} \end{matrix} = \text{Change in} \left(\begin{matrix} \text{After-tax} \\ \text{income} \end{matrix} + \text{Depreciation} - \begin{matrix} \text{Working} \\ \text{capital} \end{matrix} \right) \quad (3.1)$$

$$\Delta OCF = (\Delta REV - \Delta COST - \Delta DEP)(1 - \Delta TAX) + \Delta DEP - \Delta WC$$

where ΔREV is the change in revenues, $\Delta COST$ is the change in operating costs, ΔDEP is the change in depreciation, ΔWC is the change in working capital, and ΔTAX is the marginal income tax rate faced by the firm. All these changes are relative to the no-investment situation. Amortization of goodwill does not appear in Equation 3.1 because it is not tax deductible.

---

[4]The net income figure ignores the effects of financing costs. Alternatively, it assumes that the investment is 100% equity financed. As is shown later in this section, the required rate of return already incorporates the effects of financing charges, and so it is appropriate to ignore them in calculating operating cash flows.

Let us refer again to the Quantum Systems Co. example. The new extrusion press is expected to increase revenue by $150,000 annually. It will also reduce annual operating expenses by $180,000 because it requires only one operator instead of two, is more energy efficient, and will reduce the defect rate. In year 1, the annual depreciation charge will rise by $300,000 because depreciation for the new machine is $400,000 compared with annual depreciation of $100,000 for the old machine. According to Equation 3.1, this should result in incremental operating cash flow for year 1 of:

$$\Delta OCF = (\$150,000 + \$180,000 - \$300,000)(1 - 0.35) + \$300,000$$
$$= \$319,500$$

This operating cash flow will change from year to year in line with changes in revenue, operating costs, working capital requirements, depreciation, and the marginal tax rate. Under present assumptions, all of these parameters are assumed to remain constant except for the depreciation charge, which under current tax law will vary from year to year.

The incremental operating cash flow for year 1 can also be calculated by developing an income statement for Quantum:

	Before	After	Increments	Cash Flows
Sales	$5,000,000	$5,150,000	$150,000	+$150,000
Costs	4,000,000	3,820,000	−180,000	+180,000
Depreciation	500,000	800,000	300,000	—
Profit before tax	$500,000	$530,000	$30,000	—
Tax @ 35%	175,000	185,500	10,500	−10,500
Profit after tax	$325,000	$344,500	$19,500	—
Depreciation	500,000	800,000	300,000	—
Cash flow	$825,000	$1,144,500	$319,500	+$319,500

As before, the incremental operating cash flow is estimated to be $319,500. The incremental working capital associated with the new press is already reflected in the amount of the initial investment. To include it again here would be double counting.

Depreciation

Because depreciation is a noncash charge, its only significance lies in the fact that it reduces or *shields* taxable income and, therefore, reduces taxes. The value of the *tax shield* provided by a depreciation charge of DEP_t in year t equals $DEP_t \times TAX$, where TAX is the firm's marginal income tax rate.

Under current IRS regulations, explained at greater length in Appendix 3A, the depreciation charge for each year of the press's five-year life is set out in Exhibit 3.5.[5]

---

[5]Under current regulations, equipment is assumed to be placed in service in mid-year. Hence, a "five-year depreciation period," as in this case, actually means that depreciation deductions are taken over six taxable years. In addition, current law ignores the salvage value in computing depreciation. Thus, if Quantum Systems buys the new press for $2 million, it will have a depreciable basis of $2 million.

EXHIBIT 3.5 Year-by-Year Depreciation Tax Shield Under MACRS

Year	Depreciation Base	× Depreciation Factor =	Depreciation Write-off	× Marginal Tax Rate =	Depreciation Tax Shield
1	2,000,000	0.2	400,000	0.35	140,000
2	2,000,000	0.32	640,000	0.35	224,000
3	2,000,000	0.192	384,000	0.35	134,400
4	2,000,000	0.1152	230,400	0.35	80,640
5	2,000,000	0.1152	230,400	0.35	80,640
6	2,000,000	0.0576	115,200	0.35	40,320
		Totals	2,000,000 ×	0.35 =	700,000

Year	Depreciation Tax Shield −	Lost Depreciation Write-off =	Incremental Tax Shield
1	140,000	35,000	105,000
2	224,000	35,000	189,000
3	134,400	35,000	99,400
4	80,640	35,000	45,640
5	80,640	35,000	45,640
6	40,320	—	40,320
Totals	700,000	175,000	525,000

The value of the annual depreciation tax shield, given an assumed marginal corporate tax rate of 35%, is $0.35DEP_t$. These values are shown in Exhibit 3.5. For purposes of investment analysis, however, what really matters is the *incremental* depreciation tax shield. Because Quantum Systems loses $100,000 in annual depreciation when the old machine is scrapped, incremental depreciation in each of the first five years is actually $100,000 less than the calculations indicate. As a result, the annual net tax shield provided by the new machine is $35,000 ($100,000 × 0.35) less than the gross tax shield it provides, or $0.35DEP_t − \$35,000$.

If it buys the new machine, Quantum Systems will have annual incremental after-tax revenue plus cost reductions equal to $214,500 [($150,000 + $180,000) × (1 − 0.35)]. Assuming, as before, that working capital requirements and the marginal tax rate do not change over time, its incremental operating cash flow in year t (see Equation 3.1) will be

$$\$214,500 + 0.35\Delta DEP_t$$

where ΔDEP_t is the incremental depreciation charge in year t and $0.35\Delta DEP_t$ is the value of the incremental depreciation tax shield provided by the new machine. The incremental operating cash flows for Quantum Systems' new machine are presented in Exhibit 3.6.

Financing Costs

In estimating the operating cash flows, we left out financing costs. These costs are the payments, usually in the form of dividends and interest, to those who provided the

EXHIBIT 3.6 Calculation of Incremental Operating Cash Flows for Extrusion Press

Year	Incremental Revenues and Cost Reduction (after tax)	+	Incremental Depreciation Tax Shield	=	Incremental Operating Cash Flow
1	214,500		105,000		319,500
2	214,500		189,000		403,500
3	214,500		99,400		313,900
4	214,500		45,640		260,140
5	214,500		45,640		260,140
6	—		40,320		40,320

funds to finance the initial investment. The reason for this omission is that the required rate of return or cost of capital for the project already incorporates the cost of these funds; the higher the cost of funds for the project is, the higher the rate used to discount project cash flows will be. Subtracting interest charges and dividend payments from projected cash flows and then discounting these cash flows at the appropriate rate would be equivalent to double counting the financing costs.

At this stage of the investment analysis, we treat the project as if it were all-equity financed, assuming all cash outflows are provided by the shareholders and all cash inflows accrue to them. Other interactions between the financing and investment decisions, like the tax shield provided by interest payments, may affect the estimate of project cash flows (see Chapter 4).

ESTIMATING THE TERMINAL VALUE

A major component of the **terminal value** of the extrusion press investment is its salvage value, net of any taxes owed on the sale. The tax gains or losses on the sale would be determined in a manner similar to the tax calculations associated with the sale of the old machine as described in the section on the initial investment. For other projects, like a new product introduction, the terminal value would be based on the present value of future income expected to be earned by the product (i.e., its market value). In general, the terminal value of any asset is equal to the present value of the future cash flows generated by the asset, whether it be the scrap value of the extrusion press or the revenue produced by a product.

In addition, it is assumed that any working capital investment will be recaptured at the termination of the project. In the case of Quantum Systems' investment in the new extrusion press, this would be $45,000. The terminal value would also have to include any additional expenses required to meet environmental regulations. For example, it may cost several hundred million dollars to shut down a nuclear reactor once its useful life is over.

Suppose that the salvage value of the new extrusion press at the end of the five-year period is estimated to be $500,000, as compared with its book value of $115,200, giving rise to a taxable gain of $384,800 ($500,000 − $115,200). Assuming that the machine will be sold at that time, taxes owed on this salvage value will equal $134,680 ($384,800 × 0.35). This leaves a terminal value for the extrusion press replacement project of $410,320, the $365,320 after-tax salvage value plus the recapture of $45,000 in working capital.

Break-Even Analysis

One way to incorporate terminal value in a project analysis is to find the break-even terminal value TERM* that would just yield a zero NPV project. A terminal value in excess of TERM* would then result in a positive NPV project. Specifically, for a project with a life of n years and a discount rate of k, let H be the project NPV with a zero terminal value. If $H > 0$, the terminal value will not have a life-or-death impact on the project; in this case, the project is acceptable even with a terminal value of 0. If $H < 0$, however, then TERM* is the solution to

$$H + \frac{TERM^*}{(1+k)^n} = 0$$

or

$$TERM^* = -H(1+k)^n \qquad (3.2)$$

For example, suppose that a project's NPV—based on a required return of 12%, a 10-year life, and a terminal value of zero—is estimated at –$350,000. According to Equation 3.2, the terminal value must exceed $350,000(1.12)^{10} = $1,087,047$ for the project to be acceptable. In Section 3.3, we discuss how one might go about estimating the terminal value of a project that is expected to generate cash flows beyond the evaluation period.

CALCULATING THE PROJECT NET PRESENT VALUE

Assuming that Quantum Systems' old machine can be sold for $700,000 and that depreciation is calculated according to current tax regulations, the cash flows associated with the new machine, aside from the terminal value, are set forth in Exhibit 3.7. The calculation of the initial cash outflow of $1,415,000 is shown in Exhibit 3.3, Case 3. The operating cash flows for years 1–5 are taken from Exhibit 3.6. Exhibit 3.7 also contains the present values of these cash flows based on a discount rate of 15%. The result is a project NPV, assuming a zero terminal value, of –$347,604.

From Equation 3.2, this means that the terminal value must be greater than $347,604(1.15)^5 = $699,155$ for the new machine to have a positive NPV. We subtract the $45,000 in recaptured working capital, which leaves a required after-tax salvage value (or sale price) of $654,156. In other words,

$$\frac{\text{Sale}}{\text{price}} - \frac{\text{tax on}}{\text{sale}} = \frac{\text{Sale}}{\text{price}} - \left(\frac{\text{Sale}}{\text{price}} - \frac{\text{book}}{\text{value}}\right) \times \frac{\text{tax}}{\text{rate}} = \$654,156$$

EXHIBIT 3.7 Project Cash Flows and Their Present Values

Year	Cash Flow	+	Present Value Factor (@ 15%)	=	Present Value
0	−1,415,000		1.0000		−1,415,000
1	319,500		0.8696		277,826
2	403,500		0.7561		305,104
3	313,900		0.6575		206,394
4	260,140		0.5718		148,736
5	260,140		0.4972		129,336
			Total		−347,604

Solving this equation, given an ending book value of $115,200, yields a sale price of $944,366. In other words, the value of the new machine at the end of five years must exceed $944,366 to make it worthwhile for Quantum Systems to replace its old machine today. This high required salvage value—almost twice the expected salvage value of $500,000—makes it doubtful that the project is worth undertaking. However, as shown in Appendix 3B, this conclusion may be reversed once inflation is accounted for.

3.3 The New Product Introduction Decision

The process of estimating cash flows for replacement projects can be technically intricate given the complexities of tax law relating to depreciation schedules and the like. However, the critical elements of the analysis—the project's cost and estimated savings—can often be determined accurately by a capable manufacturing engineer. Not so with a new product introduction. Depending on whether the "new product" is a simple extension of an existing product or a true product innovation, estimates of cash flows are subject to high degrees of uncertainty.

To illustrate the challenges associated with a new product introduction, consider the following situation: The Smith Corporation is considering a major new product introduction. As a newly hired financial analyst, you have been given the estimates in Exhibit 3.8 to begin your evaluation. You have been told that the project will require capital equipment with an installed cost of $6 million. During year 7, the plant will be dismantled and sold for $1 million. For tax purposes, Smith will depreciate the investment on a straight-line basis to a zero salvage value. If Smith has a required return of 20%, should the new product be introduced?

The starting point for the analysis in Exhibit 3.8 is the sales forecast. This is an extremely difficult task since the marketing staff must not only estimate the number of units of the product Smith expects to sell but also its selling price. Where there is a possibility of a competitive response, these sales projections may be little more than educated guesses. The sales pattern in Exhibit 3.8 indicates a product life cycle where demand rises rapidly through year 4, and then declines until the product is eventually phased out by the end of the sixth year.

EXHIBIT 3.8 Smith Corporation New Product Financial Forecasts (in thousand $)

Period	0	1	2	3	4	5	6
Sales		500	5,500	8,000	14,000	7,000	4,000
Operating expenses		800	3,410	4,960	8,680	4,340	2,480
Product promotion	3,000	1,000					
Depreciation		1,000	1,000	1,000	1,000	1,000	1,000
Profit before taxes	−3,000	−2,300	1,090	2,040	4,320	1,660	520
Taxes @ 35%	−1,050	−805	382	714	1,512	581	182
Profit after taxes	−1,950	−1,495	709	1,326	2,808	1,079	338
Level of working capital		250	660	960	1,680	840	480

Once the sales forecast is developed, Smith can proceed with the tasks of identifying (1) the capital investment needed to satisfy projected demand, (2) operating costs, and (3) the project's working capital needs. This accounting-based financial forecast can then be used to identify relevant cash flows and calculate the project's NPV as shown in Exhibit 3.9.

Exhibit 3.9 displays the components of the cash flows to focus attention on the proper handling of the project's working capital requirements. The project's capital equipment needs are relatively straightforward. At time zero, Smith puts the equipment in place with an installed cost of $6 million. During year 7, after it is no longer needed to manufacture the new product, the equipment is expected to be dismantled and sold for $1,000,000. Since the equipment has been depreciated to a book value of zero, Smith will have a taxable gain of $1 million. If Smith's tax rate is 35%, taxes on that gain will be $350,000. The $650,000 cash inflow in year 7 is the difference between the $1,000,000 cash proceeds from the equipment sale, and taxes of $350,000 on the book gain.

EXHIBIT 3.9 Smith Corporation Summary of Cash Flows for New Product Introduction (in thousand $)

Year	Capital Equipment	Profit After Tax + Depreciation	Working Capital	Total Cash Flow	Present Value @ 20%
0	−6,000	−1,950		−7,950	−7,950
1	—	−495	−250	−745	−621
2	—	1,709	−410	1,299	902
3	—	2,326	−300	2,026	1,172
4	—	3,808	−720	3,088	1,489
5	—	2,079	840	2,919	1,173
6	—	1,338	360	1,698	569
7	650	—	480	1,130	315
				NPV =	−2,950

The second column takes into account the fact that while depreciation may be an expense for accounting purposes, it does not represent an expenditure of cash. Adding back depreciation to profit after taxes allows us to adjust the accounting data in Exhibit 3.8 to ultimately arrive at cash flow from operations.

The third column highlights working capital flows. The last line in Exhibit 3.8 indicates the level of working capital (i.e., accounts receivable plus inventories less accounts payable) to support the projected level of sales. In year 1, once Smith begins generating sales, working capital needs rise to $250,000. Since an increase in working capital is a use of cash, this is represented in Exhibit 3.9 as a cash outflow. Subsequent figures in this column represent the changes in working capital and reflect the fact that increases in working capital are a use of cash, while decreases in working capital are a source of cash. After the product's economic life, we assume (for simplicity) that the working capital of $480,000 remaining at the end of year 6 can be recovered in year 7 with no losses.

Once the components for each year are estimated, they are summed to give the total cash flows and multiplied by the appropriate present value factor to arrive at the present value of the cash flows in that year. The NPV can then be calculated by adding the present value of the cash inflows and outflows over the project's economic life. In the case of Smith's new product introduction, the negative NPV indicates that the project should be rejected.

ESTIMATING TERMINAL VALUES FOR NEW PRODUCT INTRODUCTIONS

The project being considered by the Smith Corporation was assumed to have a six-year product life cycle, after which the new product would be phased out. Terminal values in this example were simply (1) the salvage value of the equipment (after taxes), and (2) recovery of the project's working capital. However, many new products may have sales (and cash flows) beyond the initial evaluation period. In these cases, limiting the analysis to a set time period may seriously underestimate a project's NPV. The challenge for the financial analyst is one of capturing these postevaluation period cash flows without engaging in computational overkill.

The following variation of the constant dividend growth model can be used to conveniently estimate a project's terminal value as of the end of year n (TV_n):

$$TV_n = \frac{CF_{n+1}}{k - g} \tag{3.3}$$

where CF_{n+1} is the project's forecast cash flow one year beyond the initial evaluation period, k the required rate of return for the project, and g the projected growth rate in the project's cash flows. Equation 3.3 is a flexible tool that allows us to value: (1) growing cash flow streams ($g > 0$), (2) declining cash flow streams ($g < 0$), as well as (3) no-growth situations ($g = 0$). We can also use Equation 3.3 to perform a sensitivity analysis to determine the impact of different cash flow growth rate assumptions on the project's NPV. By calculating a project's NPV for a range of values of g, the analyst can determine the minimum cash flow growth rate that will make the NPV positive. If this "threshold" value is significantly lower than management's most pessimistic estimate, acceptance of the project will produce a positive NPV.

EXHIBIT 3.10 Smith Corporation New Product #2 Financial Forecasts (in thousand $)

Period	0	1	2	3	4	5	6
Sales		2,500	10,000	16,500	21,000	23,000	25,000
Cost of goods sold		1,625	6,500	10,725	13,650	14,950	16,250
Selling/administration expenses	3,000	3,000	3,000	3,000	3,000	3,000	3,000
Depreciation		750	750	750	750	–	–
Profit before taxes	–3,000	–2,875	–250	2,025	3,600	5,050	5,750
Taxes @ 35%	–1,050	–1,006	–88	709	1,260	1,768	2,013
Profit after taxes	–1,950	–1,869	–163	1,316	2,340	3,283	3,738
Level of working capital		750	3,000	4,950	6,300	6,900	7,500

To illustrate how Equation 3.3 can be used to evaluate cash flows beyond the initial evaluation period, let us suppose that the Smith Corporation is considering introducing a second new product in a market that already has several competitors. Smith believes that its manufacturing expertise, coupled with a well-developed global distribution system for related products, will allow it to gain a foothold in this market. Capital equipment costs are modest at $3,000,000. Even though the equipment is expected to have a 20-year economic life, Smith intends to depreciate this equipment over four years to a zero salvage value. Financial forecasts for the six-year initial evaluation period are presented in Exhibit 3.10.

This new product differs in four important respects from the one described earlier: First, sales are expected to rise steadily over time, rather than rising for several years and then declining. It appears that Smith expects that this new product will have staying power in the marketplace beyond the sixth year. Second, selling and administrative expenses are continuously high. This should come as no surprise. Breaking into a market where there are entrenched competitors typically requires heavy (and continuous) promotion and advertising expenses. Third, working capital requirements are high at 30% of sales. This reflects Smith's belief that ample inventories of finished goods must be available throughout its distribution system to provide high levels of customer service. Finally, because of the high degree of risk, the project's required return has been set at 24%.

The cash flow estimates for this new product, as well as the calculation of the project's NPV for the six-year initial evaluation period is presented in Exhibit 3.11. The NPV for this period is –$4,963,000. Even if Smith were to recover all of its working capital with no losses (a heroic assumption), and sell the equipment in year 7 at its original cost of $3 million (an even more heroic assumption), the present value of these cash flows would not be enough to make the project attractive. Clearly, the acceptance of this project will turn on its terminal value, which is the value Smith assigns to the cash flows beyond year 6. The terminal value, in turn, is dependent on how rapidly Smith believes the cash flows will grow over time. Performing a sensitivity analysis on cash flow growth rates can give Smith an indication of the minimum growth that will make the project's NPV positive.

EXHIBIT 3.11 Smith Corporation Summary of Cash Flows for New Product Introduction (in thousand $)

Year	Capital Equipment	Profit After Tax + Depreciation	Working Capital	Total Cash Flow	Present Value @ 24%
0	–3,000	–1,950	–	–4,950	–4,950
1	–	–1,119	–750	–1.869	–1,507
2	–	5,88	–2,250	–1,663	–1,081
3	–	2,066	–1,950	116	61
4	–	3,090	–1,350	1,740	736
5	–	3,283	–600	2,683	915
6	–	3,738	–600	3,138	863
				NPV =	–4,963

To illustrate the mechanics of computing terminal values, suppose that Smith wants to look at the case where the projected cash flow of $3,138,000 in year 6 will grow at 5% indefinitely. Using Equation 3.3, the terminal value (TV_6) as of year 6 will be:

$$TV_6 = \frac{\$3,138,000}{0.24 - 0.05} = \$16,515,789$$

Discounting this terminal value back to the present at Smith's 24% required rate of return yields a present value of $4,543,277. Adding this to the NPV of –$4,963,000 obtained in the initial evaluation period makes the project's NPV –$419,723—still not enough to make the project acceptable.

Terminal values and project NPV's for other growth rates are presented in Exhibit 3.12. The results of this sensitivity analysis indicates that it will take a cash flow growth rate of slightly more than 6% in order to make the project's NPV positive. Since both terminal values and project NPV's are highly sensitive to growth rate assumptions, Smith should go ahead with the project if it is confident that growth will exceed 6%. Otherwise, the company might want to put the project on hold pending further analysis.

EXHIBIT 3.12 Smith Corporation Terminal Value Sensitivity Analysis (in thousand $)

Growth Rate (%)	Terminal Value	Present Value of Terminal Value	Project NPV
3	14,943	4,111	(852)
4	15,690	4,316	(647)
5	16,516	4,543	(420)
6	17,433	4,796	(167)
7	18,459	5,078	115
8	19,613	5,395	432

3.4 Biases in Project Cash Flow Estimates

Frequently, investments that look profitable on paper wind up having negative net present values. Although many of these failures can be attributed to risk, with some projects doing better than anticipated and others doing worse, several factors contribute to the tendency of accepted projects to do less well than expected. Understanding the nature of these biases can help a firm guard against them and reduce the likelihood of accepting a project because of overly optimistic cash flow forecasts.

OVEROPTIMISM

Project sponsors are generally, and understandably, optimistic about the prospects of the projects they advocate. In addition, a manager who has spent a great deal of time and effort in developing and pushing an investment proposal is typically emotionally involved in the acceptance of the project. Furthermore, project proposals are likely to reflect any tendency by senior management to pay more attention to optimistic, rather than realistic, investment forecasts.

For example, Harold Geneen, the legendary former chairman of ITT, encouraged his people to "Think big." One outcome of this obsession with size was to drive ITT and its Rayonier subsidiary to put on their rose-colored glasses and invest in a new pulp mill in Quebec, despite an awesome collection of risks. The mill that Rayonier put at the edge of a stand of timber about the size of Tennessee was the largest the company had ever built, and it incorporated technology that was unproved. It was set in a non-English-speaking land and in a physically hostile climate with which Rayonier was unfamiliar. And finally, the market for the mill's product, chemical cellulose, was uncertain. Any one of those risks might have been the undoing of the venture; as it was, they ganged up to bury it. The result was a loss for ITT's shareholders of $600 million before tax and $475 million after tax.

For all these reasons, estimates of project cash flows are likely to be biased upwards, resulting in an overstated expected NPV. Moreover, those executives whose compensation is closely tied to the volume of the assets, sales, or earnings of the operations they manage have a vested interest in empire building, even if it means undertaking unprofitable projects. Such a situation may lead to a deliberate overstatement of a project's benefits. For example, in the case of the Florida barge canal mentioned earlier (in the section on sunk costs), the Army Corps of Engineers—whose continued high-flying existence depends on coming up with an uninterrupted stream of dams, canals, and the like to work on—was trying desperately to persuade Florida officials to complete that project. The *Wall Street Journal* reported that as part of its argument, "the Corps said it heard from 'several companies' who said they could probably benefit from the canal," but it declined to identify them.[6] In addition, the Florida Administration Department's division of state planning charged that the Corps in its report "greatly underestimated costs and inflated benefits."[7] It also said the corps's figures for abandoning the project were overstated by $13 million because that was the

---

[6,7]Montgomery, J. "Corps of Engineers Will Urge Florida to Resume Work on Controversial Canal." *Wall Street Journal*, December 16, 1976, p. 15.

cost of the right of way, already paid for (and, therefore, a sunk cost) but still included in the Corps's estimate.

Many companies are also overly optimistic about their ability to maintain a competitive edge. For example, they tend to ignore the consequences of future competitive entry into their markets. Successful products are likely to attract competitors, who will drive down prices and returns. Thus, cash flow forecasts for new-product introductions should take into account the downward adjustment of prices over time. Similarly, sales projections for improved products are often too high because they ignore the likelihood and consequences of competitors retaliating with their own improved offerings.

It is also possible to receive overly pessimistic forecasts from managers who are highly risk averse, especially if they will be penalized heavily for losers. If you are aware of these biases, it may be possible to correct for them by revising upwards or downwards the project estimates, depending on whether the figures were compiled by someone known to be consistently pessimistic or optimistic. Sometimes the estimator's idiosyncrasies are unknown. In this case, the best defense against biased forecasts is to evaluate the underlying economic basis for the project. Does the project exhibit any of the characteristics that in the past have led to positive NPV projects? These characteristics are discussed in Chapter 7.

LACK OF CONSISTENCY

Natural resource projects especially are often the victims of biased cash flow estimates. Typically, this occurs in the form of projected inflation-adjusted price increases that exceed the real interest rate. For example, suppose the nominal interest rate is 12% based on the expectation of 7% inflation. The real interest rate is, therefore, 5%. Suppose that it makes sense to develop a new oil field only if the real price of oil rises by 10% (a 17% nominal increase). Any company that projects such a steep rise in the real price of oil is mistaken. Why? Because the price of oil, or any other commodity for that matter, cannot be expected to rise by more than the real interest rate plus storage costs. Otherwise, there would be an arbitrage opportunity: Buy oil, store it, and then sell it when the price has risen. In this example, because storage costs are minimal (keep the oil in the ground), the real price of oil cannot be expected to rise by more than 5% (plus a premium for risk). Of course, after the fact, the price of oil could rise by 50%. It could also decline by 50%. But because the investment decision must be made before learning what actually will transpire, these possibilities are irrelevant except as they affect the risk of the investment.

The lesson here is that when estimating cash flows, it is necessary to be consistent with the information contained in the discount rate. If the discount rate is projecting 6% inflation and your cash flow estimates are projecting 9% price increases, be careful. Your estimates are probably wrong.

This lesson was lost on those international bankers who lent billions to oil-rich countries like Mexico, Venezuela, and Nigeria on the belief that not only would oil prices not decline but they would continue to grow forever at a real rate in excess of the real rate of interest. In short, they bet the bank that the commodity markets were inefficient! The oil glut in 1981 and the subsequent drop in oil prices revealed just how risky their gamble was.

NATURAL BIAS

Suppose project cash flows were estimated without any bias. This means that the average error associated with the cash flow forecasts would be zero. Of course, some of these cash flow estimates would be too high, whereas others would be too low, but because the future is unknown, it would be impossible to determine in advance which was which. Because of their higher predicted NPVs, however, those projects with overestimated cash flows are more likely to be chosen than are those whose cash flows are underestimated. Given this bias in the selection process, the actual NPVs of projects undertaken will generally be lower than their predicted NPVs, even if the underlying cash flow estimates are themselves unbiased.

The more projects that are investigated, the more likely it is that random error in estimating cash flows will lead to apparently profitable investments that turn out after the fact to be unprofitable. The only way to guard against this problem, aside from being aware that it exists, is to understand those circumstances under which expost positive NPV projects are likely to exist. As mentioned before, this is the subject of Chapter 7.

POSTINVESTMENT AUDIT

Once an investment has been made, it is largely a sunk cost and should not influence future decisions. Nevertheless, management wants to know when capital investment decisions have been incorrect, for two reasons:

1. Some action may be appropriate with respect to the person(s) responsible for the mistake.
2. Some safeguard to prevent a recurrence may be appropriate.

Management should conduct a **postinvestment audit** that compares actual results with *exante* budgeted figures. By reviewing the record of past investments, the firm can learn from its mistakes and its successes. For example, if a unit consistently errs in its projections, such as generally overestimating the growth of sales or underestimating the effects of inflation on costs, the firm can then include correction factors in future investment analyses. Even if estimation errors are random, a firm may be able to place bounds on the relative magnitudes of these errors and thereby supply useful inputs to an investment simulation model.

In addition to refining cash flow estimates, postinvestment audits can also help a firm improve its capital budgeting process and come up with better projects. By pinpointing the reasons for past successes and failures, the firm can learn how to structure projects better, approve them more objectively, and execute them more efficiently. In this way, the firm can repeat its successes and avoid future mistakes.

3.5 Summary and Conclusions

This chapter described some of the rules and techniques for estimating the cash flows associated with specific capital-budgeting projects. The most important rule is to include in the analysis only incremental cash flows, the difference between cash flows with the investment, and cash flows without the investment. Moreover, all these cash flows must be calculated on an after-tax basis, because only after-tax cash flows increase shareholders' purchasing power.

Project cash flows were divided into the initial cost of the investment, operating cash flows, and the terminal or ending value of the project. We examined each of these components separately, taking into account the impact of taxation at each stage of the analysis. The most important tax factor is choosing the depreciation method. Appendix 3A shows how accelerated depreciation increases the present value of the depreciation tax shield, thereby increasing the present value of the investment.

REFERENCES

Brennan, M.J., and Schwartz, E.S. "A New Approach to Evaluating Natural Resource Investments." *Midland Corporate Finance Journal*, Spring 1985, pp. 37– 47.

Kester, W.C. "Today's Options for Tomorrow's Growth." *Harvard Business Review*, March–April 1984, pp. 153–160.

SAMPLE PROBLEMS

Specialty Steel Products (SSP) is considering replacing some of its machinery with a new flexible machining center (FMC) that will permit it to respond more quickly to changes in the market-place. The price of the new equipment is $1.2 million. Base your analysis on the following data contained in SSP's capital authorization request:

(i)   Because the new system will boost output quality significantly, it is estimated that SSP's annual sales will rise somewhat, from its current level of $1.7 million to $1.8 million annually for the next five years. The before-tax and before-depreciation profit margin on SSP's sales, old and new, is estimated at 40%.

(ii) Working capital requirements are estimated to remain at 25% of sales.

(iii) The FMC will also cut overhead costs by $90,000 per year for the next five years.

(iv) The old machinery was purchased for $1 million three years ago, and is being depreciated on a straight-line basis over its five-year life. Its economic life as of today, however, is estimated to be five years. It can be sold for $300,000 today.

(v)   The FMC will be depreciated on a straight-line basis over its five-year life.

(vi) SSP faces a 34% corporate tax rate.

(vii) Given the relatively low risk of the revenue enhancement and cost savings, SSP estimates that the incremental cash flows generated by the FMC will have a cost of capital of only 10.7%, as compared to 14% for a typical company project. The risk-free interest rate is currently 8%.

(viii) SSP will receive an investment tax credit equal to 10% of the purchase price of the FMC.

(ix) The working capital will be recaptured at the end of five years.

 a. What is SSP's *net* investment required in the FMC? Assume that both pieces of equipment are being depreciated to a zero salvage value?

 b. What are the operating cash flows for each of the next five years?

 c. On the basis of the information supplied, should SSP replace its current equipment with the new system?

 d. What questions might you raise about some of the assumptions implicit in SSP's capital authorization request?

Answers

a. Net investment = Cost of FMC – ITC – Sale price – Tax benefit + Working capital

$$= \$1,200,000 - 120,000 - 300,000 - 35,000 + 25,000$$

$$= \$770,000$$

Since there are two more years to go on the old machinery, its book value is $400,000. By selling it for $300,000, SSP takes a $100,000 tax loss, which boosts its cash flow by $0.35 \times \$100,000 = \$35,000$. The investment tax credit is worth $1.2 million × 0.10 = $120,000. With a 25% working capital-to-sales ratio, the projected $100,000 rise in sales requires an additional $25,000 in working capital.

b. Operating cash flows (000 omitted)

	1	2	3	4	5
Incremental profit ($)	40	40	40	40	40
+ Cost savings	90	90	90	90	90
– Incremental depreciation	40	40	240	240	240
= EBIT	90.0	90.0	–110.0	–110.0	–110.0
– Tax (@ 35%)	–31.5	–31.5	+38.5	+38.5	+38.5
= Profit after tax	58.5	58.5	–71.5	–71.5	–71.5
+ Incremental depreciation	40.0	40.0	240.0	240.0	240.0
+ Working capital recapture	0	0	0	0	25
= Cash flow ($)	98.5	98.5	168.5	168.5	193.5

Notes: With a 40% profit margin on incremental sales, the $100,000 in incremental sales ($1.8 million – $1.7 million) generates $40,000 in incremental profit each year. It is trickier to calculate the incremental depreciation. Remember that in the absence of this new investment SSP would continue to receive $200,000 in depreciation for the next two years. Note too that the investment in working capital entails a one-time cash outflow. Once SSP has made that investment, estimated at 25% of sales or $25,000, no additional investment in working capital is necessary. At the end of year 5, SSP collects its working capital and $25,000 in cash is freed up.

c. On the basis of the numbers above, discounted at 10.7%, NPV = –$249,488. The project should be rejected because the NPV is negative.

d. Some of the implicit and questionable assumptions are:
SSP assumes that if it does not invest in this new machine, which is expected to produce a much higher quality product, its sales will stay the same. In other words, SSP is assuming that the base case is the status quo. The odds are that even if SSP does not buy the new FMC, one of its competitors will, and take market share away from SSP. The base case should, therefore, include a forecast of declining sales. Along a similar line, SSP assumes that the profit margin on sales will stay the same even though it is producing a higher quality product. More likely, the profit margin on its old sales will decline if it does not invest in the FMC.

Another questionable assumption is that the sales and cost figures will stay the same in nominal terms even though the high nominal interest rate suggests that inflation is expected to run at a rate of about 4 to 5% annually (assuming a real risk-free rate of about 3 to 4%). In other words, there is a basic conflict between the message being sent out by the risk-free interest rate (there will be inflation) and the figures used in the analysis. A more realistic assumption would be that the sales and cost savings figures will rise at about the expected rate of inflation built into the risk-free interest rate.

In addition, working capital requirements might be lower by using the FMC because higher quality output should lead to lower inventory requirements (since things will be done right the first time, reducing work-in-process inventory).

QUESTIONS

1. A new investment project is to demolish an existing gas station and construct a small shopping mall. Which of the items should be treated as incremental cash flows relevant to the investment decision?

   a. The current value of the land.
   b. The current value of the gasoline-retailing business.
   c. The cost of wrecking the gas station, digging up the tanks, and cleaning the land.
   d. The cost of new antipollution devices installed by order of the local government six months ago.
   e. Lost earnings on other real estate projects owing to staff time that will be spent if the mall is built.
   f. An allocated portion of the depreciation from the company's headquarters building.
   g. The fee that has already been paid to an architect for designing the mall.
   h. Future noncash expenses such as depreciation that will result if the mall is built.
   i. Allocation of corporate overhead to the project.

2. A soft drink bottler is trying to determine the present value of its business in an area where it forecasts no growth in unit sales. Sales this year will be $10 million and expenses will be $9 million. The present rate of return required is 20%, and inflation is expected to be 10% indefinitely.

   The company president believes that the present value of the business is $5 million, that is, $1 million per year discounted at 20%. His assistant argues that the present value is $1 million divided by 10%, the expected real interest rate. This yields an NPV of $10 million. What is the correct solution to the valuation problem?

3. In late 1985, Donald Trump, the New York real estate developer, unveiled a plan to build the tallest building in the world on Manhattan's West Side as the centerpiece of a commercial and residential complex to be known as Television City. He bought the land in 1981 for only $81 million. By 1985, its estimated value was $2 billion. "I can do things that no one else can do because I got the land so cheap," said Trump. Donald is (was?) very rich, but is he correct?

4. In May 1992, IBM announced plans to resell the ultrapowerful PCs of Parallan Computer. However, according to one analyst, "In pushing into increasingly powerful and expensive PCs, IBM runs the risk of cannibalizing its own sales of minicomputers." How should this possibility be factored into IBM's investment decision?

5. Flexible manufacturing systems enable companies to respond quickly to emerging market trends and to easily accommodate product redesigns as technology changes. What is there in

these advantages that sometimes leads companies applying the traditional discounted cash flow analysis to underinvest in such systems? That is, why do companies sometimes underestimate the value of flexible manufacturing systems in the sense of assigning negative NPVs to positive NPV projects?

6. Many companies are now installing marketing and sales productivity (MSP) systems that automate routine tasks and gather, update, and interpret data that were either scattered or uncollected before. These data include information about every sales lead generated, every sales task performed, and every customer prospect closed or terminated. Describe some of the direct costs and benefits that might be associated with an MSP system. What are some intangible benefits of an MSP system as well as some hidden costs of implementing such a system?

7. Accrued pension benefits represent an obligation of a company for the past service of its employees. No current or future action can affect this obligation. The amortization of accrued pension benefits must be recognized, however, as a current expense in the company's financial statements. Many companies turn around and allocate these costs to divisions. One company allocated these costs in proportion to pension benefits accrued by its workers. A plant with an older work force received almost all of its division's accrued pension costs, adding $4 per hour to the plant's labor cost relative to the cost of several newer plants with much younger workers.

   a. How is this allocation of accrued pension benefits likely to affect future investment decisions? The competitiveness of products manufactured by the plant?
   b. Suppose that because of its high labor costs, the company decided to shut down the older plant and shift work to the newer ones. How will this decision affect the company's competitiveness?
   c. How should the company treat accrued pension benefits for investment, product sourcing, and pricing purposes?

8. Starshine Products is considering the launch of a new line of dolls that would use an assembly line that currently has some spare capacity. Some Starshine executives argued that because the assembly line was already paid for, its cost was sunk and should not be included in the project evaluation. Others argued that the assembly line was a scarce resource and should be priced accordingly. What cost should Starshine assign to use of the excess assembly line capacity?

9. In order to produce its new line of canned foods, Hammond Foods must purchase a specialized piece of equipment that has the capacity to fill a million cans annually. Suppose Hammond plans to initially produce 150,000 cans annually. Some executives argued that the new product line should be charged for only 15% of the cost of the new equipment. Others argued that it should bear the full cost of the special-purpose machinery. Who is right? Explain.

10. Happy Tub makes traditional cast-iron bathtubs. However, the company was thinking of adopting a novel proprietary casting process to make lighter bathtubs that could compete better against plastic ones that were eating into sales, while also reducing raw materials costs. The $25 million investment seemed wise from a marketing perspective, but its NPV came to –$3 million. What other factors should you consider in light of the following assumptions that entered into this figure?

   a. The base case implicitly assumed that sales would stay the same without the new investment.
   b. Happy Tub has two plants, both running below capacity. Since just one plant would be upgraded, however, only products made at that plant would benefit from the new efficiencies. Thus, the finance director used a high discount rate to reflect the highly uncertain volumes and costs savings from using the new process.

c. Happy Tub used a standard 10-year life to evaluate the new project. Since 10 years was also the standard life over which plant and machinery were depreciated, the finance director inserted a zero terminal value for the upgraded plant.

d. Happy Tub ignored the other opportunities that the introduction of the proprietary casting process might create since these opportunities were purely speculative.

e. Although the proprietary casting process promised quality improvements, the investment analysis assumed that any sales of the new bathtub would just replace sales of Happy Tub's cast iron tubs. The analysis considered the cost savings from reduced raw materials usage to be the only source of project gains.

PROBLEMS

1. TelCo must decide whether to replace a computer system with a new model. TelCo forecasts net before-tax cost savings from the new computer over five years as given below (in $000). It has a 12% cost of capital, a 35% tax rate, and uses straight-line depreciation.

Year	1	2	3	4	5
($)	350	350	300	300	300

a. The new computer costs $1 million but TelCo is eligible for a 15% ITC in the first year. The ITC reduces TelCo's taxes by an amount equal to 15% of the equipment's purchase price. In addition, the old computer can be sold for $450,000. If the old computer originally cost $1.25 million and is three years old (depreciable, not economic, life is five years), what is the *net* investment required in the new system? Assume that there was no ITC on the old computer and that both computers are being depreciated to a zero salvage value.

b. Estimate the incremental operating cash flows associated with the new system.

c. If the new computer's salvage value at the end of five years is projected to be $100,000, should TelCo purchase it?

2. New diesel locomotives will cost a railroad $600,000 each and can be depreciated straight-line over their five-year life. Using a diesel instead of a coal-fired steam locomotive will save $12,000 annually in operating expenses. Railroads have a required rate of return of 10% and a tax rate of 40%.

a. What is the maximum price a railroad would be willing to pay for a coal-fired steam locomotive? (*Hint*: Set up the cash flows for a coal-fired locomotive at a price of P, including depreciation, and then compare them to the incremental cash flows associated with a diesel costing $600,000.)

b. Will your answer to (a) change if the railroad has enormous tax-loss carryforwards that put it in a zero taxpaying position for the foreseeable future?

3. Varico produces HO-scale trains, including a diesel locomotive that sells 100,000 units annually. Each unit requires an electric motor. Presently, these are purchased once a week from a local manufacturer for $10 apiece. However, a foreign firm has offered to sell Varico a container of 100,000 motors of like quality for only $9.50 apiece. Given an interest rate of 15%, what should Varico do?

4. To capitalize on consumers' concerns about healthful food, Specific Foods, Inc., is considering a new cereal, Veggie Crisp, which contains small bits of cooked vegetables with bran flakes. As part of its cash flow analysis, the finance department has made the following forecasts of demand and cost:

a. Sales revenue for the first year will be $200,000 and will increase to $1,000,000 the next year. Revenue will then grow by 15% a year for the next four years, remain the same in the seventh year, and then decline by 15% a year for the next three years, when the product will be terminated.

b. Cost of goods sold will be 60% of sales.

c. Advertising and general expenses will be $10,000 a year.

d. Equipment will be purchased today for $1,250,000 and will be depreciated over the 10-year project using the straight-line method. Installation cost today is $25,000, and this is depreciated over five years, also on a straight-line basis. The equipment has no salvage value. Other initial costs (which are expensed, not depreciated) total $875,000. There is no investment tax credit.

   (i) Calculate net income and operating cash flow using a 35% tax rate.
   (ii) Find the net present value of the project using a 10% cost of capital.
   (iii) In an effort to adjust for inflation, the finance department has produced an alternative estimate of cash flows. The product price will remain the same, but advertising and general expenses will grow by 5% a year from its initial level of $10,000. In addition, the cost of goods sold will grow by 20% a year from its initial level of $600,000 until year 6, remain the same in year 7, and then decline by 15% a year through year 10. What is the project's net present value under these assumptions?

5. In building a new facility for producing trucks, International Truck (IT) must estimate the total investment required. In the current year, IT estimates it will acquire land for the plant at $1,000,000 and modify existing plant equipment for $123,000. Next year, construction will begin and require $866,000, and further plant modifications will require $344,000. In addition, new equipment worth $140,000 will be purchased (with a 10% investment tax credit). The new equipment will require $250,000 of installation expense. Finally, in the next year, construction will be completed at a cost of $750,000; installation charges will total $229,000; and building modifications will require $350,000. Lastly, more new equipment will be purchased for $230,000 (with a 10% ITC). With a cost of capital of 10%, what is the present value of the initial investment required for the plant?

6. Yankee Atomic Electric Co. announced in 1992 that it would decommission its Yankee Rowe nuclear plant at an estimated cost of $247 million. The cost includes:

   a. $32 million to maintain the plant until 2000, when dismantling will begin. These expenses will accrue at the rate of $4 million a year.

   b. $56.5 million for the cost of building a facility to store its spent fuel until it is shipped in 2000 to a permanent repository. This storage facility will be depreciated straight-line over its eight-year estimated life.

   c. $158.5 million for the cost of dismantling the plant in 2000 and disposing of its nuclear wastes.

   At the same time, Yankee Atomic estimated that decommissioning the plant in 1992, eight years earlier than its planned retirement in 2000, will save it $116 million ($14.5 million a year) before tax by enabling the utility to purchase cheaper electricity than Yankee Rowe could provide. In addition, Yankee Atomic said it had accumulated $72 million in a decommissioning fund required by the Nuclear Regulatory Commission.

   a. What is the present value of Yankee's $247 million decommissioning cost? Assume a cost of capital equal to 12% and a 34% tax rate.

   b. Taking into account the savings on the purchase of cheaper electricity, and the $72 million already set aside, how much additional money does Yankee Atomic have to set aside in 1992 to have enough money to pay for the decommissioning expense?

   c. What other factors might you consider in calculating the cost of decommissioning?

7. Oldham Industries is considering replacing a five-year old machine with an original life of 10 years, a cost of $100,000, and a zero salvage value, with a new and more efficient machine. The new machine will cost $200,000 installed and will have a 10-year life. The new machine will increase sales by $25,000 and decrease scrap cost by $10,000 per year. The old machine can be sold currently at $50,000, and Oldham's marginal tax rate is 50%. Assume straight-line depreciation and a 10% investment tax credit for both the old and the new machines. A prorated portion of any investment tax credit must be returned to the IRS for equipment sold before the end of its depreciable life; that is, if half the equipment's life remains, then half the ITC is reclaimed by the IRS. Assume depreciation is taken on 100% of the cost of equipment.

   a. What is the initial cash outflow generated by the machine replacement?
   b. What are the annual operating cash flows generated by this project?
   c. What is the net present value of this replacement project, given a 12% cost of capital?

8. Molecugen has developed a new kind of cardiac diagnostic unit. Owing to the highly competitive nature of the market, the sales department forecasts demand of 5,000 units in the first year and a decrease in demand of 10% a year after that. After five years, the project will be discontinued with no salvage value. The marketing department forecasts a sales price of $15 a unit. Production estimates operating cost of $5 a unit, and the finance department estimates general and administrative expenses of $15,000 a year. The initial investment in land is $10,000, and other nondepreciable setup costs are $10,000.

   a. Is the new project acceptable at a cost of capital of 10%? (*Note*: Use straight-line depreciation over the life of the project and a tax rate of 35%.)
   b. If the marketing department had forecast a decline of 15% a year in demand, would the project be acceptable?
   c. If the marketing department had forecast a decline in sales price of 10% a year, along with the 15% annual decline in demand predicted in (b), would the project be acceptable?
   d. If prices decline by 10% a year, the marketing department estimates that demand will be a constant 5,000 units a year. Is the project acceptable?

9. Salterell Textiles is considering replacing the looming equipment in its North Carolina mill. The original purchase price was $79,300 two years ago. The machine has a useful life of 10 years and is being depreciated using the straight-line method. The old equipment can be sold today for $10,800. The new equipment costs $80,500 and has an eight-year life. Its salvage value is expected to be $8,000. The new equipment is expected to increase output and sales revenue by $9,000 a year (after tax) and reduce costs by $7,500 (after tax).

   a. With a tax rate of 25% and a 14% cost of capital, what should Salterell's decision be?
   b. Would a 10% ITC change the analysis?
   c. If an inflation rate of 7% a year must be incorporated into the decision, is the project acceptable?

10. Ross Designs is thinking of replacing its seven-year-old knitting machine with a new one that can also emboss designs on cloth. This will allow Ross to sell its textiles, which currently wholesale for $1.20 a yard, for $0.07 a yard more. The embossing should also raise sales 15%, to 2.07 million yards annually. The new machine costs $320,000, has annual operating costs of $27,000, and is expected to last for eight years. Labor, materials, and other expenses are estimated to rise by $0.02, to $1.10 per yard. Working capital requirements should remain at 30% of sales. All working capital investments will be recaptured in eight years. The current machine was purchased for $190,000 and is being depreciated on a straight-line basis assuming a 10-year life. Its economic life as of today, however, is estimated to be eight

years, the same as that of the new machine. It can be sold for $70,000 today, or for an estimated salvage value of $5,000 in eight years. The new machine will be depreciated straight line over a five-year period, and has an estimated salvage value of $20,000 in eight years. The appropriate discount rate is estimated at 12%.

a. What is the change in operating cash flows for each year? What is their present value?
b. What are the net cash flows associated with the purchase of the new knitting machine and sale of the old one?
c. What is the NPV of the investment in working capital?
d. What is the NPV of the acquisition of the new knitting machine? Should Ross buy it?
e. Suppose that all prices and costs are in nominal terms and will increase at the rate of inflation, which is projected at 4%. How does the analysis in parts (a) through (d) change? The 12% discount rate is expressed in nominal terms as well.

Appendix 3A

Current Rules for Depreciation

Depreciation is an annual income tax deduction that allows a business to recover the cost or other basis of certain property over the time it uses the property. It is an allowance for the wear and tear, deterioration, or obsolescence of the property. This appendix discusses the general rules for depreciating property. It explains what property can be depreciated, when depreciation begins and ends, what methods can be used to figure depreciation, and what the basis for depreciation is.

A business can depreciate most types of tangible property (except land), such as buildings, machinery, vehicles, furniture, and equipment. It also can depreciate certain intangible property, such as patents, copyrights, and computer software. To be depreciable, the property must meet all the following requirements:

- It must be property the business owns.
- It must be used in a business or income-producing activity.
- It must have a determinable useful life.
- It must be expected to last more than one year.
- It must not be excepted property.

Excepted property consists of the following:

- Property placed in service and disposed of in the same year.
- Equipment used to build capital improvements. You must add otherwise allowable depreciation on the equipment during the period of construction to the basis of your improvements.
- Section 197 intangibles (these include franchises, certain agreements not to compete, and the following property acquired in connection with the purchase of a business or a substantial part of a business: (a) patents and copyrights,

(b) customer or subscription lists, and (c) designs, patterns, and formats, including certain computer software). Instead of being depreciated, the cost of Section 179 intangibles must be amortized over 15 years. Amortization refers to a ratable deduction for the cost of intangible property over its useful life.

DEPRECIATION BASIS

Under current law, the estimated salvage value of an asset is *not* taken into account in computing depreciation. Thus, if Quantum Systems Co. buys the new extrusion press for $2 million, it will have a depreciable basis of $2 million for the $2 million in equipment cost.

DEPRECIATION RATE

The Modified Accelerated Cost Recovery System (MACRS) is used to recover the basis of most business and investment property placed in service after 1986. MACRS provides three depreciation methods:

- *The 200% declining balance method.* This method, also known as the **double-declining-balance method**, or DDB, means that depreciation occurs at twice the straight-line rate. For example, if the depreciable life of the asset is five years, then the depreciation factor is equal to 2/5 (instead of the 1/5 factor that would be used for straight-line depreciation). The investment base in the first year is the asset's original cost. Each year thereafter, the depreciation base is reduced by the amount of depreciation taken the year before. Thus, depreciation computed under DDB becomes progressively smaller, until depreciation figured under the straight-line method exceeds the accelerated depreciation. Then the straight-line method is used to complete depreciating the asset.

- *The 150% declining-balance method.* This method is a variation on DDB. Here the depreciation factor is 1.5 times the straight-line factor, or $1.5/n$. With a five-year life, the depreciation factor becomes 1.5/5, or 3/10. As with DDB, when depreciation figured under the straight-line method exceeds the accelerated depreciation, then the straight-line method is used to complete depreciating the asset.
- *The straight-line method.* Under this method, the annual depreciation factor is $1/n$ where n is the depreciable life of the asset. Hence, the annual depreciation charge is equal to the book value of the asset divided by the life of the asset.

The tax law specifies the circumstances under which the different accelerated methods may be used, as well as the economic lives that may be assumed for different classes of assets. The complexities associated with understanding the tax law and the complications that arise in determining what to do in a specific case are attested to by the enormous sums paid to tax experts for their detailed knowledge.

Under MACRS, there are seven classes of depreciable property, each with its own depreciable life and depreciation schedule:

- *3-year property.* This limited class includes tractor units, race horses over two years old, and certain rent-to-own property.
- *5-year property.* This class includes cars, trucks, and buses, computers and peripheral equipment, office machinery such as calculators, copiers, and typewriters, equipment used to manufacture electronic products and semiconductors, and any property used in research and experimentation.
- *7-year property.* This class includes office furniture and equipment, agricultural machinery and equipment, and any property that has not been designated by law as being in any other class.
- *10-year property.* This class includes vessels, barges, tugs, and similar water transportation equipment, any single-purpose agricultural or horticultural structures, and tree or vine bearing fruit or nuts.
- *15-year property.* This class includes roads, shrubbery, wharves, bridges, retail motor fuel outlets such as a convenience store, telephone distribution plants, and municipal wastewater treatment plants.
- *20-year property.* This specialized class is designated for farm buildings (other than single-purpose agricultural or horticultural structures).
- *25-year property.* This class includes water utility property and municipal sewers.
- *Real property, generally buildings and structures.* This class consists of residential rental property (depreciable over 27.5 years), nonresidential real property acquired before May 13, 1993 (depreciable over 31.5 years), and nonresidential real property acquired after May 13, 1993 (depreciable over 39 years).

In the case of Quantum Systems, depreciation for its new press is based on the 200% declining-balance method. The investment base in the first year is the asset's original cost of $2 million. We now derive the depreciation deductions shown in Exhibit 3.5.

To begin, a "half-year convention" applies for all depreciable business assets other than real estate. This convention—part of the MACRS depreciation rules under the Tax Reform Act of 1986—assumes that the property is depreciable for half of the taxable year in which it is placed in service. So the deduction one may take the first year is one half the amount that could be taken for a full year of depreciation. When the property is disposed of—or in the last year of service life—the last half year of depreciation can be taken. So a "five-year depreciation period," as in this case, actually means that depreciation deductions are taken over six taxable years.

Without the half-year convention, the depreciation charge for Quantum Systems' new machine in the first year under DDB would be $2,000,000 × 2/5, or $800,000. This contrasts with depreciation of $400,000 under the straight-line method with a zero salvage value. With the half-year convention, first-year depreciation would also be $400,000. In year 2, DDB depreciation would be ($2,000,000 − 400,000) × 2/5, or $640,000. Accelerated depreciation in year 3 would be ($2,000,000 − 400,000 - 640,000) × 2/5 = $384,000. In year 4, accelerated depreciation would be ($2,000,000 − 400,000 − 640,000 − 384,000) × 2/5 = $230,400, dropping to $138,240 ($345,600 × 0.4) in the fifth year. In contrast, straight-line depreciation would be $576,000 × 1/2.5 = $230,400 in both year 4 and year 5.[8] Thus, Quantum would switch to the straight-line method in year 4. Depreciation in year 6 would be $115,200, the undepreciated residual of the $2 million equipment cost after subtracting depreciation through year 5.

The sum of the cash flows under both depreciation methods is the same, but DDB permits a much faster write-off than does the straight-line method. Because a faster write-off increases the present value of the tax shield, tax-paying companies should prefer DDB depreciation.

The year-by-year depreciation tax shield associated with the new extrusion press was shown in Exhibit 3.5 under MACRS. (It is assumed that the five-year life applies.) As discussed in the body of the chapter, for purposes of investment analysis, what really matters is the *incremental* depreciation tax shield. We saw that because Quantum Systems loses $100,000 in annual depreciation when the old machine is scrapped, incremental depreciation in each of the first five years is actually $100,000 less than the calculations indicate. As a result, the annual net tax shield provided by the new machine is $35,000 ($100,000 × 0.35) less than the gross tax shield it provides.

Exhibit 3A.1 shows the year-by-year percentage depreciation charges under DDB for different asset classes ranging from 3 years to 20 years assuming the half-year convention holds. The figures are taken from IRS Publication 946 titled "How to Depreciate Property."

Appendix 3B

Incorporating Inflation in Capital Budgeting

As was noted in the chapter, capital-budgeting analyses must be consistent in the treatment of inflation. The nominal discount rate already incorporates the expected rate of inflation. To be consistent, therefore, the projected cash flows must also take into account the effects of expected inflation. Specifically, cash flow estimates should

reflect the likelihood that nominal revenues and costs will rise at about the same pace as the rate of inflation. To illustrate this principal, we return to the example of Quantum Systems' machine replacement project.

According to the analysis presented in the chapter, the high salvage value required to make the new press economically viable

---

[8]The straight-line method is applied to the book value of the depreciated asset over the remaining life of the asset. In year 4, the book value of the asset is $576,000, and the remaining life is 2.5 years. Hence, depreciation under the straight-line method is $576,000 × 1/2.5 = $230,400.

EXHIBIT 3A.1 3-, 5-, 7-, 10-, 15-, and 20-Year Property Half-Year Convention

Year	Depreciation Rate for Recovery Period					
	3-year	5-year	7-year	10-year	15-year	20-year
1	33.33%	20.00%	14.29%	10.00%	5.00%	3.750%
2	44.45	32.00	24.49	18.00	9.50	7.219
3	14.81	19.20	17.49	14.40	8.55	6.677
4	7.41	11.52	12.49	11.52	7.70	6.177
5		11.52	8.93	9.22	6.93	5.713
6		5.76	8.92	7.37	6.23	5.285
7			8.93	6.55	5.90	4.888
8			4.46	6.55	5.90	4.522
9				6.56	5.91	4.462
10				6.55	5.90	4.461
11				3.28	5.91	4.462
12					5.90	4.461
13					5.91	4.462
14					5.90	4.461
15					5.91	4.462
16					2.95	4.461
17						4.462
18						4.461
19						4.462
20						4.461
21						2.231

makes it doubtful that the project is worth undertaking. This analysis and resulting conclusion could well be wrong because of the failure to deal explicitly with inflation. Assume that Quantum Systems' replacement project has a real, or inflation-adjusted, required return of about 8%, slightly below the 8.5% real return that stocks of average riskiness have realized over the past 128 years. According to the Fisher equation, the following relation holds between the required nominal or noninflation-adjusted return r, the real return a, and the expected rate of inflation i:

$$r = a + i + ai \qquad (3B.1)$$

Turning Equation 3B.1 around, we see that given the nominal and real required returns, we can calculate the expected rate of inflation as $i = r - a$, assuming that ai is close to zero. In the example, this means that expected inflation is about $15 - 8 = 7\%$ annually.

Note the basic inconsistency here. On the one hand, the discount rate has built into it an expected annual inflation rate of about 7%. On the other hand, the cash flow analysis implicitly assumes that either (1) the expected rate of inflation is 0 or (2) inflation does not affect nominal cash flows. To be consistent, we must adjust the nominal cash flows to account for the impact of expected inflation on anticipated revenues and costs. This requires that we distinguish between contractual and noncontractual cash flows.

APPENDIX 3B.1

CONTRACTUAL VERSUS NONCONTRACTUAL CASH FLOWS

Contractual cash flows are those fixed in nominal dollar terms. Consequently, the dollar amounts of these flows are unaffected by inflation. Contractual cash flows arise from such commitments as debt, long-term leases, labor contracts (until the next contract), rents, and accounts payable and receivable. Perhaps the most important cash flow fixed in nominal terms is the tax shield provided by depreciation.

Most of a firm's revenues and costs are typically *noncontractual* in nature, however. This means that they fluctuate in line with changing market conditions. Most economists believe that by itself, inflation is neutral; that is, future real variables, including real prices, are unlikely to be significantly affected by inflation. As long as prices are free to adjust to inflation, we would expect **noncontractual cash flows** to move in line with inflation. Stated another way, a 1% increase in the price level should be matched by a 1% increase in the nominal value of noncontractual revenues and costs. Although this oversimplifies matters somewhat, over time, the prices of goods and services do seem to move in line with inflation. This evidence implies that inflation neutrality is a reasonable first approximation when performing a capital-budgeting analysis.

Returning to the example of Quantum Systems, we see that the contractual cash flows are the depreciation tax shield and the working capital to be recaptured on project termination. Noncontractual cash flows include the cost savings and the additional revenues to be received from investing in the new extrusion press. Moreover, because working capital is assumed to equal 30% of sales, as sales rise, so must the investment in working capital.

Base incremental sales and cost savings from investing in the new body stamping machine were assumed to be $150,000 and $180,000, respectively. These are noncontractual cash flows, however, and should

therefore be adjusted for the anticipated 7% rate of inflation. Performing this adjustment leads to expected first-year revenues and cost savings of $160,500 ($150,000 × 1.07) and $192,600 ($180,000 × 1.07), respectively. After tax, the nominal increases will be $6,825 ($10,500 × 0.65) and $8,190 ($12,600 × 0.65), given the assumed 35% marginal corporate tax rate. Furthermore, the inflation-induced sales increase of $10,500 during the first year will require an additional investment of $3,150 ($10,500 × 0.30) in working capital. The depreciation charge is fixed in nominal terms and so remains the same regardless of the rate of inflation. Accordingly, the incremental project cash flow in the first year resulting from the adjustment for inflation is $11,865 ($6,825 + $8,190 − $3,150). Exhibit 3B.1 contains projected cash flows for all five years revised to reflect a 7% rate of inflation.

The project NPV of −$210,178, taking inflation into account, is $137,426 greater than the previously calculated NPV of −$347,604, which ignored inflation. Applying Equation 3.2 as before, we find that the terminal value at the end of five years must be greater than $210,178(1.15)^5 = $422,743 for the project to have a positive NPV. If we subtract the $63,100 in recovered working capital, this will require an after-tax salvage value of the new machine in five years in excess of $359,643.

This means that the sales price must exceed ($359,643 − 115,200)/0.65 + $115,200 = $491,266 before tax, taking into account the 35% tax on the salvage value in excess of its $115,200 book value. Unless the machine can be sold for more than $491,266 at the end of year 5, the project will not be acceptable.

In estimating the likelihood of a sales price this high, we must take into account the effects of inflation on the nominal value of the machine. Earlier, we assumed that in the absence of inflation, the value of the

EXHIBIT 3B.1 Project Analysis Incorporating 7% Inflation

Year	0	1	2	3	4	5
1. Sales		160.5	171.7	183.8	196.6	210.4
2. Cost savings		192.6	206.1	220.5	235.9	252.5
3. Incremental depreciation		300.0	540.0	284.0	130.4	130.4
4. Pretax incremental profit (1 + 2 – 3)		53.1	–162.2	120.3	302.2	332.4
5. Tax @ 35%)		18.6	–56.8	42.1	105.8	116.4
6. Profit after tax (4 – 5)		34.5	–105.4	78.2	196.4	216.1
7. Operating cash flow (3 + 6)		334.5	434.6	362.2	326.8	346.5
8. Working capital (0.3 × sales)		48.2	51.5	55.1	59.0	63.1
9. Change in working capital)		3.2	3.4	3.6	3.9	4.1
10. Initial investment	–1,415.0					
11. Net cash flow (7 – 9 + 10)	–1,415.0	331.4	431.2	358.6	322.9	342.4
12. Present value @ 15%	–1,415.0	288.1	326.1	235.8	184.6	170.2
Net present value = –$210,178						

machine will be $500,000 in five years. In other words, $500,000 is its assumed *real* value. If inflation is neutral, the real value of the machine will remain at $500,000. This means that the nominal value of the machine will appreciate at the rate of inflation each year. On the basis of the anticipated 7%

annual inflation rate, the nominal sales price of the machine at the end of year 5 should be $500,000(1.07)^5 = $701,276. This exceeds by $210,010 the $491,266 salvage value required for the new extrusion press to have a positive NPV. The extrusion press replacement project is now economically viable.

APPENDIX 3B.2

INFLATION AND TAXATION

Although it may not be apparent through all the numbers, inflation does have a harmful effect on projects, especially those with long economic lives and depreciation that stretches years into the future. This is because the current tax system taxes nominal income rather than real income. The distinction between nominal and real values is especially important when recording depreciation and gains or losses on the salvage value of assets.

Depreciation, Inflation, and Taxation. Because the tax shield associated with the depreciation charge is fixed in nominal terms, its real value declines as the rate of

inflation rises. In the case of the new extrusion press, the $230,400 depreciation charge recorded in year 5 provides a nominal tax shield worth $80,640 ($230,400 × 0.35). With an assumed 7% annual rate of inflation, however, the real value of this tax shield will be only $57,495 [$80,640/(1.07)^5]. Thus, during inflationary times, the use of historical cost accounting to measure depreciation causes the true amount of depreciation to be understated and profits to be overstated. The result is higher taxes and a reduction in real cash flows.

Salvage Values, Inflation, and Taxation. We saw before that if the real salvage value of the machine remains at $500,000, its nominal value will rise by $201,276 to $701,276 in five years. Quantum Systems will have to pay a tax of $70,446 ($201,276 × 0.35) on this phantom gain. It is a phantom gain because with 7% annual inflation, $701,276 in five years will be worth no more than $500,000 is worth today. Thus, if the before-tax real value of the machine is $500,000 in five years, its after-tax real value will decline to $449,773 [($701,276 − $70,446)/(1.07)^5].

The net effect of combining inflation with a tax system geared toward nominal, instead of real, gains or losses is to reduce the real cash flows associated with depreciable assets. This distorts investment decisions by reducing the attractiveness of capital-intensive projects, especially those with long economic lives, relative to other projects as well as relative to consumption. The end result is less investment and more consumption.

A p p e n d i x   3 C

Analyzing Foreign Investments

Multinational corporations evaluating foreign investments find their analyses complicated by a variety of problems that domestic firms rarely, if ever, encounter. This appendix examines several such problems, including differences between project and parent company cash flows, foreign tax regulations, expropriation, blocked funds, exchange rate changes and inflation, project-specific financing, and differences between the basic business risks of foreign and domestic projects. The analysis of a foreign project raises two additional issues other than those dealing with the interaction between the investment and financing decisions:

1. Should cash flows be measured from the viewpoint of the project or that of the parent?
2. Should the additional economic and political risks that are uniquely foreign be reflected in cash flow or discount rate adjustments?

APPENDIX 3C.1

ISSUES IN FOREIGN INVESTMENT ANALYSIS

We now address these issues in foreign investment analysis and suggest ways in which to deal with them. We then examine an example that illustrates the application of these approaches.

PARENT VERSUS PROJECT CASH FLOWS

A substantial difference can exist between the cash flow of a project and the amount that is remitted to the parent firm because of tax regulations and exchange controls. In addition, project expenses such as management fees and royalties are returns to the parent company. Furthermore, the incremental revenue contributed to the parent MNC by a project can differ from total project revenues if, for example, the project involves substituting local production for parent company exports or if transfer price adjustments shift profits elsewhere in the system.

Given the differences that are likely to exist between parent and project cash flows, the question arises as to the relevant cash flows to use in project evaluation. Economic theory has the answer to this question. According to economic theory, the value of a project is determined by the net present value of future cash flows back to the investor. Thus, the parent MNC should value only those cash flows that are, or can be, repatriated net of any transfer costs (such as taxes) because only accessible funds can be used for the payment of dividends and interest, for amortization of the firm's debt, and for reinvestment.

A Three-Stage Approach. A three-stage analysis is recommended for simplifying project evaluation. In the first stage, project cash flows are computed from the subsidiary's standpoint, exactly as if the subsidiary were a separate national corporation. The perspective then shifts to the parent company. This second stage of analysis requires specific forecasts concerning the amounts, timing, and form of transfers to headquarters, as well as information about what taxes and other expenses will be incurred in the transfer process. Finally, the firm must take into account the indirect benefits and costs that this investment confers on the rest of the system, such as an increase or decrease in export sales by another affiliate.

Estimating Incremental Project Cash Flows. Essentially, the company must estimate a project's true profitability. **True profitability** is an amorphous concept, but basically it involves determining the marginal revenue and marginal costs associated with the project. In general, as mentioned earlier, incremental cash flows to the parent can be found only by subtracting worldwide parent company cash flows (without the investment) from postinvestment parent company cash flows. This estimating entails the following:

1. Adjust for the effects of transfer pricing and fees and royalties.

- Use market costs/prices for goods, services, and capital transferred internally.
- Add back fees and royalties to project cash flows because they are benefits to the parent.
- Remove the fixed portions of such costs as corporate overhead.

2. Adjust for global costs/benefits that are not reflected in the project's financial statements. These costs/benefits include:

- cannibalization of sales of other units;
- creation of incremental sales by other units;
- additional taxes owed when repatriating profits;
- foreign tax credits usable elsewhere;
- diversification of production facilities;
- market diversification;
- provision of a key link in a global service network;
- knowledge of competitors, technology, markets, and products.

The second set of adjustments involves incorporating the project's strategic purpose and its impact on other units. These strategic considerations embody the factors that are discussed in Chapter 7. For example, AT&T is investing heavily in the ability to provide multinational customers with seamless global telecommunications services.

Although the principle of valuing and adjusting incremental cash flows is itself simple, it can be complicated to apply. Its application is illustrated in the case of taxes.

Tax Factors. Because only after-tax cash flows are relevant, it is necessary to determine when and what taxes must be paid on foreign-source profits. The following example illustrates the calculation of the incremental tax owed on foreign-source earning. Suppose an affiliate remits after-tax earnings of $150,000 to its U.S. parent in the form of a dividend. Assume that the foreign tax rate is 25%, the withholding tax on dividends is 4%, and excess foreign tax credits are unavailable. The marginal rate of additional taxation is found by adding the withholding tax that must be paid locally to the U.S. tax owed on the dividend. Withholding tax equals $6,000 (150,000 × 0.04), and U.S. tax owed equals $14,000. This latter tax is calculated as follows. With a before-tax local income of $200,000 (200,000 × 0.75 = 150,000), the U.S. tax owed would equal $200,000 × 0.35, or $70,000. The firm then receives foreign tax credits equal to $56,000—the $50,000 in local tax paid and the $6,000 dividend withholding tax—leaving a net of $14,000 owed to the IRS. This calculation yields a marginal tax rate of 13.33% on remitted profits, as follows:

$$\frac{6,000 + 14,000}{150,000} = 0.1333$$

If excess foreign tax credits are available to offset the U.S. tax owed, then the marginal tax rate on remittances is just the dividend withholding tax rate of 4%.

POLITICAL AND ECONOMIC RISK ANALYSIS

All else being equal, firms prefer to invest in countries with stable currencies, healthy economies, and minimal political risks, such as expropriation. All else is usually not equal, however, and so firms must assess the consequences of various political and economic risks for the viability of potential investments.

The three main methods for incorporating the additional political and economic risks, such as the risks of currency fluctuation and expropriation, into foreign investment analysis are (1) shortening the minimum payback period, (2) raising the required rate of return of the investment, and (3) adjusting cash flows to reflect the specific impact of a given risk.

Adjusting the Discount Rate or Payback Period. The additional risks confronted

abroad are often described in general terms instead of being related to their impact on specific investments. This rather vague view of risk probably explains the prevalence among multinationals of two unsystematic approaches to account for the added political and economic risks of overseas operations. One is to use a higher discount rate for foreign operations; another is to require a shorter payback period. For instance, if exchange restrictions are anticipated, a normal required return of 15% might be raised to 20%, or a five-year payback period might be shortened to three years.

Neither of the aforementioned approaches, however, lends itself to a careful evaluation of the actual impact of a particular risk on investment returns. Thorough risk analysis requires an assessment of the magnitude and timing of risks and their implications for the projected cash flows. For example, an expropriation five years hence is likely to be much less threatening than one expected next year, even though the probability of its occurring later may be higher. Thus, using a uniformly higher discount rate simply distorts the meaning of the present value of a project by penalizing future cash flows relatively more heavily than current ones, without obviating the necessity for a careful risk evaluation. Furthermore, the choice of a risk premium is an arbitrary one, whether it is 2 or 10%. Instead, adjusting cash flows makes it possible to fully incorporate all available information about the impact of a specific risk on the future returns from an investment.

Adjusting Expected Values. The recommended approach is to adjust the cash flows of a project to reflect the specific impact of a given risk, primarily because there is normally more and better information on the specific impact of a given risk on a project's cash flows than on its required return. The cash flow adjustments presented in this chapter employ only expected values; that is, the analysis reflects only the first moment of the probability distribution of the impact of a given risk. Although this procedure does not assume that shareholders are risk-neutral, it does assume either that risks such as expropriation, currency controls, inflation, and exchange rate changes are unsystematic or that foreign investments tend to lower a firm's systematic risk. In the latter case, adjusting only the expected values of future cash flows will yield a lower bound on the value of the investment to the firm.

Although the suggestion that cash flows from politically risky areas should be discounted at a rate that ignores those risks is contrary to current practice, the difference is more apparent than real: Most firms evaluating foreign investments discount most-likely (modal) cash flows rather than expected (mean) cash flows at a risk-adjusted rate. If an expropriation or currency blockage is anticipated, then the mean value of the probability distribution of future cash flows will be significantly below its mode. From a theoretical standpoint, of course, cash flows should always be adjusted to reflect the change in expected values caused by a particular risk; however, only if the risk is systematic should these cash flows be further discounted.

Exchange Rate Changes and Inflation. The present value of future cash flows from a foreign project can be calculated using a two-stage procedure: (1) Convert nominal foreign currency cash flows into nominal home currency terms, and (2) discount those nominal cash flows at the nominal domestic required rate of return. In order to properly assess the effect of exchange rate changes on expected cash flows from a foreign project, one must first remove the effect of offsetting inflation and exchange rate changes. It is worthwhile to analyze each effect separately because different cash flows may be differentially affected by inflation. For example, the **depreciation tax shield** will not rise with inflation, while revenues and variable costs are likely to rise in line with inflation. Or local price controls may not permit internal price adjustments. In practice, correcting for these effects means first adjusting the foreign currency cash flows for inflation and then converting the projected cash flows back into dollars using the forecast exchange rate.

Illustration. Factoring in Currency Depreciation and Inflation. Suppose that with no inflation the cash flow in year 2 of a new project in France is expected to be €1 million, and the exchange rate is expected to remain at its current value of €1 = $0.85. Converted into dollars, the €1 million cash flow yields a projected cash flow of $850,000. Now suppose that French inflation is expected to be 6% annually, but project cash flows are expected to rise only 4% annually because the depreciation tax shield will remain constant. At the same time, because of purchasing power parity (and U.S. inflation of 1%), the euro is expected to depreciate at the rate of 5% annually—giving rise to a forecast exchange rate in year 2 of $0.85 \times (1 - 0.05)^2 = \$0.7671$. Then the forecast cash flow in year 2 becomes €1,000,000 $\times 1.04^2 = $ €1,081,600, with a forecast dollar value of $829,722 $(0.7671 \times 1,081,600)$.

An alternative approach to valuing a foreign project's future cash flows is to (1) discount the nominal foreign currency cash flows at the nominal foreign currency required rate of return, and (2) convert the resulting foreign currency present value into the home currency using the current spot rate. These two different approaches to valuing project cash flows should give the same results if the international Fisher effect is assumed to hold.

APPENDIX 3C.2

FOREIGN PROJECT APPRAISAL: THE CASE OF INTERNATIONAL DIESEL CORPORATION

This section illustrates how to deal with some of the complexities involved in foreign project analysis by considering the case of a U.S. firm with an investment opportunity in England. International Diesel Corporation (IDC-U.S.), a U.S.-based multinational firm, is trying to decide whether to establish a diesel manufacturing plant in the United Kingdom (IDC-U.K.). IDC-U.S. expects to significantly boost its European sales of small diesel engines (40–160 hp) from the 20,000 it is currently exporting there. At the moment, IDC-U.S. is unable to increase exports because its domestic plants are producing to capacity. The 20,000 diesel engines it is currently shipping to Europe are the residual output that it is not selling domestically.

IDC-U.S. has made a strategic decision to significantly increase its presence and sales overseas. A logical first target of this international expansion is the European Community (EC). Market growth seems assured by recent large increases in fuel costs and the advent of Europe 1992 and European Monetary Union. IDC-U.S. executives believe that manufacturing in England will give the firm a key advantage with customers in England and throughout the rest of the EC.

England is the most likely production location because IDC-U.S. can acquire a 1.4-million-square-foot plant in Manchester from British Leyland (BL), which used it to assemble gasoline engines before its recent closing. As an inducement to locate in this vacant plant and thereby ease unemployment among autoworkers in Manchester, the National Enterprise Board (NEB) will provide a five-year loan of £5 million ($10 million) at 3% interest, with interest paid annually at the end of each year and the principal to be repaid in a lump sum at the end of the fifth year. Total acquisition, equipment, and retooling costs for this plant are estimated to equal $50 million.

Full-scale production can begin six months from the date of acquisition because IDC-U.S. is reasonably certain it can hire BL's plant manager and about 100 other former employees. In addition, conversion of the plant from producing gasoline engines to producing diesel engines should be relatively simple.

The parent will charge IDC-U.K. licensing and overhead allocation fees equal to 7% of sales in pounds sterling. In addition, IDC-U.S. will sell its English affiliate valves, piston rings, and other components that account for approximately 30% of the total amount of materials used in the manufacturing process. IDC-U.K. will be billed in dollars at the current market price for this material. The remainder will be purchased locally. IDC-U.S. estimates that its all-equity nominal required rate of return for the project will equal 12%, based on an anticipated 3% U.S. rate of inflation and the business risks associated with this venture. The debt capacity of such a project is judged to be about 20% — that is, a debt-to-equity ratio for this project of about 1:4 is considered reasonable.

To simplify its investment analysis, IDC-U.S. uses a five-year capital-budgeting horizon and then calculates a terminal value for the remaining life of the project. If the project has a positive net present value for the first five years, there is no need to engage in costly and uncertain estimates of future cash flows. If the initial net present value is negative, then IDC-U.S. can calculate a break-even terminal value at which the net present value will just be positive. This break-even value is then used as a benchmark against which to measure projected cash flows beyond the first five years.

We now apply the three-stage investment analysis outlined in the preceding section: (1) Estimate project cash flows; (2) forecast the amounts and timing of cash flows to the parent; and (3) add to, or subtract from, these parent cash flows the indirect benefits or costs that this project provides the remainder of the multinational firm.

ESTIMATION OF PROJECT CASH FLOWS

A principal cash outflow associated with the project is the initial investment outlay, consisting of the plant purchase, equipment expenditures, and working-capital requirements. Other cash outflows include operating expenses, later additions to working capital as sales expand, and taxes paid on its net income.

IDC-U.K. has cash inflows from its sales in England and other EC countries. It also has cash inflows from three other sources:

- The tax shield provided by depreciation and interest charges
- Interest subsidies
- The terminal value of its investment, net of any capital gains taxes owed upon liquidation.

Recapture of working capital is not assumed until eventual liquidation because this working capital is necessary to maintain an ongoing operation after the fifth year.

Initial Investment Outlay. Total plant acquisition, conversion, and equipment costs for IDC-U.K. were previously estimated at $50 million. The plant and equipment will be depreciated on a straight-line basis over a five-year period, with a zero salvage value.

Of the $50 million in net plant and equipment costs, $10 million will be financed by NEB's loan of £5 million at 3%. The remaining $40 million will be supplied by the parent in the form of equity capital.

Working-capital requirements—comprising cash, accounts receivable, and inventory—are estimated at 30% of sales, but this amount will be partially offset by accounts payable to local firms, which are expected to average 10% of sales. Therefore, net investment in working capital will equal approximately 20% of sales. The transfer price on the material sold to IDC-U.K. by its parent includes a 25% contribution to IDC-U.S.'s profit and overhead. That is, the variable cost of production equals 75% of the transfer price. Lloyds Bank is providing an initial working-capital loan of £1.5 million ($3 million). All future working-capital needs will be financed out of internal cash flow. Exhibit 3C.1 summarizes the initial investment.

Financing IDC-U.K. On the basis of the information just provided, IDC-U.K.'s initial balance sheet, in both pounds and dollars, is presented in Exhibit 3C.2. The debt ratio (debt to total assets) for IDC-U.K. is 33:53, or 62%.

The tax shield benefits of interest write-offs are represented separately. Assume that IDC-U.K. contributes $10.6 million to its

---

EXHIBIT 3C.1 Initial Investment Outlay in IDC-U.K. (£ 1 = $2)

	£ (Millions)	$ (Millions)
Plant purchase and retooling expense	17.5	35
Equipment		
Supplied by parent (used)	2.5	5
Purchased in the United Kingdom	5	10
Working capital		
Bank financing	1.5	3
Total initial investment	£ 26.5	$53

EXHIBIT 3C.2 Initial Balance Sheet of IDC-U.K. (£ 1 = $2)

	£ (Millions)	$ (Millions)
Assets		
Current assets	1.5	3
Plant and equipment	25	50
Total assets	26.5	53
Liabilities		
Loan payable (to Lloyds)	1.5	3
Total current liabilities	1.5	3
Loan payable (to NEB)	5	10
Loan payable (to IDC-U.S.)	10	20
Total liabilities	16.5	33
Equity	10	20
Total liabilities plus equity	£ 26.5	$53

parent's debt capacity (0.2 × $53 million), the dollar market rate of interest for IDC-U.K. is 8%, and the U.K. tax rate is 40%. This calculation translates into a cash flow in the first and subsequent years equal to $10,600,000 × 0.08 × 0.40, or $339,000. Discounted at 8%, this cash flow provides a benefit equal to $1.4 million over the next five years.

Interest Subsidies. On the basis of a 5% anticipated rate of inflation in England and on an expected annual 2% depreciation of the pound relative to the dollar, the market rate on the pound loan to IDC-U.K. would equal about 10%. Thus, the 3% interest rate on the loan by the National Enterprise Board represents a 7% subsidy to IDC-U.K. The cash value of this subsidy equals £350,000 (£5,000,000 × 0.07, or approximately $700,000) annually for the next five years, with a present value of $2.7 million.[9]

Sales and Revenue Forecasts. At a profit-maximizing price of £250 per unit in the first year ($490 at the projected year 1 exchange rate), demand for diesel engines in England and the other EC countries is expected to increase by 10% annually, from 60,000 units in the first year to 88,000 units in the fifth year. It is assumed here that purchasing power parity holds with no lag and that real prices remain constant in both absolute and relative terms. Hence, the sequences of nominal pound prices and exchange rates, reflecting anticipated annual rates of inflation equaling 5% and 3% for the pound and dollar, respectively, are

Year	Price (pounds)	Exchange rate (dollars)
0	—	2.00
1	250	1.96
2	278	1.92
3	308	1.89
4	342	1.85
5	380	1.82

---

[9]The present value of this subsidy is found by discounting it at 10% and then converting the resulting pound present value into dollars at the current spot rate of $2/£. The appropriate discount rate is 10% because this is a pound loan. The exact present value of this subsidy is given by the difference between the present value of debt service on the 3% loan discounted at 10% and the face value of the loan.

It is also assumed here that purchasing power parity holds with respect to the euro and other currencies of the various EC countries to which IDC-U.K. exports. These exports account for about 60% of total IDC-U.K. sales. Disequilibrium conditions in the currency markets or relative price changes can be dealt with by explicitly developing scenarios of exchange rate and price changes.

In the first year, although demand is at 60,000 units, IDC-U.K. can produce and supply the market with only 30,000 units (because of the six-month start-up period). IDC-U.S. exports another 20,000 units to its English affiliate at a unit transfer price of £250, leading to no profit for IDC-U.K. Because these units would have been exported anyway, IDC-U.K. is not credited from a capital-budgeting standpoint with any profits on these sales. IDC-U.S. ceases its exports of finished products to England and the EC after the first year. From year 2 on, IDC-U.S. is counting on an expanding U.S. market to absorb the 20,000 units. Based on these assumptions, IDC-U.K.'s projected sales revenues are shown in Exhibit 3C.3, line C.

In nominal terms, IDC-U.K.'s pound sales revenues are projected to rise at a rate of 15.5% annually, based on a combination of the 10% annual increase in unit demand and the 5% annual increase in unit price ($1.10 \times 1.05 = 1.155$). Dollar revenues will increase at about 13% annually, due to the anticipated 2% annual rate of pound depreciation.

Production Cost Estimates. On the basis of the assumptions that relative prices will remain constant and that purchasing power parity will hold continually, variable costs of production, stated in real terms, are expected to remain constant, whether denominated in pounds or in dollars. Hence, the pound prices of both labor and material sourced in England and components imported from the United States are assumed to increase by the rate of British inflation, or 5% annually. Unit variable costs in the first year are expected to equal £140, including £30 ($60) in components purchased from IDC-U.S.

In addition, the license fees and overhead allocations, which are set at 7% of sales, will rise at an annual rate of 15.5% because pound revenues are rising at that rate. With a full year of operation, initial overhead expenses would be expected to equal £1,100,000. Actual overhead expenses incurred, however, are only £600,000 because the plant does not begin operation until midyear. These expenses are partially fixed, so their rate of increase should be about 8% annually.

The plant and equipment, valued at £25 million, can be written off over five years, yielding an annual depreciation charge against income of £5 million. The cash flow associated with this tax shield remains constant in nominal pound terms but declines in nominal dollar value by 2% annually. With a 3% rate of U.S. inflation, its real value is, therefore, reduced by 5% annually, the same as its loss in real pound terms.

Annual production costs for IDC-U.K. are estimated in Exhibit 3C.3, lines D–I. It should be realized, of course, that some of these expenses, like depreciation, are a non-cash charge or, like licensing fees, a benefit to the overall corporation.

Total production costs rise less rapidly each year than the 15.5% annual increase in nominal revenue. This situation is due both to the fixed depreciation charge and to the semifixed nature of overhead expenses. Thus, the profit margin should increase over time.

Projected Net Income. Net income for years 1 through 5 is estimated on line L of Exhibit 3C.3. The effective tax rate on corporate income faced by IDC-U.K. in England is estimated to be 40%. The £2.8 million loss in the first year is applied against income in years 2, 3, and 4, reducing corporate taxes owed in those years.

EXHIBIT 3C.3 Present Value of IDC-U.K.: Project Viewpoint

				Year			
	0	1	2	3	4	5	5+
A. Sales (units)		30,000	66,000	73,000	80,000	88,000	
B. Price per unit (£)		250	263	276	289	304	
C. Sales revenue (£ millions)		7.5	17.3	20.1	23.2	26.7	
D. Variable cost per unit (£)		140	147	154	162	170	
E. Total variable cost (£ millions)		4.2	9.7	11.3	13.0	15.0	
F. Licensing fees and royalties (0.07 × line C, in £ millions)		0.5	1.2	1.4	1.6	1.9	
G. Overhead expenses (£ millions)		0.6*	1.2	1.3	1.4	1.5	
H. Depreciation (£ millions)		5.0	5.0	5.0	5.0	5.0	
I. Total expenses (E + F + G + H, in £ millions)		10.3	17.1	19.0	21.0	23.3	
J. Profit before tax (C − I, in £ millions)		−2.8	0.2	1.2	2.2	3.4	
K. U.K. corporate income taxes @ 40% = 0.40 × J**		0.0	0.0	0.0	0.3	1.4	
L. Net profit after tax (J − K, in £ millions)		−2.8	0.2	1.2	1.9	2.0	
M. Terminal value for IDC-U.K. [2.7 × (L + H), for year 5, in £ millions]							19.0
N. Initial investment, including working capital (£ millions)	−26.5						
O. Working capital investment at 20% of revenue (0.2 × C, in £ millions)		1.5	3.5	4.0	4.6	5.3	
P. Required addition to working capital (line O for year t − line O for year t − 1; t = 2, . . . , 5, in £ millions)	0.0	2.0	0.6	0.6	0.7		
Q. IDC-U.K. net cash flow (L + H + M + N − P, in £ millions)	−26.5	2.2	3.3	5.6	6.3	6.3	19.0
R. £ exchange rate ($)	2.00	1.96	1.92	1.89	1.85	1.82	1.82
S. IDC-U.K. cash flow (Q × R, in $ millions)	−53.0	4.3	6.3	10.6	11.6	11.5	34.5
T. Present value factor at 12%	1.0	0.8929	0.7972	0.7118	0.6355	0.5674	0.5674
U. Present value (S × T, in $ millions)	−53.0	3.8	5.0	7.5	7.4	6.5	19.6
V. Cumulative present value ($ millions)	−53.0	−49.2	−44.2	−36.7	−29.3	−22.8	−3.2

*Represents overhead for less than one full year.

**Loss carryforward from year 1 of £ 2.8 eliminates tax for years 2 and 3 and reduces tax for year 4.

Additions to Working Capital. One of the major outlays for any new project is the investment in working capital. IDC-U.K. begins with an initial investment in working capital of £1.5 million ($3 million). Working-capital requirements are projected at a constant 20% of sales. Thus, the necessary investment in working capital will increase by 15.5% annually, the rate of increase in pound sales revenue. These calculations are shown on lines O and P of Exhibit 3C.3.

Terminal Value. Calculating a terminal value is a complex undertaking, given the various possible ways to treat this issue. Three different approaches are pointed out. One approach is to assume that the investment will be liquidated after the end of the planning horizon and to use this value. However, this approach just takes the question one step further: What would a prospective buyer be willing to pay for this project? The second approach is to estimate the market value of the project, assuming that it is the present value of remaining cash flows. Again, however, the value of the project to an outside buyer may differ from its value to the parent firm, owing to parent profits on sales to its affiliate, for instance. The third approach is to calculate a break-even terminal value at which the project is just acceptable to the parent and then use that as a benchmark against which to judge the likelihood of the present value of future cash flows exceeding that value.

Most firms try to be quite conservative in estimating terminal values. IDC-U.K. calculates a terminal value on the basis of the assumption that the market value of the project will be 2.7 times the net cash flow in year 5 (net income plus depreciation), or £19.0 million.

Estimated Project Present Value. We are now ready to estimate the net present value of IDC-U.K. from the viewpoint of the project. As shown in Exhibit 3C.3, line V, the NPV of project cash flows equals –$3.2

million. Adding to this amount the $2.7 million value of interest subsidies and the $1.4 million present value of the tax shield on interest payments yields an overall positive project net present value of $0.9 million. The estimated value of the interest tax shield would be correspondingly greater if this analysis were to incorporate benefits derived over the full 10-year assumed life of the project, rather than including benefits from the first five years only. Over 10 years, the present value of the tax shield would equal $2.3 million, bringing the overall project net present value to $1.8 million. The latter approach is the conceptually correct one.

Despite the favorable net present value for IDC-U.K., it is unlikely that a firm would undertake an investment that had a positive value only because of interest subsidies or the interest tax shield provided by the debt capacity of the project. However, this is exactly what most firms do if they accept a marginal project, using a weighted cost of capital. On the basis of the debt capacity of the project and its subsidized financing, IDC-U.K. would have a weighted cost of capital of approximately 10%. At this discount rate, IDC-U.K. would be marginally profitable.

It would be misleading, however, to conclude the analysis at this point without recognizing and accounting for differences between project and parent cash flows and their impact on the worth of investing in IDC-U.K. Ultimately, shareholders in IDC-U.S. will benefit from this investment only to the extent that it generates cash flows that are, or can be, transferred out of England. The value of this investment is now calculated from the viewpoint of IDC-U.S.

Estimation of Parent Cash Flows. From the parent's perspective, additional cash outflows are recorded for any taxes paid to England or the United States on remitted funds. IDC-U.S. has additional cash inflows as well. It receives licensing and overhead allocation fees each year for which it incurs no additional expenses. If it did, the expenses would have to be charged against the fees. IDC-U.S. also profits from exports to its English affiliate.

Loan Payments. IDC-U.K. will first make all necessary loan repayments before paying dividends. Specifically, IDC-U.K. will repay the £1.5 million working-capital loan from Lloyds at the end of year 2 and NEB's loan of £5 million at the end of the fifth year. Their dollar repayment costs are estimated at $2.9 million and $9.3 million, respectively, based on the forecasted exchange rates. These latter two loan repayments are counted as parent cash inflows because they reduce the parent's outstanding consolidated debt burden and increase the value of its equity by an equivalent amount. Assuming that the parent would repay these loans regardless, having IDC-U.K. borrow and repay funds is equivalent to IDC-U.S. borrowing the money, investing it in IDC-U.K., and then using IDC-U.K.'s higher cash flows (because it no longer has British loans to service) to repay IDC-U.S.'s debts.

Remittances to IDC-U.S. IDC-U.K. is projected to pay dividends equal to 100% of its remaining net cash flows after making all necessary loan repayments. It also pays licensing and overhead allocation fees equal, in total, to 7% of gross sales. On both of these forms of transfer, the English government will collect a 10% withholding tax. These remittances are shown in Exhibit 3C.4. IDC-U.S., however, will not owe any further tax to the IRS because the company is assumed to have excess foreign tax credits. Otherwise, IDC-U.S. would have to pay U.S. corporate income taxes on the dividends and fees it receives, less any credits for foreign income and withholding taxes already paid. In this case, IDC-U.K. losses in the first year, combined with the higher British corporate tax rate, will assure that IDC-U.S. would owe minimal taxes to the IRS even if it did not have any excess foreign tax credits.

Earnings on Exports to IDC-U.K. With a 25% margin on its exports, and assuming it has sufficient spare-parts manufacturing capacity, IDC-U.S. has incremental earnings on sales to IDC-U.K. equaling 25% of the value of these shipments. After U.S. corporate

EXHIBIT 3C.4 Dividends and Fees and Royalties Received by IDC-U.S. (U.S. $ MILLIONS)

	Year					
	1	2	3	4	5	5+
A. Net cash flow to IDC-U.K., (from Exhibit 3C.3, line S)	4.3	6.3	10.6	11.6	11.5	34.5
B. Loan repayments by IDC-U.K.		2.9			9.3	
C. Dividend paid to IDC-U.S. (A–B)	4.3	3.3	10.6	11.6	2.2	34.5
D. Fees and royalties (Exhibit 3C.3, line F × line G)	1.0	2.3	2.7	3.0	3.4	15.5*
E. Withholding tax paid to England @ 10% = 0.10 × (C + D)	0.5	0.6	1.3	1.5	0.6	5.0
F. Net income received by IDC-U.S. (C + D – E, in $ millions)	$4.8	$5.1	$11.9	$13.1	$5.1	$45.0
G. Exchange rate	$1.96	$1.92	$1.89	$1.85	$1.82	$1.82

*Estimated present value of future fees and royalties. These were not incorporated in the terminal value figure of $25 million.

EXHIBIT 3C.5 Net Cash Flows from Exports to IDC-U.K.

	1	2	3	4	5	5+
			Year			
A. Sales (units)	30,000	66,000	73,000	80,000	88,000	88,000
B. Components purchased from IDC-U.S.						
1. Unit price ($)	60.0	61.8	63.7	65.6	67.5	67.5
2. Total export revenue (A × B1 in $ millions)	1.8	4.1	4.6	5.2	5.9	5.9
C. After-tax cash flow (0.165 × B2 in $ millions)	$0.3	$0.7	$0.8	$0.9	$1.0	$1.0

tax of 35%, IDC-U.S. generates cash flows valued at 16.5% (25 × 65%) of its exports to IDC-U.K. These cash flows are presented in Exhibit 3C.5.

Estimated Present Value of Project to IDC-U.S. In Exhibit 3C.6, all the various cash flows are added up, net of tax and interest subsidies on debt, and their present value is calculated at $13.0 million. Adding the $5 million in debt-related subsidies ($2.4 million for the interest tax shield and $2.6 million for the NEB loan subsidy), brings this value up to $18.0 million. It is apparent

EXHIBIT 3C.6 Present Value of IDC-U.K.: Parent Viewpoint (U.S. $ Millions)

	0	1	2	3	4	5	5+
				Year			
A. Cash inflows							
1. Loan repayments by IDC-U.K. (from Exhibit 3C.4, line B)			2.9			9.3	
2. Dividends paid to IDC-U.S. (from Exhibit 3C.4, line C)		4.3	3.3	10.6	11.6	2.2	34.5
3. Fees and royalties paid to IDC-U.S. (from Exhibit 3C.4, line D)		1.0	2.3	2.7	3.0	3.4	15.5
4. Net cash flows from exports (from Exhibit 3C.5, line C)		0.3	0.7	0.8	0.9	1.0	4.1*
5. Total cash inflows		5.6	9.3	14.0	15.4	15.9	54.1
B. Cash outflows							
1. Plant and equipment	50						
2. Working capital	3						
3. Withholding tax paid to U.K. (from Exhibit 3C.4, line E)		0.5	0.6	1.3	1.5	0.6	5.0
4. Total cash outflows	53	0.5	0.6	1.3	1.5	0.6	5.0
C. Net cash flow (A5–B4)	−53	5.1	8.7	12.7	14.0	15.3	49.1
D. Present-value factor at 12%	1.0	0.8929	0.7972	0.7118	0.6355	0.5674	0.5674
E. Present value (C × D)	−53	4.5	6.9	9.0	8.9	8.7	27.9
F. Cumulative present value ($ millions)	−$53	−$48.5	−$41.5	−$32.5	−$23.6	−$14.9	$13.0

*Estimated present value of future earnings on export sales to IDC-U.K..

that, despite the additional taxes that must be paid to England and the United States, IDC-U.K. is more valuable to its parent than it would be to another owner on a stand-alone basis. This situation is due primarily to the various licensing and overhead allocation fees received and the incremental earnings on exports to IDC-U.K.

Lost Sales. There is a circumstance, however, that can reverse this conclusion. This discussion has assumed that IDC-U.S. is now producing at capacity and that the 20,000 diesel engines currently being exported to the EC can be sold in the United States, starting in year 2. Should this assumption not be the case (that is, should 20,000 units of IDC-U.K. sales just replace 20,000 units of IDC-U.S. sales), then the project would have to be charged with the incremental cash flow that IDC-U.S. would have earned on these lost exports. We now see how to incorporate this effect in a capital-budgeting analysis.

Suppose the incremental after-tax cash flow per unit to IDC-U.S. on its exports to the EC equals $180 at present and that this contribution is expected to maintain its value in current dollar terms over time. Then, in nominal dollar terms, this margin grows by 3% annually. If we assume lost sales of 20,000 units per year, beginning in year 2 and extending through year 10, and a discount rate of 12%, the present value associated with these lost sales equals $19.5 million. The calculations are presented in Exhibit 3C.7. Subtracting the present value of lost sales from the previously calculated present value of $18.0 million yields a net present value of IDC-U.K. to its parent equal to –$1.5 million (–$6.5 million ignoring the interest tax shield and subsidy).

This example points up the importance of looking at incremental cash flows generated by a foreign project rather than total cash flows. An investment that would be marginally profitable on its own, and quite profitable when integrated with parent activities, becomes unprofitable when taking into account earnings on lost sales.

EXHIBIT 3C.7 Value of Lost Export Sales

	Year								
	2	3	4	5	6	7	8	9	10
A. Lost unit sales	20,000	20,000	20,000	20,000	20,000	20,000	20,000	20,000	20,000
B. Cash flow per unit*	185.4	191.0	196.7	202.6	208.7	214.9	221.4	228.0	234.9
C. Total cash flow from exports (A × B)	3.7	3.8	3.9	4.1	4.2	4.3	4.4	4.6	4.7
D. Present value factor at 12%	0.7972	0.7118	0.6355	0.5674	0.5066	0.4523	0.4039	0.3606	0.3220
E. Present value (C × D)	3.0	2.7	2.5	2.5	2.1	1.9	1.8	1.6	1.5
F. Cumulative present value ($)	3.0	5.7	8.2	8.2	12.6	14.5	16.3	18.0	19.5

*The figures in this row grow by 3% each year. So, 185.4 = 180(1.03), and so on.

CHAPTER

Real Options and Project Analysis

How many ages hence
Shall this lofty scene be acted over
In states unborn and accents still unknown!
    —SHAKESPEARE,
    Julius Caesar

The discounted cash flow (DCF) analysis presented so far treats a project's expected cash flows as given at the outset. This approach presupposes a static approach to investment decision making: It assumes that all operating decisions are set in advance. In reality, though, the opportunity to make decisions contingent on information to become available in the future is an essential feature of many investment decisions. Depending on the project's outcome (e.g., the success of a new model in the case of a car factory) and the operating environment at that time (e.g., the level of factor costs and product prices), the rate of output may be speeded up or slowed down, and the facility may be expanded, temporarily closed, or even abandoned. Indeed, in the case of an investment in research and development, a plant may not be built if the outcome is not commercially feasible. In all these cases, the optimal operating policy depends on outcomes that are not known at the project's inception. The ability of companies to change course in response to changing circumstances create what are often termed **real**, or **growth**, **options**.

4.1 Option Valuation and Investment Decisions

The corporation must value the set of available investment projects in order to decide which are worth undertaking. As we saw in Chapter 2, the standard approach is to estimate the cash flows that a project is expected to generate and to discount them at a risk-adjusted cost of capital. However, many investments have very uncertain payoffs that are best valued with an options approach.

Consider a firm that must decide whether to make a $50,000 down payment on an undeveloped piece of land. The down payment will permit the firm to purchase the property outright by paying an additional $500,000 at any time during the next six months. If the additional payment is not made, the $50,000 will be forfeited. The down payment agreement is a call option, with the $50,000 down payment equivalent to the option price; the extra money needed to complete the deal ($500,000) is the strike price; and the uncertain value of the land after it is developed is the "stock" price. The decision to "exercise the option," that is, to pay the additional $500,000 to own the land, depends on whether the value of the land exceeds $500,000 at the time the agreement is about to expire. Before entering into this agreement and spending the $50,000 option price, the company must determine whether $50,000 is a fair price for the option. Clearly, the Black–Scholes formula could be used for this purpose. Exhibit 4.1 shows how the value of this option varies with the price of the land in six months.

Other explicit and implicit contracts to which a firm is a party and involve investment decision making can be thought of (and valued) as options. A lease with an option to cancel can be viewed as a put option. If the value of leasing the property drops below the value of the lease payments, the lease will be canceled and the property will be "returned" to its owner, just as a stock will be sold to a put writer if its value drops sufficiently low. For example, a federal crop price support program is equivalent to issuing put options to farmers. A farmer would prefer to sell his crop at a higher price in the market but can always sell to the government at the guaranteed price if the market price plummets. The purchase of an insurance policy on property can also be thought of as a put: If the property is not damaged and remains valuable, the insurance contract will not be used; if a fire or earthquake damages the property, it will be forfeited in return for the contracted insurance payoff. It is analogous to exercising a put option when the price of the stock drops below the exercise price.

Any investment that requires an additional infusion of funds for its completion and offers an uncertain payoff can be viewed as an option. Consider the value of a patent on an untested cure for cancer. The price of obtaining the patent is the option price; the cost of developing, producing, and marketing the drug is the striking price; and the market value of profits on sales of the drug is equivalent to the stock price. The extra funds required to start production will be invested only if this cost is less than the payoff in the form of subsequent profits from the sale of the drug.

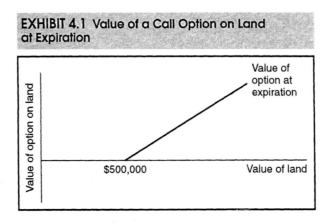

EXHIBIT 4.1 Value of a Call Option on Land at Expiration

The opportunities that a firm may have to increase the profitability of its existing product lines and benefit from expanding into new products or markets may be thought of as **growth options**.[1] Similarly, a firm's ability to capitalize on its managerial talent, its experience in a particular product line, its brand name, or its other resources, may provide valuable but uncertain future prospects. Growth options are of great importance to new firms. New ventures often have few, if any, tangible assets; their assets consist primarily of the knowledge and skills of an entrepreneur. Yet such firms have value because of the profitable possibilities their intangible assets provide. As we will see in Section 4.4, these growth options may constitute a large fraction of firm value. For example, Genentech, a gene-splicing company, had a stock market value of over $3 billion in late 1986, even though its earnings for the year were only $11 million, giving it a P/E ratio of over 270 to 1. Clearly, the market was valuing Genentech's future ability to capitalize on its research in areas like anticancer therapy and blood clot dissolvers for heart attack victims.

Any firm that faces a continuing series of operating decisions may be thought of as having investment options. The owners of a gold mine, for example, may increase or decrease the mine's gold output depending on the current price of gold and expectations of future gold prices. The mine can be shut down and then reopened when production and market conditions are more favorable, or it can be abandoned permanently. Each decision is an option from the viewpoint of the mine's owners. The value of these options, in turn, affects the value of the mine.

BOX 4.1

APPLICATION: VALUING A GOLD MINE

Consider the decision of whether to reopen a gold mine. The cost of doing so is expected to be $1 million. There are an estimated 40,000 ounces of gold remaining in the mine. If the mine is reopened, the gold can be removed in one year at a variable cost of $390 per ounce. Assuming an expected gold price in one year of $400 per ounce, the expected profit per ounce mined is $10. Clearly, the expected cash inflow (ignoring taxes) of $400,000 next year ($10 × 40,000) is far below that necessary to recoup the $1 million investment in reopening the mine, much less to pay the 15% yield required on such a risky investment. But intuition—which suggests a highly negative project NPV (net present value) of –$652,174 (–$1,000,000 + 400,000/1.15)—is wrong in this case. The reason is that the cash flow projections underlying the classical DCF analysis ignore the option *not* to produce gold if it is unprofitable to do so.

The following is a simple example that demonstrates the fallacy of always using expected cash flows to judge an investment's merits. Suppose there are only two possible gold prices next year: $300 per ounce and $500 per ounce, each with probability 0.5. The expected gold price is $400 per ounce, but this expected price is irrelevant to

---

[1]Growth options are synonymous with real options.

the optimal mining decision rule: Mine gold if, and only if, the price of gold at year's end is $500 per ounce. Exhibit 4.2 shows the cash flow consequences of that decision rule. Closure costs are assumed to be zero.

Incorporating the mine owner's option *not* to mine gold when the price falls below the cost of extraction reveals a positive net present value of $913,043 for the decision to reopen the gold mine:

$$\begin{array}{c}\text{NPV of gold mine} \\ \text{investment}\end{array} = -\$1,000,000 + \frac{\$2,200,000}{1.15}$$

$$= \$913,043$$

In option pricing terms, the current value of the mine can be thought of as a call option on the value of the gold in the mine: The strike price equals the cost of reopening, and the stock price equals the value of the gold that could subsequently be produced. For valuation purposes, we used the decision rule to reopen the mine only if the value of the gold to be mined exceeds the cost of reopening, just as a call option will be exercised only if the stock price exceeds the exercise price.

With regard to investments already under way, firms have three choices: Continue to invest in the project; abandon the project; or delay it. The flexibility to change course in mid-stream, rather than continue down a losing path, has value. How much value depends on a variety of factors, including the amount of uncertainty surrounding the project's economics, the cost of changing, and payoff associated with the change.

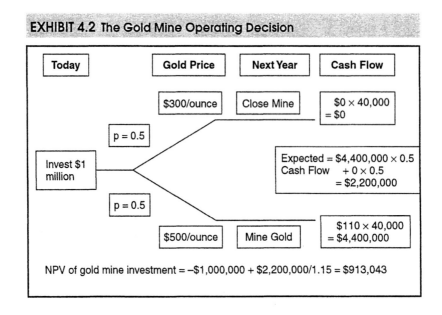

EXHIBIT 4.2 The Gold Mine Operating Decision

BOX 4.2

APPLICATION: MICRON SLOWS THINGS DOWN

In early 1996, Boise, Idaho-based Micron Technology, Inc. faced a glut in the market for computer chips, which caused the prices of Micron's products to slide. In response, the company announced it would postpone completion of a chip plant in Lehi, Utah, after it had already invested $400 million in the project. The partially completed chip plant gave Micron "a leg up on the next 'up' cycle," according to Kipp Bedard, the firm's vice president of corporate affairs.[2] Instead of starting from scratch, Micron could complete its unfinished plant when demand picked up.

4.2 Evaluating R&D Investments Using an Option Valuation Approach

As the case of the gold mine investment demonstrates, the ability to alter decisions in response to new information may contribute significantly to the value of a project. Such investments bear the characteristics of options on securities and should be valued accordingly. Just as a call option gives the holder the right to acquire shares at a fixed exercise price, an investment in research and development gives the investor the right to acquire the outcomes of the R&D at the cost of commercialization. Similarly, the owner of a mine has the right to acquire the mine's output at the variable cost of production ($390 per ounce in the case of the gold mine). In addition, both the investor in R&D and the mine owner have put options; they can abandon their projects at an exercise price equal to the costs of shutdown. By contrast, the traditional approach to investment analysis, which ignores management's ability to respond to future operating conditions, may be likened to valuing a stock option contract while ignoring the holder's right not to exercise when it is unprofitable (e.g., the mine owner's right not to produce when the price of gold falls below $390 per ounce). By failing to take into account the benefits of operating flexibility and potentially valuable add-on projects, the traditional DCF will tend to understate project values.

Consider, for example, an investment in developing a new product and bringing it to market. The product development phase is expected to cost $5 million a year from 2005 through 2007. At that time, the company will build a plant costing $100 million to manufacture the new product. On the basis of the new product's anticipated properties and the projected competition, the annual cash flow from year-end 2008 through 2017 is expected to be $13 million. The terminal value of the project as of year-end 2017 is projected at $105 million. These data are summarized in Exhibit 4.3.

The present values of these cash flow items as of January 1, 2005, and January 1, 2008, if we use an assumed discount rate of 14%, are shown in Exhibit 4.4. They indicate

---

[2]"Know When To Say No," *Investors Business Daily*, March 28, 1996.

**EXHIBIT 4.3 Expected Cash Flows from New Product Development*
($ millions)**

R&D Expense		Cost of New Plant		Operating Cash Flows			Terminal Value
2005	2006	2007	2008	2008	2009	...	2017
−5	−5	−5	−100	13	13	...	105

*Costs are assumed to occur at the start of the year and operating cash flows at the end of the year.

EXHIBIT 4.4 Present Values of Cash Flow Items for New Product Development ($ millions)

	Present Value as of January 1	
Cash Flow Item	2005	2008
Research and development expense	−13.2	—
Plant cost (2008, beginning of year)	−67.5	−100.0
Post-2007 operating cash flows (2008–2017)	45.8	67.8
Terminal value (2017)	16.8	28.3
Net present value	−18.2	−3.9

a highly negative project NPV. But as in the case of the gold mine, the numbers are misleading.

The problem with the analysis is that it assumes the plant will be built regardless of the outcome of the product development effort and the market conditions prevailing in 2007. By ignoring the option not to build the plant, standard DCF analysis projects a negative NPV of –$3.9 million as of 2008. Option valuation allows for the decision *not* to build the plant and also values only those outcomes that will follow if the plant is built. Clearly, if the R&D investment does not pan out or if market conditions are unfavorable, the plant will not be built.

Exhibit 4.5 shows the probability distribution of possible outcomes of the R&D investment as of 2008, according to both the traditional DCF valuation method and the option valuation method, and also illustrates the sharp contrast between these methods. Note that the option valuation approach properly values only *positive* net present value outcomes, whereas the traditional DCF analysis values *all* outcomes, negative as well as positive.

Exhibit 4.6 shows how the different assumptions underlying the two methods affect their estimates of expected cash flows and project NPVs. The analysis considers only four possible scenarios, each with probability 0.25 of occurring (in contrast with the continuous probability distribution shown in Exhibit 4.5). Even though the expected payoff from undertaking the project remains at $96.1 million as of 2008, the figures in Exhibit 4.6 show that the possible payoffs can vary from $223.9 million down to $8.6 million. The variability in possible payoffs means that the plant is worth

EXHIBIT 4.5 Probability Distribution of Outcomes Under DCF Valuation and Option Valuation

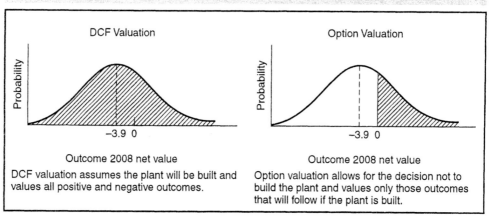

DCF Valuation assumes the plant will be built and values all positive and negative outcomes.

Option valuation allows for the decision not to build the plant and values only those outcomes that will follow if the plant is built.

EXHIBIT 4.6 DCF Valuation versus Option Valuation ($ millions)

Present Value on January 1		2005 R&D Expense	2008 Plant Cost	2008 Possible Payoff	2005 Project NPV
DCF Analysis		−13.2	−100.0	96.1	−18.2
Assumes one outcome, measured as expected value of all possible outcomes					
Option Analysis	I	−13.2	−100.0	223.9	70.4
Assumes many possible outcomes and measures each one separately	II	−13.2	−100.0	118.1	−1.0
	III	−13.2	−	33.9	−13.2
	IV	−13.2	−	8.6	−13.2

building under some scenarios and not under others. Under scenarios III and IV, the option valuation approach assumes the plant will not be built because the present values of the possible payoffs are negative. In these cases, the project's NPV is just −$13.2 million, the cost of the R&D investment.

Unlike the DCF analysis, in which the net present value is calculated as −$18.2 million, the option valuation approach recognizes that the expected NPV of the new product development project cannot fall below −$13.2 million. The expected project payoff in 2008 of $96.1 million used in the DCF analysis is a weighted average of the four possible outcomes. However, this number is irrelevant to the investment decision because the company will not build the plant unless the future payoff is at least equal to its $100 million cost. Hence, the possible outcomes of $33.9 million and $8.6 million can be disregarded.

EXHIBIT 4.7 Expected NPV of R&D Investment in 2008 ($ millions)

Scenario	Decision	Cost	Payoff	NPV	× Probability	=	Value
I	Build plant	−100.0	223.9	123.9	0.25		31.0
II	Build plant	−100.0	118.1	18.1	0.25		4.5
III	Don't build	0	0	0	0.25		0
IV	Don't build	0	0	0	0.25		0
							35.5

Note: Because the R&D investment will have already been made by 2008, it is a sunk cost and so does not affect the calculated NPV.

To conclude this example, Exhibit 4.7 shows that the expected project NPV in 2008 valuing only favorable outcomes is $35.5 million. This yields a present value in 2005 of $24.0 million. Subtract the $13.2 million present value of the R&D investment, and the result is a highly acceptable project with a $10.7 million net present value. By contrast, the traditional DCF analysis, which yields an estimated project NPV of −$18.2 million, gives a reject decision. The correct decision is to invest in new product development and exercise the option of proceeding further in 2008 if the outcome looks favorable. Otherwise, the project should be abandoned at that point.

4.3 Strategic Investments and Growth Options

The problem of undervaluing investment projects using the standard DCF analysis is particularly acute for strategic investments. Many strategically important investments, such as investments in R&D, factory automation, a brand name, or a distribution network, provide growth opportunities because they are often but the first link in a chain of subsequent investment decisions. For example, companies that invested in automatic and electronically controlled machine tools in the 1970s were ideally positioned to exploit the microprocessor-based revolution and capabilities (higher performance at a much lower cost) that hit during the 1980s. Since machine operators, maintenance personnel, and process engineers were already comfortable with electronic technology, it was relatively easy to retrofit existing machines with the new technology. Companies that had deferred their investment in the latest technology, fell behind in the 1980s.

The investment in R&D frequently provides growth opportunities since they are the first link in a chain of investments that can create competitive advantage. Such follow-up projects, which create options on investments in other products, markets, or production processes, are sometimes referred to as **growth options** and may be an important component of firm value. Viewing these projects in isolation ignores their ability to create options on future products, markets, and production technologies.

BOX 4.3

APPLICATION: WESTERN FIRMS INVEST IN EASTERN EUROPE

The investments that many Western companies are now considering in Eastern Europe can be thought of as growth options. Some view investments there as a way to gain entry into a potentially large market. Others see Eastern Europe as an underdeveloped area with educated and skilled workers but low wages, and view such investments as a low-cost backdoor to Western European markets. In either case, companies who invest there are buying an option that will pay off in the event that Eastern European markets boom or that Eastern European workers turn out to be much more productive with the right technology and incentives than they have been under communism.

To illustrate the nature of these strategic options, consider the case of Bubbly Beverage, Inc., a soft drink manufacturer thinking about entering the fruit drink segment with its Delightfully Delicious line. The firm is already a world leader in carbonated beverages, and believes that its soft drink marketing expertise, coupled with its global distribution network will provide it with a long-term competitive advantage. Entering the fruited beverage segment will not be costless since Bubbly would face formidable competition from a number of entrenched smaller firms that have been in this market for a number of years. However, not entering the fruited beverage market at this time might preclude entry at a later date if one of the existing fruit beverage firms were acquired by Kampy Kola, Bubbly's major competitor in the carbonated beverage market. This would not only foreclose future product extensions but might make Bubbly vulnerable if soft drink demand shifted dramatically from carbonated to noncarbonated beverages.

Using standard DCF techniques, Bubbly develops its initial cash flow estimates, which are presented in Exhibit 4.8.

EXHIBIT 4.8 Bubbly Beverage Company Summary of Cash flows for Delightfully Delicious Line ($ millions)

Year	1	2	3	4	5
After-tax operating cash flow*	−140	−120	50	100	100
Capital investment	−80	−	−	−	−
Working capital changes	−20	−30	−30	−20	−
Terminal value**	−	−	−	−	500
Net cash flow	−240	−150	20	80	600
Present value @ 20%	−240.0	−125.0	13.9	46.3	289.4
NPV @ 20% = − $15.5 million					

*Equal to net profit after taxes plus depreciation. After-tax operating cash flow is negative in years 1 and 2 because of heavy promotion and advertising expenses.

**Cash flows beyond year 5 are assumed to be $100 million per year into the indefinite future. Discounting this cash flow stream by 20% yields the $500 million terminal value.

As Exhibit 4.8 indicates, traditional techniques show that, contrary to management's gut feel, the fruited beverage line should not be introduced because the project does not meet Bubbly's required rate of return of 20%, and has a negative NPV of $15.5 million. However, this analysis does not come close to capturing the project's strategic value. For example, if the Delightfully Delicious line is successful, Bubbly could follow-up with a low calorie version. A product extension such as this would, in all likelihood, require lower market development costs because the brand name is already established. With two lines in place, vertical integration into the fruit juice business and/or related diversification into wine coolers becomes a possibility. While these future investments may be risky, Bubbly does not have to commit additional resources today until it sees how the initial investment turns out. Moreover, since option values increase with risk, the speculative nature of these future ventures enhances the value of the option to invest in these potential new products. For a large firm like Bubbly, the $15.5 million negative NPV associated with the initial offering of Delightfully Delicious may be a small price to pay for a set of options to enter new markets if conditions are favorable.

Valuing investments that embody discretionary follow-up projects requires an expanded net present value rule that considers the attendant options. More specifically, the value of an option to undertake a follow-up project equals the expected project NPV using the conventional DCF analysis plus the value of the discretion associated with undertaking the project. This is shown in Exhibit 4.9. According to option pricing theory, the latter element of value (the discretion to invest or not invest in a project) depends on:

1. *The length of time the project can be deferred.*   The ability to defer a project gives the firm more time to examine the course of future events and to avoid costly

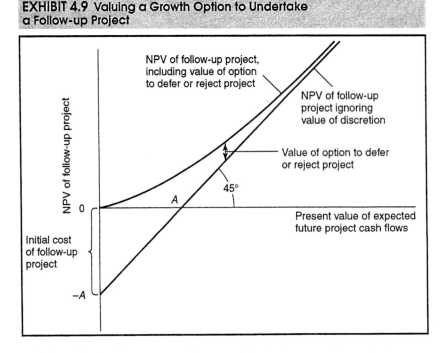

EXHIBIT 4.9 Valuing a Growth Option to Undertake a Follow-up Project

errors if unfavorable developments occur. A longer time interval also raises the odds that a positive turn of events will dramatically boost the project's profitability and turn even a negative NPV project into a positive one.

2. *The risk of the project.* Surprisingly, the riskier the investment is, the more valuable an option on it will be. The reason is the asymmetry between gains and losses. A large gain is possible if the project's NPV becomes highly positive, whereas losses are limited by the option not to exercise when the project NPV is negative. The riskier the project is, the greater the odds will be of a large gain without a corresponding increase in the size of the potential loss.

3. *The level of interest rates.* Although a high discount rate lowers the present value of a project's future cash flows, it also reduces the present value of the cash outlay needed to exercise an option. The net effect is that high interest rates generally raise the value of projects that contain growth options.

4. *The proprietary nature of the option.* Consideration of competitive conditions is what separates growth options from stock options. Growth options are valuable because they allow the firm to delay investments to learn more about the value of the underlying growth opportunities. But because these options are (1) often shared with other competitors and (2) cannot generally be traded, competition provides an incentive to exercise the option early and invest in the opportunity before competitors do. This is equivalent to the early exercise of an option on a dividend-paying stock. An exclusively owned option is clearly more valuable than one that is shared with others. The latter might include the chance to enter a new market or to invest in a new production process. Shared options are less valuable because competitors can replicate the investments and drive down returns.

BOX 4.4

APPLICATION: FORD MOTOR CO. GIVES UP ON SMALL-CAR DEVELOPMENT

In late 1986, Ford gave up on small-car development in the United States and handed over the job to Japan's Mazda. Although seemingly cost effective in the short run (Ford should save about $500 million in development costs for one car model alone), such a move—which removed a critical mass from Ford's own engineering efforts— could prove dangerous in the longer term. Overcoming engineering obstacles unique to subcompact cars—for example, the challenges of miniaturization—enhances engineers' skills and allows them to apply innovations to all classes of vehicles. By eroding its technological base, Ford may have yielded the option of generating ideas that can be applied elsewhere in its business. Moreover, the cost of reentering the business of in-house design can be substantial. The abandonment decision is not one to be taken lightly.

Some American consumer electronics companies, for example, are learning the penalties of ceding major technologies and the experiences that come from working with these technologies on a day-to-day basis. Westinghouse Electric, after quitting the development and manufacture of color television tubes in 1976, later decided to get back into the color-video business. But because it had lost touch with the product, Westinghouse was able to reenter only by way of a joint venture with Japan's Toshiba.

The video recorder is a classic example of how production know-how can yield important technical advances. Sony, along with Matsushita Electric and its partner, Japan Victor Corp. (JVC), redesigned a professional-use product from the United States that cost $20,000 or more and turned it into a $1,500 home product with a relatively small market. Japanese designers then worked closely with factory personnel to make every component smaller and less expensive.

Cooperation between Matsushita's design teams and employees on the shop floor eliminated more than three quarters of the product's cost while dramatically improving its quality. In the process, the company turned a niche product into the consumer electronics mass-market success story of the 1980s.

Moreover, in ceding to the Japanese development of videocassette recorders, as well as laser video disk players, RCA and other U.S. manufacturers lost more than these products alone. Each technology has since spawned entirely new, popular product lines — from video cameras to compact disk players — in which U.S. companies are left with nothing to do beyond marketing the Japanese-made goods.

Even those companies that merely turn to outside partners for technical help could nevertheless find their skills atrophying over the years as their partners handle more of the complex designing and manufacturing. Such companies range from Boeing, which has enlisted three Japanese firms to help engineer a new plane, to Honeywell, which is getting big computers from NEC. The corresponding reduction in in-house technological skills decreases the value of the option these firms have to develop and apply new technologies in novel product areas.

Unfortunately, estimating the value of a growth option is an all-but-impossible task since it depends on unknowable future events. A recommended approach is to estimate the NPV ignoring any growth options. If the resulting NPV is positive, then the project is acceptable; consideration of growth options would just increase its value. But if the NPV is negative, say, –$5 million, management must then decide whether it would be willing to spend $5 million (the amount necessary to yield a zero NPV) to acquire the growth options that the project may give rise to. Such a question is easier to answer than the one that asks "How much are these growth options worth?

4.4 Investment Decisions and Real Options

The preceding suggests that the existence of strategic options increases the value of a project. In general, the value of a project (*VPROJ*) can be viewed as follows:

$$VPROJ = VDCF + VSTRAT \qquad (4.1)$$

where *VDCF* is the project's value using traditional DCF techniques, and *VSTRAT* is the value of the strategic options. While the value of the strategic options may be difficult (if not impossible) to assess, their presence can be treated as qualitative factors in making decisions. Further, the value of an option increases with uncertainty. Since an option represents a right, but not the obligation, to buy or sell an asset, there is no commitment to future investments unless conditions are favorable. In this way, a company can exploit a project's upside potential without incurring significant downside risks.

There are many classes of investment decisions containing embedded options. The potential for product line extensions for Bubbly Beverage's Deliciously Delightful fruit drink is an example of a growth option, which is essentially an option to change output in response to changes in product demand. A variation on this theme is the decision to build a pilot plant to manufacture a new product. While pilot plant operations, in general, do not exploit economies of scale, they do mitigate losses if sales are disappointing. On the other hand, if sales take off, the firm can invest in a higher capacity plant that would be more efficient.

In some cases, the firm may also have the option to abandon a project after it is undertaken. This may consist of simply selling the assets for cash or redeploying the assets in some other area of the business thereby eliminating the requirements for additional cash outlays. Effectively, the ability to abandon a project represents a put option for the firm. Whether we are dealing with a single piece of equipment, or whether the firm is considering a divestiture of an entire product line or division, the decision rule is the same: A project should be abandoned if the abandonment value exceeds the present value of subsequent cash flows.

Although we do not usually think about it this way, the flexibility of a project represents a set of options made available to management if the project is accepted. Baldwin, Mason, and Ruback refer to such options as "operating options," which may be inherent in some large-scale production projects.[3] For example, the management of an electric utility may face the choice of building a power plant that burns only oil or one that is capable of burning both oil and coal. While the latter facility would cost more to build, it also provides greater flexibility because management now has the option to switch back and forth between fuel sources based on prices in the energy markets. Operating options also exist in production facilities like oil refineries and chemical plants where the firm can use different raw material mixes to produce the same final product, or the same inputs (e.g., crude oil) to produce a variety of outputs (e.g., gasoline, heating oil). In an environment characterized by highly variable commodity prices, such operating options can be extremely valuable.

Other operating options include the following:

- Reducing or increasing output in response to changing demand.
- Changing marketing (pricing/promotion) strategies.
- Redesigning a product in response to changing demand or input costs.
- Changing the mix of products made at a plant (see the refinery example above).
- Temporarily closing a plant in response to a decline in demand.

The examples presented above represent a "short list" of situations where there are options imbedded in an investment project. As a practical matter, valuing these

---

[3]Operating options are also called **managerial options**. See Baldwin, C.Y., Mason, S.P., and Ruback, R.S. *Evaluation of Government Subsidies to Large Scale Energy Projects: A Contingent Claims Approach.* Harvard Business School Working Paper, 1983.

options may be extremely difficult; however, ignoring their existence can lead to the rejection of strategically valuable—and value-adding—projects. Thus, while DCF analysis represents a useful starting point for determining a project's value, its results should be tempered by the existence of real options.

One approach to incorporating options in a capital-budgeting analysis would be to first estimate the value of a project using DCF. If the project has a positive net present value ignoring the value of its strategic options, there is no need to engage in costly and uncertain estimates of their value; the project is acceptable regardless of the value of the strategic options imbedded in it. On the other hand, if the project's NPV is negative, then management would have to decide whether they would be prepared to pay X dollars to acquire the strategic options associated with it, where NPV(project) + X = 0; that is, X is the added value that would just yield a zero NPV for the project. This type of break-even analysis avoids forcing managers to determine the actual value of the options. Instead, they can focus on whether the options are likely to be worth more or less than X, an easier decision.

The use of real options evaluation techniques appears to be more widespread by corporate America than one might think given the complexity of the methodology. In their previously referenced survey of capital-budgeting techniques, Graham and Harvey report that more than one-fourth of the companies claimed to be using real options evaluation techniques.[4] However, they state that the dominant corporate use of real options probably remains as a qualitative strategic planning tool rather than a valuation technique.

4.5 Summary and Conclusions

The standard approach to investment decision making involves forecasting future project cash flows and then discounting them back to their present value. The underlying assumption is that all decisions are made at the outset, with no subsequent changes. Such an approach, however, fails to account for the flexibility that companies often have to change their decisions in response to new information and changing circumstances. This flexibility gives companies what have come to be termed real, or growth, options.

Options are valuable because they allow the holder to defer a decision until a later date, by which time more information will have been acquired about what is best to do. The more uncertain the future, the more valuable the ability to delay decisions will be. What this means is that the cash flows associated with growth options are contingent on how the world evolves and whether it makes sense to exploit the growth opportunities that may appear.

Failure to account for the options available to managers to adjust the scope or scale of a project will lead to a downward bias in estimating project cash flows. These options include the possibility of expanding or contracting the project, speeding it up or slowing it down, or abandoning it altogether, the chance to employ radical new process technologies by utilizing skills developed from implementing the project, and the possibility of entering the new lines of business to which a project may lead. Except

---

[4]Graham, J., and Harvey, C. "How Do CFOs Make Capital Budgeting and Capital Structure Decisions?" *Journal of Applied Corporate Finance*, Spring 2002, pp. 8–23.

in very special circumstances, valuing these real options precisely is a task beyond our current capabilities. However, ignoring them altogether will result in a downwards biased estimate of a project's value.

REFERENCES

Brennan, M.J., and Schwartz, E.S. "A New Approach to Evaluating Natural Resource Investments." *Midland Corporate Finance Journal*, Spring 1985, pp. 37– 47.

Kester, W.C. "Today's Options for Tomorrow's Growth." *Harvard Business Review*, March–April 1984, pp. 153–160.

QUESTIONS

1. Imagine that the price of copper rises to the point that the copper value of a penny is worth more than $0.01. As a result, pennies disappear from circulation. Your firm uses copper in its production process, and you can melt pennies down and retrieve their copper content at zero cost. At present, you have a six-month supply of copper reserves and you have also managed to collect 1 million pennies. Should you melt the pennies down and add the copper to your stockpile? Why or why not?

2. .Will a gold mine ever be shut permanently? Why or why not?

3. Some economists have stated that too many companies are not calculating the cost of *not* investing in new technology, world-class manufacturing facilities, or market position overseas. What are some of these costs? How do these costs relate to the notion of growth options discussed in the chapter?

4. In December 1989, General Electric spent $150 million to buy a controlling interest in Tungsram, the Hungarian state-owned light bulb maker. Even in its best year, Tungsram earned less than a 4% return on equity (based on the price GE paid). What might account for GE's decision to spend so much money to acquire such a dilapidated, inefficient manufacturer?

PROBLEMS

1. A biotech firm must decide whether to purchase the patent to a new food additive, a low-cal starch substitute. It is estimated that the funds required to bring the additive to the market can be as high as $50 million or as low as $25 million. The payoff is uncertain as well: The present value of profits could be as high as $500 million or as low as $30 million. The risk-free rate is 10%, and the standard deviation of rate of return on biotech products is 35%. The patent's life is estimated at one year.

   a. In a worst-case scenario, how much is the patent worth?
   b. In a best-case scenario, how much is the patent worth?

2. The managers of a firm are asked to consider two possible new product lines for the firm. Project 1 is quite risky and may result in a market value for the firm of $50 million in two years, or nothing. Project 2 is much more certain in outcome and may result in a firm market value as high as $25 million or as low as $15 million.

   The face value of the company's debt, payable in two years, is $20 million.
   a. What are the possible payoffs to the bondholders under projects 1 and 2?
   b. What are the possible payoffs to the shareholders under projects 1 and 2?
   c. Which will the shareholders favor? The bondholders?

3. Eastern Shallow, Ltd., is a gold mining company operating a single mine. The present price of gold is $300 an ounce and it costs the company $250 an ounce to produce the gold. Last

year, 50,000 ounces were produced and engineers estimate that at this rate of production the mine will be exhausted in seven years. The required rate of return on gold mines is 10%.

a. What is the value of the mine?

b. Suppose inflation is expected to increase the cost of producing gold by 10% a year but the price of gold does not change because of large sales of stockpiled gold by foreign governments. Furthermore, imagine that the inflation raises the required rate of return to 21%. Now, what is the value of the mine?

c. Suppose the company may shut, reopen, or abandon the mine in response to fluctuations in the price of gold. Can the NPV method be used to value the mine under these conditions?

4. G.D. Sorrell is developing an anticancer drug. The project is in its preliminary stage. G.D.S. must decide whether to initiate a large-scale drug test costing $1.5 million a year for two years. If the test results are positive, a $17.5 million plant to produce the drug for commercial trials will be built at the end of the testing period. If commercial sales of the drug meet the company's forecast for the next two years, a second, larger plant costing $50 million will be built to produce the drug in quantity. The cash flows resulting from this larger plant are expected to be $76 million for eight years after it is built. The following are the relevant cash flows associated with the three possible scenarios.

	Year 0	1	2	3	4	5–12
Scenario 1	($1,500)	($1,500)	Unsuccessful			
Scenario 2	(1,500)	(1,500)	(17,500)	$3,000	$2,000	Unsuccessful
Scenario 3	(1,500)	(1,500)	(17,500)	5,000	7,500	9,500
					(50,000)	

a. With a cost of capital of 10%, value the research project using DCF analysis. Is the project acceptable? (Assume the two plants are built.)

b. Assuming that the three possible scenarios have equal probability, is the project acceptable? (*Hint:* Value this project as a growth option.)

5. An oil company has paid $100,000 for the right to pump oil on a plot of land during the next three years. A well has already been sunk and all other necessary facilities are in place. The land has known reserves of 60,000 barrels. The company wishes to know the market value of this operation. The interest rate is 8% and the marginal cost of pumping is $8 per barrel. Both these costs are expected to remain unchanged over the three-year period. The current price of oil is $10 per barrel. Company economists have estimated the following:

(i) Oil will increase in price by 10% with a probability of 40%, or decrease in price by 12% with a probability of 60% during each of the next three years.

(ii) The cost of storing oil in above-ground tanks is $0.50 per year.

(iii) The company can pump a maximum of 20,000 barrels per year at the site.

(iv) The site may be shut down for a year and then reopened at a cost of $2,000.

Determine the market value of the operation ignoring taxes. Assume that all cash flows occur at the end of each year. (*Hint:* Chart all possible sequences of oil prices, and calculate the optimal production decisions and payoffs associated with each sequence.)

Risk Analysis in Capital Budgeting

The race is not to the swift, nor the battle to the strong, neither yet bread to the wise, nor yet riches to men of understanding, nor yet favour to men of skill; but time and chance happen to them all.

—ECCLESIASTES 9:11

The best laid schemes o' mice and men
Gang aft a-gley.

—ROBERT BURNS

Chapters 2 and 3 showed how to conduct a capital-budgeting analysis when a firm has detailed information about the timing and magnitude of the project's cash flows. This chapter shows how the analytical techniques developed for the case of complete certainty can be modified to deal with the more realistic situation in which project returns are highly uncertain. Risk analysis is increasingly important as the economic environment has become more uncertain—with developments halfway around the world affecting the survival of companies in their domestic markets—and the stakes higher—with multimillion- or billion-dollar investments in plant and equipment or research and development projects on the line.

Consider, for example, the following investment decision under uncertainty facing the new president of Beech Aircraft Corp.:[1] Should he gamble the company's future by spending $250 million to develop a brand-new executive airplane that promises a revolution in performance and economy? The eye-catching plane, built mostly of plastic materials reinforced with graphite fibers, is the Starship—an eight-passenger turboprop that looks more like a Hollywood vision of interstellar space travel than an earthbound airplane. (Because its stretched wings supposedly resemble those of a flying duck, its design type is known as a *canard*, the French word for duck.)

---

[1]Although the Starship is a real-world example, the financial data presented here are illustrative only.

The Starship will fly almost as fast as a jet and, at a $2.7 million projected price, would cost as much as some jets. But it is supposed to be 40% more fuel-efficient than are jets of comparable size and will provide an extremely comfortable ride. The first deliveries to customers are scheduled in three years.

As with all such bold ventures, there were a number of unknowns. Aside from the technical problems, of which there were several, the major uncertainties were in the area of marketing. These included both the size of the executive aviation market in three years and the Starship's likely share of that market. The latter depended on whether executives would entrust their lives to such a different type of airplane. Beech was gambling for extremely high stakes. If the plane succeeded, Beech could lead the industry for the next generation. If it failed, the firm would have a very turbulent future.

Although Beech's venture is riskier than most corporate projects, risk is present in all investments, especially, it seems, in those projects promising the highest returns. Thus, managers responsible for evaluating capital expenditure proposals should "pray for the best but prepare for the worst." This requires an ability to understand the different sources of uncertainty and how they might influence the value of proceeding with a given project.

Companies have responded to the added uncertainty they face by devoting more resources to the general area of risk analysis. The payoff from this effort is readily apparent: Companies are becoming more sophisticated in analyzing project risk, largely because of the increasingly powerful techniques made possible by a combination of new theoretical developments, high-powered computers, and the legions of business school graduates who understand the nature and application of these techniques.

The purpose of this chapter is to present and evaluate the techniques that firms use to incorporate risk in the capital-budgeting process. Section 5.1 reviews fundamental concepts of risk and discusses three possible ways of measuring project risk. Section 5.2 uses sensitivity analysis to assess the consequences for project profitability of variations in certain key parameters, and Section 5.3 shows how computer simulation can be used to determine the risk profile of a given investment. Section 5.4 shows how project risk can be accounted for within the basic capital-budgeting framework supplied by present value analysis. In Section 5.5, we see how decision tree analysis can be employed to evaluate the consequences of alternative marketing and cost assumptions on project present values and thereby aid the decision-making process. Chapter 6 discusses how the capital asset pricing model can be used to determine the returns required for projects of varying risk.

5.1 Measuring Project Riskiness

Risk is normally measured as the variability of possible returns. The same factors that affect the variability of security returns also affect the variability of project returns. Macroeconomic risk factors, which affect all firms to a greater or lesser degree, include changes in the growth rate of the economy, the inflation rate, and the level of real interest rates. Risk factors that are company and project specific include competitor actions, shifting consumer tastes, technological uncertainty, uncertain exploration costs, and changing input costs and output prices. Macroeconomic risk factors are the primary source of systematic or beta risk, whereas firm-specific risk factors result in unsystematic risk.

Project risk is not an unambiguous concept. It can be measured relative to the project itself, the firm, or a well-diversified investor. Thus, in discussing project risk, one must distinguish among three separate types of risk: (1) total project risk, which is based on the variability of project returns, (2) company risk, which is measured by the contribution of project risk to the variability of total company returns, and (3) systematic risk, which is based on the project's beta, as measured by the correlation between project returns and returns on the market portfolio.

PROJECT RISK

The business risk of a project is primarily determined by the variability of sales and costs. The latter include both the initial investment cost and subsequent production costs. Natural resource projects are also affected by uncertainty over the location and magnitude of mineral deposits. Regardless of the source of the risk — whether from macroeconomic or project-specific factors — operating leverage magnifies its impact.

Operating Leverage

Any time a firm uses assets for which it must pay a fixed charge, regardless of the volume of production, it has **operating leverage**. These fixed costs include the opportunity cost of the funds tied up in the assets, economic depreciation of the plant and equipment, property taxes, insurance, management expenses, and a portion of the utility bills. By contrast, variable costs — including direct labor, raw materials, energy, sales commissions, and most utility bills — vary directly with the level of production and sales. Once the plant is built, the opportunity cost of funds is no longer a relevant fixed cost; it is now a sunk cost, unless the firm is considering selling the plant.

Firms pay careful attention to operating leverage in deciding the trade-off between more automated, capital-intensive production facilities with lower unit costs and more labor-intensive production facilities with higher unit costs. Suppose, for example, that a firm is trying to decide between two different microprocessor assembly facilities — facility A, which is highly automated, and facility B, which is less automated and more labor intensive. Facility A is expected to have fixed costs of $8 million annually and unit variable costs of $4. In contrast, B's fixed costs are expected to be only $4 million annually but its variable costs are $10 per unit. To summarize,

	Facility A	Facility B
Fixed costs ($)	8 million	4 million
Variable costs ($)	4/unit	10/unit

The microprocessor is expected to sell for $20. We can study the relationship among profits, volume, and the different cost structures by means of the break-even charts in Exhibits 5.1(a), 5.1(b), and 5.1(c).

The intersection of the total revenue line with the total cost line is the point at which the project just breaks even, that is, the volume of sales at which project revenue just covers all project costs. This point is reached when

$$\text{Total revenue} = \text{Total cost}$$

$$P \times Q = F + V \times Q \tag{5.1}$$

EXHIBIT 5.1 (a) Break-Even Analysis for Facility A

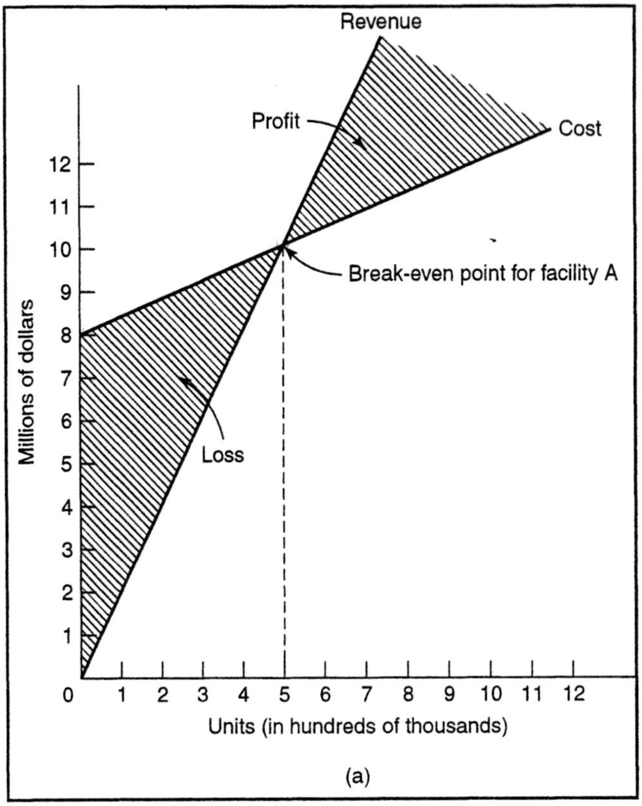

(a)

where

P = sales price per unit
Q = unit volume
F = fixed costs
V = unit variable cost

By rearranging terms, we can solve Equation 5.1 for the break-even quantity

$$Q^* = \frac{F}{(P - V)} \tag{5.2}$$

Applying Equation 5.2, we obtain the break-even point of 500,000 units for facility A (8,000,000/16) and 400,000 units for facility B (4,000,000/10). This is shown in Exhibits 5.1(a) and 5.1(b). Thus, if there is substantial risk that sales will be below 500,000 units annually, facility B will clearly be preferable. In fact, facility B is more profitable until annual sales reach 667,000. This can be seen by solving for the sales quantity at which A's profits are just equal to B's profits. The subscripts on the fixed

EXHIBIT 5.1   (b) Break-Even Analysis for Facility B

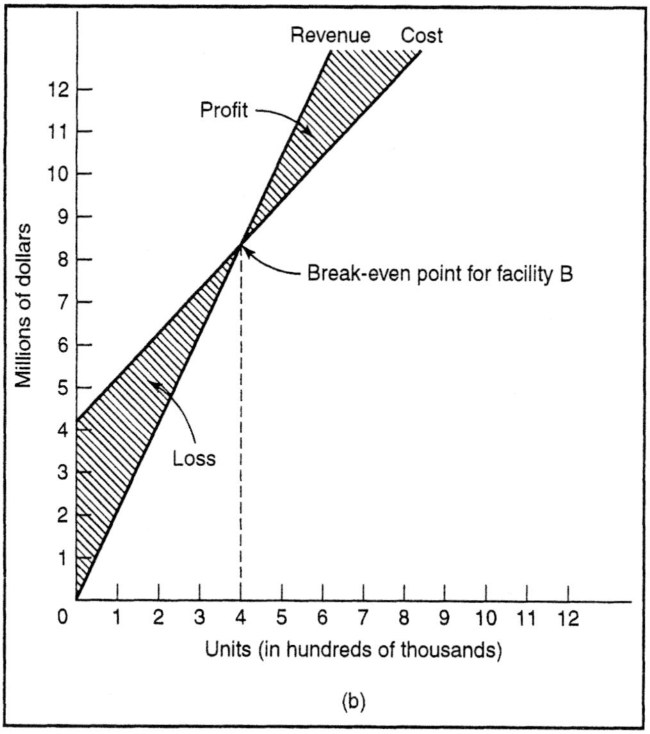

(b)

and variable costs refer to costs for A and B:

$$\text{Profit for A } = \text{ Revenue } - \text{ Cost } = \text{ Profit for B } = \text{ Revenue } - \text{ Cost}$$

$$P \times Q - F_A - V_A \times Q = P \times Q - F_B - V_B \times Q$$

$$20Q - 8,000,000 - 4Q = 20Q - 4,000,000 - 10Q$$

or

$$Q = 667,000$$

Beyond this level of sales, shown in Exhibit 5.1(c), facility A becomes increasingly profitable relative to facility B because the incremental profit on each additional unit sold
by facility A is $16 in comparison with B's incremental profit of $10. The reason for
facility A's higher incremental profit, of course, is that A's unit variable cost is $6 lower
than B's unit variable cost.

As sales expand beyond the break-even level, profit increases. This is represented
by the shaded area to the right of the break-even point for each facility, as seen in
Exhibits 5.1(a) and 5.1(b). On the other hand, the shaded areas to the left of the break-
even points show the losses associated with each level of sales below these points. The
higher is the ratio of fixed to variable costs, the more sensitive that profit will be to a

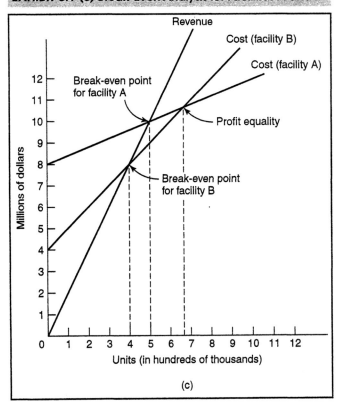

EXHIBIT 5.1 (c) Break-Even Analysis for Facilities A and B

(c)

change in sales. Similarly, an increase in the ratio of price to unit variable cost increases the sensitivity of profit to fluctuations in the quantity sold.

In general, the advantage of a labor-intensive process is that labor is typically a variable cost and can be reduced if demand falls off. Not so with capital equipment, for which the firm must continue to bear the opportunity cost of the funds tied up in it along with the cost of economic depreciation.

The logic of this analysis breaks down in the case of those Japanese firms adhering to a system of lifetime employment. For them, labor is treated as a fixed cost, giving these firms far greater operating leverage than firms that can easily adjust their work forces to changes in economic conditions. The same is true for firms located in those countries that restrict or prohibit layoffs—which these days include most countries aside from the United States. Viewing labor as a fixed cost helps explain why, once a plant is built and workers hired, Japanese firms and others that are unable to adjust their work force tend to keep producing at close to capacity even at low prices that do not come close to covering their costs.

Clearly, operating leverage does not cause variation in profit. But it can exacerbate any profit variation that does exist. The more fixed costs a project has, the more its profits will fluctuate with a given change in sales volume (i.e., all other things being equal, higher operating leverage leads to greater project risk).

The Relevance of Project Risk

Although most risk analysis techniques focus on the total risk of the project standing on its own, this emphasis is somewhat misplaced. Any single project is just one of the collection of projects that make up the firm, each with its own uncertain return. It is the overall riskiness of this project portfolio—which we will call *firm risk*—that matters to top management, not the riskiness of any individual project. Management pays attention to firm risk because this is what determines the possibility of financial distress and, ultimately, bankruptcy. Thus, project risk will be of concern to top management only to the extent that it affects the variability of total corporate returns.

From the even broader perspective of a well-diversified investor, the firm itself is just one of numerous firms, each with its own project portfolio. What matters to the well-diversified investor, therefore, is the project's contribution to *total* portfolio risk. Of course, the manager who is in charge of the project and who will be judged according to its results, will be quite concerned with total project risk. This may lead to risk-averse behavior that is suboptimal from the standpoint of the firm and its investors.

Companies do pay attention to project risk because it serves as a proxy for the project's contribution to firm risk. In the presence of uncertainty, it is often difficult to figure out just how much of a project's return variability will be diversified away. In general, though, the riskier the project is on its own, the more risk it is likely to contribute to firm risk. This contribution will not be one for one, however, as is evident from the following example.

FIRM RISK

A project that is highly risky in and of itself, like drilling for oil, may be of minimal risk from the firm's standpoint. For example, suppose the cost of drilling a well is $3 million and the chance of finding a commercial quantity of oil (an amount that makes the well economic to develop) is 10%. At the current price of oil, a successful well will yield an average net profit after development costs of $35 million. Although the firm has only a one-in-ten chance of striking oil, if it drills 100 wells, it is almost certain to be successful 10 times. As long as the price of oil is stable, the firm's expected profit will be $50 million with very little risk. The expected profit per well drilled will be $0.5 million. The more wells that are drilled, the lower the average risk will be per well. Thus, from the firm's standpoint, the incremental risk associated with drilling one more well is minimal.

No matter how many wells the firm drills, however, it still faces a major risk—the risk of fluctuations in the price of oil. The $0.5 million expected profit per well drilled is predicated on a specific price of oil. If the price of oil changes, the net profit per well will also change. Thus, drilling numerous wells can eliminate most of the *discovery risk*—uncertainty as to the quantity of oil that will be found—but it cannot eliminate the *price risk*—uncertainty about the price at which the oil will sell in the market.

Total Risk versus Systematic Risk

According to the capital asset pricing model (CAPM) and the more recent arbitrage pricing theory (APT), which are discussed in Chapter 6, even the firm risk of a project is irrelevant except that it affects the firm's systematic risk. This is true but in a limited sense. Both the CAPM and the APT demonstrate that under reasonable circumstances, diversifiable risks are not priced and hence do not affect the required rate of return on risky investments. Systematic risks are priced; but because the price of risk is the same for all market participants, or so the story goes, there is no gain to shareholders from "laying them off" to financial markets. And yet corporations are major purchasers of insurance, heavy use commodity, financial futures, and forward contracts; sign long-term purchase and sales contracts; and engage in a wide variety of other behavior, all designed to avoid or reduce total risk.

One explanation for this behavior, which is consistent with both shareholder wealth maximization and the focus of asset pricing models on systematic risk, is that reducing total risk can increase expected cash flows. This explanation does not conflict with either the CAPM or APT, both of which say that only the systematic component of total risk affects investors' required returns; the unsystematic or *avoidable* component is irrelevant. These models are concerned only with the effect of risk on market discount rates; for the most part, they ignore its effect on expected cash flow. To the extent that an increase in total risk can lower the firm's expected future cash flows, however, it makes sense to reduce total risk. The distinction between the effects of systematic risk and the effects of total risk on the value of the firm is shown in Exhibit 5.2.

How does a higher total risk lower the expectations of future cash flows? Firms with a higher total risk, all else being equal, are more likely to find themselves in financial distress. Thus, total risk, by increasing the threat of financial difficulties, can affect the level of future corporate cash flows by influencing the willingness of customers, suppliers, and employees to commit themselves to relationships with the firm, thereby affecting future sales, operating costs, and financing costs.[2] It can also affect the firm's ability to take full advantage of tax credits and write-offs. In addition, an increase in total risk may result in management actions detrimental to shareholder interests.

Impact of Total Risk on Sales

Reducing total risk can aid a firm's marketing efforts by providing greater assurance to potential customers that the company will be around in the future to service and upgrade its products. Purchasers of long-lived capital assets are especially concerned about the seller's longevity. They want to know if the manufacturer will be there to service the equipment and supply new parts as old ones wear out. If the original supplier goes

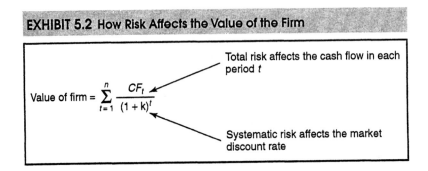

EXHIBIT 5.2 How Risk Affects the Value of the Firm

$$\text{Value of firm} = \sum_{t=1}^{n} \frac{CF_t}{(1+k)^t}$$

Total risk affects the cash flow in each period t

Systematic risk affects the market discount rate

---

[2]The effects of total risk on sales and costs are explored in more detail in Shapiro, A.C., and Titman, S. "An Integrated Approach to Corporate Risk Management." *Midland Corporation Finance Journal,* Summer 1985, pp. 41–56.

out of business, parts and repairs may become a problem. Potential buyers of Chrysler cars in the late 1970s, for example, were understandably nervous about purchasing a product that they might have difficulty getting serviced if Chrysler went bankrupt.

Customers of products like computers that are undergoing rapid technological change are also very concerned about producers' staying power. For example, IBM exploits buyers' fears—of getting stuck with obsolete equipment and having to write off the associated nontransferable investments in software and learning—with the message, "What people want most from a computer company is a good night's sleep." Such fears hastened the downfall of Wang Laboratories, the pioneer of word-processing computers. As its financial outlook worsened, customers who feared becoming techno-logical orphans took their business elsewhere, eventually forcing Wang into bank-ruptcy.

Fortunately for Beech, it was an affiliate of Raytheon—a profitable defense elec-tronics company with "deep pockets"—that could afford to take some risks. This gave potential customers greater assurance that the company would be around in the future to supply parts and provide service for the Starship. Were this not the case, it is doubt-ful that Beech would have gone ahead and developed the plane on its own.

Impact of Total Risk on Operating Costs

A firm's cost of doing business is, in part, a function of its suppliers' view of the com-pany's long-run prospects. A firm struggling to survive is unlikely to find suppliers bending over backwards to provide it with specially developed products or services, particularly if those products or services are unique—like special dies or castings—and suitable for use only by the firm in question.

In general, the value of investing in a long-term relationship with a customer will depend on whether the customer is expected to survive in the long run. The lower the likelihood is of future survival, the more of these relationship costs the customer will have to bear up front in the form of higher prices or less closely tailored services and products. Lower-risk firms also have an easier time attracting and retaining good personnel.

Impact of Total Risk on Taxes

As the variability of operating profits increases, so does the probability that a firm will be unable to fully utilize its tax credits and depreciation and interest expense tax write-offs. Because the resale market in tax credits and tax write-offs is imper-fect, as indicated by the discount taken when tax benefits are sold, an increase in total risk will lead to a reduction in expected corporate cash flows. If the tax credit or tax loss is carried forward, the relevant cost will be the reduction in the present value of the tax benefit. By reducing its total risk, a firm can increase the expected value of its tax credits and tax write-offs and thereby increase its expected future cash flows.

Perhaps the costliest aspect of financial distress stems from the firm's loss of oper-ating and investment flexibility owing to the constraints imposed by lenders. The riskier a firm is perceived to be, the more stringent will be the restrictions on the oper-ating policies and the investment projects that it can pursue. For example, lenders may veto high-risk projects with positive net present values.

Decreasing total risk can reduce or eliminate some of the more onerous debt restrictions and covenants. Investment and operating policies with fewer restrictions on them should increase expected future cash flows and shareholder wealth.

SYSTEMATIC RISK

From the perspective of a well-diversified investor, the total firm risk associated with a project does not affect the expected return that the investor demands for undertaking the project. All that matters to such an investor is the project's contribution to the risk of the investor's portfolio. Clearly, the fraction of risk that is relevant from the standpoint of a well-diversified investor is less than that which is relevant to corporate management, which, in turn, is less than that of the project's management.

Consider, for example, the systematic risk of the general aviation business. This is the systematic risk that faces Beech Aircraft's new Starship venture, and it primarily depends on the state of the national economy. In a healthy economy, with expanding business activity, executives are more likely to travel, and so the value to their companies of investing in corporate planes will rise. Sales of executive aircraft, therefore, pick up during prosperous times and fall off during recessions.

Other risks faced by Beech's Starship project, including the uncertainty of its appeal to business executives and the possibility of competitors' developing their own canards, are unsystematic in nature. This is evident from the fact that a well-diversified investor, whose portfolio includes the securities of competitor general aviation manufacturers, can fully avoid these risks.

According to the CAPM, the systematic risk of a project—as measured by the correlation between the returns on the project and returns on the market portfolio—will affect the required return on the project. The important point here is that the required return on a project is a function of the riskiness of the project itself, not of the riskiness of the firm undertaking the project. This means that each project has its own cost of capital, which is independent of the firm investing in the project. Thus, when Coca-Cola entered the motion picture business through its acquisition of Columbia Pictures, its required return on this investment was determined by the risk of making films, not the risk of being in the soft drink business.

To summarize, only the project's systematic risk will determine its required return, but total risk could affect the project's actual cash flows through its impact on the expectations of customers, suppliers, employees, and creditors. Even the diversified investor, therefore, will be interested in the project's total risk to the extent that it is likely to affect the project's *actual* return.

5.2 Sensitivity Analysis

As we will see in the next section, most techniques for factoring risk into a capital-budgeting analysis reduce all uncertainties to just a single value for the risk-adjusted NPV. This is done by using the expected values of sales and costs and ignoring any variations in those numbers. The advantage of using a single number to represent the impact of risk is that it simplifies the decision process. If the calculated NPV is positive, the project should be undertaken; if it is negative, it should be rejected. Often, however, this single number hides a great deal of information about the riskiness of the proposed project: Because the future is unknowable, it is evident that today's estimates of future project prices, costs, and volumes are going to be wrong. It is natural, therefore, for decision makers to want to study, in advance, how potential estimation errors will affect the project NPV.

Moreover, before conducting a project risk analysis, it makes sense to see whether the risk has a significant impact on the project's net present value. There is no sense in doing a thorough risk analysis if the risk is not material. An important means of going beyond the information conveyed by a risk-adjusted NPV is sensitivity analysis.

Sensitivity analysis is a procedure to study systematically the effect of changes in the values of key parameters—including R&D costs, plant construction cost, market size, market share, price, and production costs—on the project NPV. It is best suited to address a series of "what if" questions, like the ones contained in the following quotation from the *Wall Street Journal*:

> The Chrysler Corp. of 10 years ago wouldn't have had any trouble making the decision that is occupying a good deal of top-executive time at the No. 3 auto maker: whether to invest some $350 to $400 million to expand production of the company's fast-selling minivans.
>
> Chrysler has the capacity at its Windsor, Ontario, plant to build 270,000 minivans a year, and it's currently producing them at that rate. But before adding the capacity to build about 150,000 more each year, Chrysler has asked itself some rough questions about the vehicle's market and potential.
>
> What if, as some predict, the economy should turn sour next year or the year after, just about the time the new capacity would be coming on stream? What if the minivans that General Motors Corp. and Ford Motor Co. are introducing later this year saturate the market or even eat into Chrysler's current share?
>
> Ultimately, Chrysler resolved those doubts to its satisfaction. In essence, top Chrysler executives have concluded that the minivan has a niche in a market that probably will continue to grow.[3]

The first step in a sensitivity analysis usually is to have the engineering, marketing, and production people specify pessimistic, most likely, and optimistic values for each of these variables. Then a series of project NPVs is calculated on the basis of setting each variable at its most pessimistic or optimistic value while holding all the other variables equal to their expected values. The purpose is to see how sensitive the project returns are to different cost and marketing assumptions.

---

[3]Lehner, U.C. "Chrysler Seen Spending $350 Million or More on Minivan, but Step Is Careful." *Wall Street Journal*, March 23, 1984, p. 6.

BOX 5.1

APPLICATION: CRYSTAL GLASS'S NEW PLATE GLASS PLANT

Crystal Glass Co. is thinking of building a plate glass plant in eastern Michigan. The plant, with an annual capacity of 100,000 tons, will cost $100 million to construct. The $100 million plant cost is regarded as pretty certain because it is guaranteed by fixed price contracts with the equipment manufacturer and the construction company. Profits on the project are assumed to be taxed at a combined federal and state rate of 50%.

Revenues. The glass plant is designed to capitalize on the rapidly growing market for high-quality plate glass within its sales territory. Total plate glass consumption in the plant's market area is currently running at 800,000 tons annually. This figure is expected to grow to 832,000 tons by next year, a 4% annual growth rate. Crystal Glass expects its new plant to produce about 90,000 tons of plate glass annually, an average of 90% of rated capacity. This would give it an approximate 11% market share in the first year of operation and annual revenues of $59.4 million. This revenue figure is based on an estimated $660 price per ton of glass sold by Crystal Glass, a price net of transportation charges.

Depending on market conditions, however, yearly production could rise to 100,000 tons or fall to 80,000 tons. Similarly, the price of plate glass could climb as high as $700 per ton or sink as low as $600 per ton.

Depreciation. For the sake of simplicity, the cost of the plant, $100 million, is assumed to be depreciated on a straight-line basis over 10 years, for an annual depreciation charge of $10 million.

Operating costs. Operating costs are divided into fixed costs and variable costs. Fixed costs include payroll costs, maintenance, repairs, supplies, and overhead expenses such as selling, general, and administrative costs. These costs are expected to average $12 million annually. Depending on current labor negotiations and other factors, however, these costs could be as low as $10 million or as high as $15 million. Payroll costs are treated as fixed costs here because the labor input does not vary with output.

Variable production costs—which include the costs of raw materials and power—are expected to average $140 per ton. Possible fluctuations in energy costs could reduce these costs to $110 a ton or raise them to as much as $170 a ton.

From these data, we can calculate the yearly cash flows for this project, along with its net present value and internal rate of return. The required return for this project is taken to be 15% because of the high degree of systematic risk associated with such a cyclical product as plate glass. As shown in the following table, the project NPV is $12.4 million. The term $PVIFA_{15,10}$ refers to the present value of an annuity of $1 for 10 years discounted at 15%. Its value is 5.0188.

Projected Cash Flows for Crystal Glass' New Plate Glass Plant

	Year 0	Years 1–10
Initial investment	−$100,000,000	
Sales		
Tons sold		90,000
Price		× $660
Revenue		$59,400,000
Costs		
Variable costs (90,000 × $140)		12,600,000
Fixed costs		
Depreciation		12,000,000
Total costs		10,000,000
Net income		34,600,000
Taxes (@ 50%)		$24,800,000
After-tax income		12,400,000
Depreciation		$12,400,000
Operating cash flow		10,000,000
Net cash flow		$22,400,000
	−$100,000,000	22,400,000

Net present value (@ 15%) = −$100,000,000 + $PVIFA_{15,10}$ × $22,400,000

= $12.4 million

The following table shows what will happen to the NPV of Crystal Glass' proposed new plant when each variable is set, in turn, to its pessimistic and optimistic values, while simultaneously holding all other variables at their expected values. For example, if fixed costs rise to $15 million annually (a jump of $3 million from their expected value of $12 million), then the plant's annual operating cash flow will decline by $1.5 million (the after-tax increase in cost is half the before-tax increase because of the 50% tax rate) to $20.9 million. The project net present value, using the same 15% discount rate as before, drops to

$$NPV = -\$100,000,000 + PVIFA_{15,10} \times \$20,900,000$$

$$= -\$100,000,000 + 5.0188 \times \$20,900,000$$

$$= \$4,892,920$$

The value of $5 million shown for this scenario in the following table is rounded to the nearest million.

Sensitivity Analysis of Crystal Glass' Proposal Plate Glass Plant					
	Value for each variable under alternative scenarios			Project NPV under each scenario rounded to nearest million[*]	
Variable	Pessimistic	Expected	Optimistic	Pessimistic	Optimistic
Demand (tons)	80,000	90,000	100,000	0	25
Price per ton ($)	600	660	700	−1	21
Fixed cost ($)	15,000,000	12,000,000	10,000,000	5	17
Variable cost per ton ($)	170	140	110	6	19

[*]Discount rate is 15%.

The numbers from the sensitivity analysis in the table above indicate that the project is likely to be successful, even though its value is sensitive to changes in all the key variables. Only if the price drops to $600 a ton will the project have a negative NPV, and even then it will be just –$1 million.

But this analysis is somewhat misleading. It assumes that demand and price are independent of each other, a highly unlikely scenario. Typically, high demand and high prices go hand in hand, as do low demand and low prices. To see the effect of a low-demand, low-price scenario, rework the calculations to incorporate simultaneously, both a $600 per ton price and sales of 80,000 tons. This will produce a yearly operating cash flow of $17.4 million and a project NPV equal to –$12.7 million. Thus, the project turns out to be riskier than the simple sensitivity analysis indicates. We will explore further what happens when more than one variable is allowed to change at the same time in the section on simulation.

BREAK-EVEN ANALYSIS

In deciding whether to go ahead with a project, the real concern for investors is the possibility of losing money. Because production costs generally are fairly predictable, the key to making or losing money on most projects is the level of sales revenue. The major contributor to revenue uncertainty is uncertainty over the sales volume, Q. One approach to use in figuring this element of project risk is **break-even analysis**. This involves determining the quantity of sales, Q^*, at which the project NPV is just zero. If sales exceed Q^*, the project will have a positive NPV, whereas if sales are less than Q^*, the project NPV will be negative. The value of break-even analysis is that it is normally easier and requires less information to ascertain whether Q is less than or greater than Q^* than to decide on the absolute level of Q. For example, if $Q^* = 300,000$, then it is unnecessary to spend time worrying whether actual sales will be, say, 375,000 or 400,000, because the result will not affect the decision (which is to accept the project).

Consider, for example, the Starship project described earlier. As you may recall, Beech's initial investment is expected to be $250 million and it plans on setting the price at $2.7 million apiece. Suppose the fixed costs of production are $15 million annually and the variable costs are $1.5 million per plane. At the time of the project, Beech was eligible to receive a 10% investment tax credit (ITC). The present value of the ITC and the accelerated depreciation write-offs taken together is assumed to be $120 million, based on an estimated 10-year project life and federal and state taxes of 50%. Hence, the initial investment net of the present value of the tax savings associated with the investment is $130 million. Exhibit 5.3 summarizes these data, and Exhibit 5.4 shows the cash flow estimates for the project and its net present values under various sales assumptions. The discount rate is set at 10%.

As expected, the NPV will be highly negative if Beech sells no Starships. With annual sales of 50 planes, the project NPV will be slightly positive and so will be acceptable; the NPV will be highly positive if annual sales are 75 planes. This suggests that the break-even sales point—the point at which the project NPV is just 0—is slightly fewer than 50 planes annually.

EXHIBIT 5.3 Summary of Data for the Starship Project

Initial investment: gross	$250,000,000
PV of investment tax benefits	120,000,000
Initial investment: net	$130,000,000
Price per plane	2,700,000
Variable cost per plane	1,500,000
Fixed costs	15,000,000

EXHIBIT 5.4 Break-even Analysis for the Starship ($ millions)

Annual Plane Sales	0	50	75
Revenue	0	135.0	202.5
Variable cost	0	75.0	112.5
Fixed cost	15.0	15.0	15.0
Net income*	−15.0	45.0	75.0
Taxes @ 50%	−7.5	22.5	37.5
After-tax income	−7.5	22.5	37.5
Present value @ 10%	−46.1	138.3	230.4
Initial investment	130.0	130.0	130.0
Project NPV @ 10%	−176.1	8.3	100.4

*Depreciation is already included in estimating the net investment required

The actual break-even sales quantity of 48 Starships annually is shown in Exhibit 5.5. It is the point at which the present value of future project cash flows just equals the $130 million net initial investment. Although the cost figures presented here are just estimates, they illustrate the application of this powerful technique.

In general, the NPV of a project—assuming that annual fixed cash costs (which excludes depreciation), variable cash costs, prices, and quantities are constant—is:

$$NPV = -I_0 + D + [Q(P - V) - F](1 - t)\, PVIFA_{r,n} \tag{5.3}$$

where

I_0 = the initial investment
D = the present value of the depreciation write-off and any investment tax credits
Q = annual sales
P = unit sales price
V = unit variable cost
F = annual fixed cost
t = tax rate
n = project life
r = discount rate

EXHIBIT 5.5 Break-Even Analysis for Starship Project

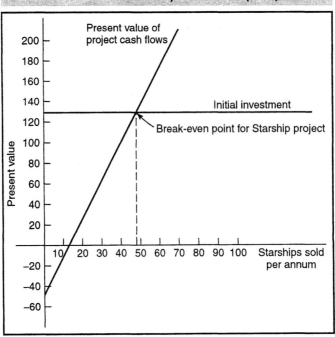

We can find the break-even sales quantity by substituting Q^* for Q in Equation 5.3, setting NPV equal to 0, and solving for Q^*. This yields

$$Q^* = \frac{I_0 - D}{PVIFA_{r,n}(P - V)(1 - t)} + \frac{F}{P - V} \tag{5.4}$$

Applying Equation 5.4 to the various parameters for the Starship project, we see, as before, that the break-even level of annual Starship sales is

$$Q^* = \frac{250 - 120}{6.1446 \times (2.7 - 1.5) \times 0.5} + \frac{15}{2.7 - 1.5}$$

$$= 48$$

Of course, once the investment of $250 million has been made, and it becomes a sunk cost, the break-even point is lowered dramatically, to 13 (15/1.2 = 12.5) Starships annually.

Misuse of Break-Even Analysis

Some firms misuse break-even analysis by calculating the break-even point as that level of sales at which cumulative revenues just equal the sum of all development and production costs. This is known as the **accounting break-even point**. It can be converted to an annual basis by depreciating the initial investment on a straight-line basis and then finding the number of units that must be sold each year for the accounting profit to equal zero.

If we ignore the tax credit, this would mean an annual depreciation charge of $25 million for Beech's Starship project, given the initial project cost of $250 million and its 10-year life. With annual sales of Q planes, therefore, Beech's accounting profit (in millions) will be ($2.7 – $1.5)$Q$ – $15 – $25. Setting this profit figure equal to zero yields the accounting break-even point of 33 Starships per annum (40/1.2). At this level of sales, revenues will be just sufficient to cover all operating costs as well as recover the initial investment of $250 million. But unlike the NPV break-even analysis, the accounting break-even analysis makes no allowance for the *opportunity cost* of the funds tied up in the project. Hence, it is not surprising that the resulting break-even estimate of 33 is substantially below the NPV break-even estimate of 48 planes.

As a general rule, projects that break even on an accounting basis are sustaining an economic loss equal to the opportunity cost of the funds tied up in them. The case of Lockheed provides a dramatic illustration of the disastrous consequences that failure to heed this rule can have.[4] In 1971, Lockheed requested a federal guarantee for $250 million in additional bank debt to complete its L-1011 Tri Star program. A key issue during the resulting congressional debate was whether this program was economically viable. Lockheed's chief executive argued that sales would eventually reach or exceed the estimated break-even level of about 200 Tri Stars, making the program commercially

---

[4]This example is elaborated in Reinhardt, U.E. "Break-even Analysis for Lockheed's Tri Star: An Application of Financial Theory." *Journal of Finance*, September 1973, pp. 821–838.

sound. This break-even point, however, excluded the opportunity cost of the estimated $1 billion in project development and facilities costs. Had Lockheed allowed for this cost, its break-even sales level would have been closer to 500 aircraft, a number generally regarded as unattainable. This opportunity cost was irrelevant, of course, for that portion of the costs already incurred. This is in line with the proper focus on incremental cash flows pointed out in Chapter 3.

5.3 Simulation Analysis

Sensitivity analysis is a valuable technique for project risk analysis, and as such, it is widely used by business. Despite this, sensitivity analysis does have its limitations. Even if a project is very sensitive to changes in a particular variable, that variable may be very unlikely to change. Sensitivity analysis, however, ignores probabilities. In addition, it focuses on the effect of variations in one key parameter at a time instead of studying the effect on the value of the project of simultaneous changes in several key variables.

In contrast, computer simulation represents a project's NPV by a probability distribution rather than by a single number. In order to conduct a **simulation analysis**, you must first estimate probability distributions for each variable that will affect the project's cash inflows and outflows. For a new product introduction (e.g., Beech's Starship), these variables include the initial investment outlay (which determines not only the upfront cost but also the amount of depreciation recognized for tax purposes), market size, growth of the market, price, market share, variable costs, fixed costs, life of the project, and the project's terminal value. Some of these probability distributions, like the ones describing the initial investment cost and production costs, can be estimated with more confidence than can others, like the distributions for price and market share.

The next step is to program the computer to select at random one value apiece from each of these probability distributions. These values—for market size, market share, variable costs, and the like—are then used to calculate the net cash flow for each period. As each scenario is generated—a scenario being a particular set of values for the relevant project variables—the project NPV associated with that particular combination of parameter values is calculated and stored. This process is repeated, say, 600 times by the computer. The stored NPVs (all 600 of them) are then printed out by the computer in the form of a frequency distribution, along with the expected NPV and its standard deviation.

One caveat: *In calculating these NPVs, the cash flows should be discounted at the risk-free rate.* Using the opportunity cost of capital instead implicitly assumes that we already know what the project's risk is. And of course, if we knew that, we would not need to perform a simulation. Thus, assuming we are trying to evaluate project risk, we use the discount rate solely as a means to take into account the time value of money.

At each iteration, we could compute the project's IRR instead of its NPV. The result would be a frequency distribution for the project's rate of return. This frequency distribution could then be used to evaluate the expected return on the project and the standard deviation of that return. Many managers find this probability distribution more informative than the distribution of project NPVs.

To illustrate the simulation process, suppose the estimated probability distribution for the size of the executive aviation market is as follows:

Market size	200	250	300	350	400	450	500	550	600	650	700
Probability	0.02	0.05	0.08	0.10	0.15	0.20	0.15	0.10	0.08	0.05	0.02

The expected number of planes that will be sold is 450, but sales can range from 200 to 700 planes. To begin the simulation, the computer assigns numbers 1 to 100 to the different market sizes in proportion to their probabilities of occurrence. Specifically, numbers 1 and 2 are assigned to a market size of 200 planes, the next five digits to a market size of 250 planes, numbers 8 through 15 represent a market size of 300 planes, and so on. The computer's random number generator, which is like a roulette wheel with 100 slots, then selects a number at random from 1 to 100. Suppose it selects 37. This corresponds to a market size of 400 planes. Similarly, probability distributions and associated numbers are assigned to the other key variables.

The computer then picks values (listed in parentheses) for each of the other factors associated with the Starship, including market share (10%), price ($2.5 million), fixed costs ($12 million) and variable costs ($1.2 million), the initial investment outlay ($280 million), terminal value (0), and project life (10 years). On the basis of this particular scenario, annual sales are 40 Starships at a price of $2.5 million apiece. Thus, annual after-tax operating cash flows (excluding depreciation) are equal (in $ millions) to $40(2.5 - 1.2)0.5 - 12 = 14$. Discounting at the assumed risk-free rate of 6% yields a present value of $147 million over the 10-year life of the project. The initial investment net of tax credits and the present value of depreciation, discounted at 6%, is estimated at $140 million. For this scenario, therefore, the project NPV is $7 million.

PROBLEMS WITH SIMULATION ANALYSIS

Despite its appeal as a highly sophisticated, technologically advanced tool for evaluating project risk, simulation analysis is a controversial technique. Its difficulties are both theoretical and practical. Here are three potential problems.

Interdependencies

One major stumbling block to simulation analysis is that the more realistic the simulation is, the more complex it will turn out to be in practice. This is clearly shown in the case of interdependencies among the variables.

Our analysis so far has implicitly assumed that what happens in one period is independent of what happens in all the other periods. This is clearly unrealistic: A higher market share in one period is likely to mean better consumer acceptance and, therefore, a higher market share in subsequent periods. Similarly, lower-than-expected costs in one period will likely imply lower costs in the future.

This simulation process also assumes that within each period the variables are independent of one another. But as pointed out in the case of Crystal Glass' new glass plant, it is unrealistic to suppose that, for example, sales volume and sales price are unrelated to each other. In general, we would expect strong demand and high prices and weak demand and low prices to go together.

These interdependencies should be reflected in the simulation analysis. For example, if a high value for sales in the early years is selected, implying market acceptance, then higher sales volumes in subsequent years should also be selected. Similarly, within each period, higher prices should be used in conjunction with the higher sales volumes. Although specifying these interdependencies is difficult, ignoring them will render less valuable the resulting frequency distributions.

No Clear-Cut Decision Rule

The second problem is both practical and theoretical. After conducting a simulation analysis, you are left staring at a frequency distribution for either the project NPV or IRR. Should you accept or reject the project on the basis of this distribution? Simulation analysis gives no guidance in resolving what is ultimately the only important capital-budgeting issue—specifying an acceptable trade-off between project risk and return. By contrast, the NPV rule is quite specific: If the project NPV is positive when using the systematic risk-adjusted discount rate, accept the project; otherwise, reject it.

Disregards Diversification

The third basic problem is that the description of risk provided by a simulation analysis ignores the opportunities available to both the firm and its investors to diversify away a good portion of that risk. To the extent that the project returns are not highly correlated with returns on the rest of the firm's assets, the incremental risk of the project to the firm may be substantially lower than the project's total risk. Similarly, the less highly correlated the project's returns are with stock market returns, the less risky the project will be to highly diversified investors.

SURVEY OF RISK ASSESSMENT TECHNIQUES USED IN PRACTICE

The survey of corporate capital-budgeting practices by Graham and Harvey referenced in Chapter 2 also generated data on the risk assessment techniques used in practice.[5] These data show that about 53% of respondents used sensitivity analysis and 14% used simulation analysis to measure risk.

An earlier survey of risk assessment techniques used by companies was undertaken by Suk Kim, Trevor Crick, and Seung Kim.[6] These data are displayed in Exhibit 5.6. If the responses are taken at face value, 21% of the 367 firms surveyed ignore risk in evaluating projects. Another 52% assess risk subjectively, which could mean anything (see the application of Alaska Interstate for one such approach). These numbers indicate a major problem with such surveys: They are either unbelievable, or they raise more questions than they answer.

Consistent with the more recent survey by Graham and Harvey, the only risk assessment technique that is widely used is sensitivity analysis. Some companies use more than one technique, as is evidenced by the fact that the numbers in Exhibit 5.6 sum to more than 100%. Decision tree analysis is discussed in Section 5.5. The low incidence of quantitative technique usage could reflect skepticism over the value of these techniques. But more likely, they reflect a lack of faith in the data inputs that drive these methods.

---

[5]Graham, J., and Harvey, C. "How Do CFOs Make Capital Budgeting and Capital Structure Decisions?" *Journal of Applied Corporate Finance*, Spring 2002, pp. 8–23.

[6]Suk, H.K, Crick, T., and Seung, H.K. "Do Executives Practice What Academics Preach?" *Management Accounting*, November 1986, pp. 49–52.

BOX 5.2

APPLICATION: ALASKA INTERSTATE

Diana Harrington described how one company, Alaska Interstate (AKI, its stock market symbol), a diversified company with holdings consisting of oil and gas ventures, a public utility, and an agricultural equipment manufacturer, tried to quantify risk and factor consideration of it into the strategic planning process.[7] AKI's 14-member top-management group first forecast the expected returns of each business unit by analyzing the market environment, competitive position, and available resources of each unit.

Next, AKI's top management turned to the question of expected risk. The group considered not only each unit's past history but also the various factors that could affect future returns, including the quality of management, the health of the industry, the unit's position in the industry, and the economic and political environments anticipated. Every one of the 14 officers estimated each unit's susceptibility to every factor identified, the importance of each factor, and — from these estimates — rated the risk of the unit on a scale of 1 to 10. The group aggregated these rankings to come up with an average projected risk for each unit.

AKI's risk assessment procedure, although subjective, included the best judgment of the most knowledgeable people. Moreover, the process of obtaining information in a systematic way forced managers to perform their evaluations with care. The end result was greater understanding by top management of the risks facing AKI and its business units. One outcome of this process was top management's decision to sell off all its nonoil and nongas businesses because the projected returns in those businesses did not compensate for their anticipated risks.

EXHIBIT 5.6 Risk Assessment Techniques Used by Respondents

Technique	Percentage
No method is used	21
Risk is determined subjectively	52
Standard deviation (variance)	4
Decision trees*	3
Computer simulations	7
Sensitivity analysis	27
Others	10

Source: Survey data from Suk H. Kim, Trevor Crick and Seung H. Kim. Do Executives Practice What Academies Preach? Management Accounting, November 1986, pp. 49–52.
Copyright IMA. Reprinted with permission from the Institute for Management Accountants, Montvale, N.J. www.imanet.org.

*Decision trees are covered in Section 5.5.

---

[7]Harrington, D.R. "Stock Prices, Beta, and Strategic Planning." *Harvard Business Review*, May–June 1983, pp. 157–164.

5.4 Adjusting for Project Risk

So far we have seen how to assess the riskiness of a given project. This section discusses various methods of factoring risk into a capital-budgeting analysis. The principal means of incorporating project risk include adjusting the payback period, using a risk-adjusted discount rate, adjusting cash flows, and calculating certainty equivalents for the cash flows.

ADJUSTING THE PAYBACK PERIOD

Many firms treat risk in a subjective way instead of dealing with its impact on specific investments. This rather vague view of risk probably accounts for firms' frequent use of the somewhat haphazard requirement that riskier projects have shorter payback periods. For example, a project that is riskier than average may have a three-year payback requirement instead of the usual five-year requirement. But why three years? Why not four years or three and a half years? The arbitrariness of this procedure is evident.

Even in the absence of risk, we have already seen in Chapter 2 that payback is an inappropriate technique to use in investment analysis. Consequently, we shall not discuss this method further.

ADJUSTING THE DISCOUNT RATE

Another approach used to account for varying risks is to employ a risk-adjusted discount rate. This method is theoretically correct, but too often it is applied in an *ad hoc* manner. For example, a normal required return of 15% might be increased to 20% for a riskier project. Again, the question can be raised of why 20%? Why not 17% or 21.3%? In addition, when applying this method, decision makers often fail to distinguish between the project's total risk and the systematic component of that risk. Which is the relevant risk, and how should it be reflected in the discount rate? Chapter 6 shows how the CAPM can be used to supply the theoretically correct discount rate.

ADJUSTING CASH FLOWS

Most firms discount most-likely (modal) cash flows rather than expected (mean) cash flows. If a major new risk is anticipated, the mean value of the probability distribution of future cash flows will be significantly below its mode. Consider, for example, a proposed copper mining venture by Anaconda in Indonesia for which both the mean and mode of future cash flows are projected at $20 million annually. Suppose now that a change in government raises the possibility that the mine will be nationalized with no compensation paid to Anaconda. If the probability of nationalization is 25%, the mean value of future annual cash flows will decline to $15 million ($20 × 0.75 + $0 × 0.25); the modal value will remain at $20 million.

When faced with such a risk, many companies will apply one of the two methods discussed to the $20 million modal value, either shortening the payback period or raising the discount rate. Neither of these two approaches, however, lends itself to a careful evaluation of the actual impact of a particular risk on investment returns. Thorough risk analysis requires an assessment of the magnitude and timing of risks and their implications for the projected cash flows. In the case of the copper mine, the impact of the risk is to convert a $20 million expected cash flow into a $0 cash flow. Taking into account the likelihood of the risk's materializing reduces the expected cash flow to $15 million. In addition, both the payback and the risk-adjusted discount rate methods ignore the matter of timing. Nationalization five years hence is likely to be much less threatening than one expected next year, even though the probability of its occurring later may be higher.

In such a situation, using a uniformly higher discount rate just distorts the meaning of the present value of a project by penalizing future cash flows relatively more heavily than current ones; it does not avert the need for a careful risk evaluation. Instead, adjusting cash flows makes it possible to incorporate all available information about the impact of a specific risk on the future returns from an investment.

The method of cash flow adjustment requires that cash flows be adjusted to reflect the year-by-year expected effects of a given risk. Suppose, for instance, that nationalization of Anaconda's copper mine—should it occur—will not take place until year 4 at the earliest. If the venture is expected to have a seven-year life, then the expected year-by-year cash flows under this scenario will be

Year	1	2	3	4	5	6	7
Expected cash flow ($ millions)	20	20	20	15	15	15	15

If the additional risk being incorporated is systematic in nature, then the discount rate should also be adjusted to reflect the change in the project's systematic risk. This issue is discussed further in Chapter 6. Risks like nationalization, or most other project-specific risks—such as the possibility, when investing in new product development, that a competitor will come out with a similar product—are likely to be unsystematic in nature. Thus, when accounting for these risks, only the expected cash flows need be adjusted; there is no need to adjust the discount rate further.

USING CERTAINTY EQUIVALENTS

It is unlikely that management will be concerned solely with the systematic component of total risk—nor, as pointed out, should it be. An alternative approach is to use the certainty-equivalent method of Alexander Robichek and Stewart Myers, in which risk-adjusted cash flows are discounted at the risk-free rate r_f.[8]

The **certainty equivalent** of a risky cash flow is defined as that certain amount of money that the decision maker would just be willing to accept in lieu of the risky amount. For example, suppose a person would be willing to trade for $15,000, a lottery ticket having a 25% chance of winning $100,000 and a 75% chance of winning nothing (an expected value of $25,000). We would say that the certainty equivalent of this lottery ticket is $15,000.

This method is implemented by converting each expected cash flow into its certainty equivalent, by using a conversion factor that can range from 0 to 1.0. Specifically, the expected cash flow for period t, CF_t, is multiplied by the conversion factor for period t, a_t, and the resulting number, $a_t CF_t$, is the certainty-equivalent cash flow. The more certain the expected future cash flow is, the closer to 1.0 the value of a_t will be. Equivalently, a high a_t implies a more certain and, therefore, more valuable expected

---

[8]Robichek, A.A., and Myers, S.C. *Optimal Financing Decisions*. Prentice Hall: Englewood Cliffs, N.J., 1965.

cash flow. Less certain cash flows are valued less highly and, accordingly, have lower conversion factors.

The certainty-equivalent conversion factors are calculated as follows:

$$a_t = \frac{\text{Certain cash flow}}{\text{Expected cash flow}}$$

In the example of the lottery ticket, the conversion factor is 0.6 ($15,000/$25,000).

The certainty-equivalent cash flows, $a_t CF_t$, are then discounted at the risk-free rate of return to yield a certainty-equivalent net present value:

$$\text{Certainty-equivalent } NPV = -a_0 I_0 + \sum_{t=1}^{n} \frac{a_t CF_t}{(1 + r_f)^t}$$

where n is the expected life of the project and r_f is the risk-free rate.

To illustrate the application of the certainty-equivalent method, consider a project with a five-year life that has the expected cash flows and associated certainty-equivalent factors depicted in Exhibit 5.7. On the basis of a 9% risk-free rate of return, the calculations in Exhibit 5.7 show that the project has a net present value equal to $1,505.

The initial outlay is assumed to be known with certainty and so has a certainty-equivalent factor of 1.0. Subsequent cash flows, being risky, have certainty-equivalent factors of less than 1.0 but more than 0 because some return is expected; although they are risky, these returns have value. Note that the certainty-equivalent factors decrease over time. This is the typical pattern and reflects the greater risk associated with more distant cash flows. Despite this, the expected future cash flows are sufficiently large, relative to the initial investment of $15,000, so that the project is acceptable.

The certainty-equivalent method is considered by many financial theorists to be conceptually superior to the risk-adjusted discount rate method for several related reasons:

1. When valuing future cash flows, it is necessary to account for both the time value of money and risk. Adding a risk premium to the risk-free rate—which is what is done when using a risk-adjusted discount rate—may produce a present value factor that is not very meaningful. The certainty-equivalent method, on the other

EXHIBIT 5.7 Calculation of Certainty-Equivalent NPV

Year	Expected Cash Flow	Conversion Factor	Certainty-Equivalent Cash Flow	Present Value Factor @ 9%	Present Value
0	−15,000	1.0	−15,000	1.0	−5,000
1	8,000	0.8	6,400	0.9174	5,872
2	9,000	0.7	6,300	0.8417	5,303
3	6,000	0.6	3,600	0.7722	2,780
4	5,000	0.5	2,500	0.7084	1,771
5	3,000	0.4	1,200	0.6499	780
				Certainty-equivalent NPV =	1,505

hand, differentiates between the two distinct factors. It uses the discount rate to account for the time value of money and the certainty-equivalent factor to account for the riskiness of each individual cash flow.

2. The certainty-equivalent method allows each period's cash flow to be adjusted separately for its own degree of risk. It allows for different time patterns of risk, unlike the risk-adjusted discount rate method. Although the risk-adjusted discount rate method can also employ a time-varying risk premium, this procedure is considered to be more awkward.

3. With this method, decision makers can incorporate their own risk preferences directly in the analysis. This process increases the meaningfulness of the net present value number to the decision maker, even if this approach, by substituting managerial preferences for shareholder preferences, does not lead to shareholder wealth maximization.

Despite its conceptual superiority, however, the certainty-equivalent method is rarely used in practice. The main reason that it is not used is that no satisfactory procedure has yet been developed to generate the necessary certainty-equivalent factors. Moreover, it means losing some information about the valuation of future cash flows that is provided by shareholders in the form of their required yield on a typical firm investment.

SURVEY OF RISK ADJUSTMENT TECHNIQUES USED IN PRACTICE

The survey of corporate capital-budgeting practices by Kim, Crick, and Kim provide information on the risk adjustment techniques used in practice (unfortunately, the more recent survey by Graham and Harvey contains no information on this subject[9]). These data are summarized in Exhibit 5.8. The numbers in the table sum to more than 100%, indicating that some companies use more than one risk adjustment technique. Eighty-six percent of the 367 respondents claimed that their firms factored risk into the investment decision. But their methods for doing so vary.

EXHIBIT 5.8 Risk Adjustment Techniques Used by Respondents

Technique	Percentage
No adjustment is made	14
Adjustment is made subjectively	48
Certainty-equivalent method	7
Risk adjusted discount rate	29
Shortening payback period	7
Others	5

Source: Survey data from Suk. H. Kim, Trevor Cock, and Seung H. Kim, *Do* Executives Practice What Academics Preach? *Management Accounting,* November, 1986, pp. 49–52. Copyright IMA. Reprinted with permission from the Institute for Management Accountants, Montvale, N.J. www.imanet.org.

---

[9]Graham and Harvey point out that 51% of respondents said they would always or almost always use a risk-matched discount rate. However, it is not clear whether the risk adjustment is *ad hoc* or based on the CAPM.

It is unclear what "subjective adjustment" means, but this was the overwhelming favorite method. The risk-adjusted discount rate is also popular, but it is not clear whether the risk premium is subjectively assigned or is based on the CAPM. The odds are that the risk premium is decided on in an *ad hoc* manner. It is surprising that so few firms use payback to account for risk when so many use it as their primary or secondary capital-budgeting technique. Not surprisingly, given its difficulty in application, few respondents use the certainty-equivalent approach.

5.5 Decision Trees

Investment decisions are often not quite so cut-and-dried as the examples used so far would seem to indicate. Instead, as we saw in Chapter 4, many investment opportunities require a sequence of decisions through time, with each subsequent decision depending both on earlier decisions as well as the actual outcomes of those decisions. Consequently, what you plan to do today will often depend on what you plan to do in the future.

A useful aid in solving problems involving sequential decisions is to diagram the alternatives and their possible consequences. The resulting chart or graph is known as a **decision tree**, so called because it has the appearance of a tree with branches. A decision tree enables managers to visualize quickly the possible future events, their probabilities, and their financial consequences. It also helps in selecting the optimal sequence of decisions by facilitating the calculation of the NPVs associated with the alternative decision paths.

BOX 5.3

APPLICATION: PROCTER & GAMBLE'S NEW SOFT DRINK PLANT

To take a hypothetical example, suppose Procter & Gamble (P&G) has developed a new soft drink but is uncertain whether demand for the product will be high or low. P&G estimates that there is a 60% chance that demand will be high in the first year. High initial demand is a good omen; it raises the probability of high demand in the second and subsequent years to around 80%. On the other hand, if initial demand is low (with a 40% probability), there is a 70% chance that future demand will also be low.

Because of competitive pressures, P&G has decided to build a plant immediately to produce the drink rather than to spend additional time testing the product's market acceptance. It is uncertain, however, whether the plant should be large or small. If P&G constructs a large plant, at a cost of $15 million, it will keep the plant regardless of subsequent demand. Alternatively, P&G could build a smaller plant today (time 0) for $10 million, and then in the next year, if demand warrants, it could enlarge the plant at an additional cost of $7 million. (Thus, building a large plant at the outset is $2 million less expensive than building a small one initially and having to expand it later.)

The decision tree in Exhibit 5.9 on page 136 displays the choices available to P&G, along with their potential consequences. The squares represent decision points, and the circles represent chance events. After each decision has been made, fate selects the actual level of demand. This is represented by the branches of the decision tree. Each branch has its probability of occurrence written on it, along with the payoff associated with that combination of plant size and demand.

The sequence of events depicted by the tree is as follows: P&G builds a plant at time 0, after which fate selects either a high or a low demand. Each of the four possible combinations of plant size and demand level during that first year generates a different cash flow. At time 1 (the end of year 1), the small plant can be expanded (if it were the time 0 choice). Unfortunately, the permanent level of demand is still unknown at this point, although there exists somewhat less uncertainty about what it will be. Thus, in year 2, fate once more selects a high or a low level of demand. The resulting payoff again depends on the particular demand-plant size combination involved. It is clear that the demand probabilities in year 2 depend on actual demand in year 1. For example, the probability of a high demand in year 2, given a high demand in year 1, is 0.8, but only 0.3 if year 1 demand was low. The chance of high demand in both years is 0.6 × 0.8 = 0.48.

Note that there are two points in time at which P&G can make decisions, now (time 0) and next year (time 1). The first decision is whether to build a large or a small plant. If the large plant is built, P&G's course is set—it can only hope that demand is high and remains high. If the time 0 decision is to build the small plant, P&G has another decision to make at time 1: Should it expand the small plant or should it sit tight? This decision depends on what the first-year demand turns out to be.

The problem confronting P&G today is whether to build a small or a large plant now. One solution procedure is to make the more distant decision first—the choice of whether P&G should expand its small plant next year—and then work backward to the present. This requires that we determine the expected net present value of expansion, given that the first-year demand turns out to be high or low. According to the numbers provided in Exhibit 5.9 on page 136, expansion when demand is low has an expected NPV of –$3,601,000. This is clearly dominated by the expected NPV of $1,780,000 for the no-expansion choice.

Expansion subsequent to high demand in year 1 has an expected NPV of $6,858,000. Alternatively, the no-expansion decision has an expected NPV of $4,979,000. Hence, the decision rule at time 1 is clear: If year 1 demand is high, expand; if it is low, do not expand. Now that we know the optimal decisions at time 1, conditional on year 1 demand, we can determine P&G's optimal decision at time 0.

The expected NPV at time 0 for a small plant, given that time 1 decisions are made optimally, is $4,827,000. If year 1 demand is low, we use the expected NPV associated with maintaining the small plant. If year 1 demand is high, we use the expected NPV associated with expansion at time 1. By contrast, the expected NPV associated with building the large plant initially is $4,557,000.

Thus, the expected NPV for building a small plant initially exceeds that for building a large plant by $270,000. But if there were no option to expand, the expected NPV of the small plant would be only $3,699,400 (0.6 × 4,979,000 + 0.4 × 1,780,000), and it would be optimal to build the large plant. This means that the option to expand, once the small plant is built, is worth $1,127,600 ($4,827,000 – $3,699,000). Before any investment, the option to expand has an expected NPV of $270,000, the difference between the expected NPVs of the optimal decisions with and without the expansion option ($4,827,000 – $4,557,000).

EXHIBIT 5.9 Decision Tree Analysis for P&G's Soft Drink Plant

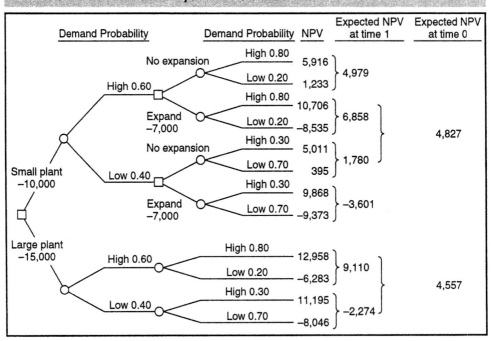

5.6 Summary and Conclusions

Uncertainty of investment cash flows is an all-pervasive element in the capital-budgeting process, but it affects differently the riskiness of the project, the firm, and well-diversified investors. In this chapter, therefore, we identified three different types of risk associated with a project: (1) total project risk, which is based on the variability of project returns, (2) firm risk, which is measured by the contribution of project risk to the variability of total firm returns, and (3) systematic risk, which is based on the project's beta coefficient, as measured by the correlation between project returns and returns on the market portfolio. Although type 1 and type 2 risks should not affect the required return on a project, we have seen that these risks could affect project revenues and costs and, hence, alter actual project returns. Thus, it makes sense to incorporate total risk as well as systematic risk into capital-budgeting analyses.

This chapter described some of the methods that firms use to factor risk into their project analyses. These methods include adjusting the discount rate, adjusting project cash flows, and using certainty-equivalent cash flows. The end result of these analyses is the risk-adjusted project net present value. We have already seen that if calculated correctly, this number is sufficient to describe the relative desirability of each project.

Rather than settle for just one number, however, many firms also perform sensitivity analyses on project cash flows to appraise the effect of varying the values of certain key parameters on the project NPV, including construction costs, R&D costs, market size and share, price, and production costs. In addition, the advent of low-cost, high-powered computers and computer modeling techniques has encouraged a number of firms to simulate the effects of changing several of these parameters simultaneously, while taking into account the probability of these changes actually occurring. The output from a simulation analysis is a probability distribution of project NPVs. Finally, we considered the evaluation of projects in which a sequence of decisions must be made at different points in time, with each subsequent decision being affected by earlier decisions and the outcomes of those decisions. A useful aid in such situations, which is known as decision tree analysis, is to graph the alternatives and their possible consequences.

Although none of these techniques for assessing project risk and incorporating risk in a project analysis is perfect, some useful information may be gained from each. Employing several techniques in combination is likely to prove the most fruitful approach in practice.

REFERENCES

Hertz, D.B. "Risk Analysis in Capital Investment." *Harvard Business Review*, January–February 1964, pp. 95–106.

Hertz, D.B. "Investment Policies That Pay Off." *Harvard Business Review*, January–February 1968, pp. 96–108.

Magee, J. "How to Use Decision Trees in Capital Investment." *Harvard Business Review*, September–October 1964, pp. 79–96.

Reinhardt, U.E. "Break-Even Analysis for Lockheed's Tri Star: An Application of Financial Theory." *Journal of Finance*, September 1973, pp. 821–838.

Shapiro, A.C., and Titman, S. "An Integrated Approach to Corporate Risk Management." *Midland Corporate Finance Journal*, Summer 1985, pp. 41–56.

SAMPLE PROBLEMS

1. Calculate the NPV of an investment project with the following characteristics:

   Units sold per year: 55,000

   Price per unit: $800

   Variable cost per unit: $720

   Fixed cost: 0

   Initial cost: $20 million

   Life of project: 10 years

   Discount rate: 10%

   Depreciation: straight-line

   Tax rate: 34%

   Answer: $NPV = -PV(\text{cost}) + PV(\text{depreciation tax shield}) + PV(\text{operating cash flows})$

   $$PV(\text{cost}) = \$20,000,000$$

   With a depreciable life of 10 years, annual depreciation is $2,000,000. This results in an annual depreciation tax shield of $2,000,000 \times 0.34 = \$680,000$. Hence,

   $$PV(\text{depreciation tax shield}) = \$680,000 \times PVIFA_{10,10}$$
   $$= 680,000 \times 6.1446 = \$4,178,328$$

$$PV(\text{operating cash flows}) = (\text{Price} - \text{Cost})(\text{Units})(1 - \text{tax rate})PVIFA_{10,10}$$
$$= (800 - 720)(55,000)(0.66)(6.1446) = \$17,843,918$$
$$NPV = -\$20,000,000 + 4,178,328 + 17,843,918 = \$2,022,246$$

a. Suppose an additional investment of $5 million would reduce the variable cost per unit to $700. Calculate the *NPV* of this alternative.

Answer: $PV(\text{cost}) = \$25,000,000$ (25% more than above)

$PV(\text{depreciation tax shield}) = \$5,222,882$ (25% more)

$$PV(\text{operating cash flows}) = (800 - 700)(55,000)(0.66)(6.1446)$$
$$= \$22,304,898$$
$$NPV = -25,000,000 + 5,222,882 + 22,304,898$$
$$= \$2,527,780$$

b. What is the break-even (*NPV*) number of units for the two alternatives?

Answer: Break-even occurs when

$$PV(\text{operating cash flows}) = PV(\text{cost}) - PV(\text{depreciation tax shield})$$

For the prior case,

$$(800 - 720)(X)(0.66)(6.1446) = 15,821,694.37$$
$$\text{Break-even } X = 48,767 \text{ units}$$

For part (a),

$$(800 - 700)(X)(0.66)(6.1446) = 19,777,117.96$$
$$\text{Break-even } X = 48,767 \text{ units}$$

The break-even quantities are identical. However, for any sales beyond 48,767 units, profits rise faster once the additional investment has been made. For sales less than break-even, losses mount more quickly if the investment is undertaken.

2. Multifoods, a retail grocery chain, is considering entering the fast-growing bulk food retail area. Although Multifoods is uncertain as to what its costs and revenues will be, it estimates that each of the relevant project parameters can take on only one of two possible values. Given below are the best estimates of the project's four parameters and their possible values over its five-year life:

Revenue/year	$100,000	$125,000
Fixed cost/year	20,000	15,000
Variable cost/year	10,000	5,000
Depreciation/year	10,000	10,000

Each parameter value has a 50% probability of being selected, and the selection of one parameter value is independent of the selection of any of the other parameter values.

a. Construct a probability distribution of the NPV for the project. Multifoods has a tax rate of 35% and a cost of capital of 12%. The initial investment is $150,000. (*Hint:* Since each of the four parameters can take on either of two values with probability 0.5, there are eight possible scenarios to examine.)

Answer: The eight (equally likely) scenarios are reported below:

Scenario 1 2 3 4 5 6 7 8

Revenue	100.00 100.00 100.00 100.00 125.00 125.00 125.00 125.00
– Fixed cost	20.00 15.00 20.00 15.00 20.00 15.00 20.00 15.00
– Variable cost	10.00 10.00 5.00 5.00 10.00 10.00 5.00 5.00
– Depreciation	10.00 10.00 10.00 10.00 10.00 10.00 10.00 10.00
= Taxable income	60.00 65.00 65.00 70.00 85.00 90.00 90.00 95.00
– Tax	21.00 22.75 22.75 24.50 29.75 31.50 31.50 33.25
= After-tax income	39.00 42.25 42.25 45.50 55.25 58.50 58.50 61.75
+ Depreciation	10.00 10.00 10.00 10.00 10.00 10.00 10.00 10.00
= Cash flow	49.00 52.25 52.25 55.50 65.25 68.50 68.50 71.75
$\times PVIFA_{12,5} =$	176.63 188.34 188.34 200.06 235.21 246.92 246.92 258.64
– Investment	150.00 150.00 150.00 150.00 150.00 150.00 150.00 150.00
= NPV	26.63 38.35 38.35 50.07 85.21 96.93 96.93 108.64

The expected NPV of Multifoods' project, given these eight scenarios with equal probability of being realized, equals 67.64, with a standard deviation of 30.44.

b. If Multifoods prepared estimates of five alternative values for each parameter, how many possible outcomes would have to be considered?
Answer: The number of alternative scenarios would equal $5 \times 5 \times 5 = 125$.

QUESTIONS

1. Comment on the following statements:
   a. "Because our new expansion project has the same systematic risk as the firm as a whole, we need do no further risk analysis on the project."
   b. "Our company should accept the new potash mine project at Moosejaw. The cost of additional loans to fund the project is 12%, and our simulations lead us to expect a 14% return from the project."
   c. "It is difficult to decide whether to spend $10 million to reopen our mine because the price of gold is so uncertain. However, if we assume the price of gold grows at an average of 5% a year with a standard deviation of 20% a year, simulation indicates the mine has an average NPV of $500,000. Therefore, we should reopen."

2. Assess the impact of the following events on a firm's operating leverage:
   a. an increase in output price due to increased demand.
   b. a decrease in fixed cost.
   c. negotiation of a new contract with suppliers leading to higher commitments to purchase raw materials.
   d. lowered variable labor costs per unit of output.
   e. installation of new machine tools that lower variable production costs per unit of output.

3. Consider two firms, one American and the other Japanese, using identical production processes; that is, they use the same equipment and hire the same number of workers. However, the Japanese firm follows a no-layoff policy, whereas the American firm is willing to alter its work force in line with changing market conditions. Which company will have the larger amount of operating leverage? Why? How will the difference in amounts of operating leverage affect their marketing and production decisions and strategies?

4. The CAPM and the APT argue that only systematic risk matters; risk that is diversifiable is irrelevant to the well-diversified investor. Yet this chapter has argued that total risk matters, not just systematic risk. Is there an inconsistency here? Explain.

5. What is the advantage of using certainty-equivalent cash flows instead of risk-adjusted discount rates to calculate the NPV of an investment project?

PROBLEMS

1. Suppose that Bethlehem Steel has a current sales level of $2.5 billion, variable costs of $2 billion, and fixed costs of $400 million. If sales rise by 15%, how much will pre-tax profit increase in dollar terms? What will be the percentage increase in pre-tax profit? What explains the relationship between the percentage change in sales and the percentage change in pre-tax profit for Bethlehem?

2. In early 1990, Boeing Co. decided to gamble $4 billion to build a new long-distance, 350-seat wide-body airplane called the Boeing 777. The price tag for the 777, scheduled for delivery beginning in 1995, is about $120 million apiece. Assume that Boeing's $4 billion investment is made at the rate of $800 million a year for the years 1990 through 1994 and that the present value of the tax write-off associated with these costs is $750 million. On the basis of estimated annual fixed costs of $100 million, variable production costs of $90 million apiece, a marginal corporate tax rate of 34% and a discount rate of 14%, what is the break-even quantity of annual unit sales over the Boeing 777's projected 15-year life? Assume that all cash inflows and outflows occur at the end of the year.

3. The recently opened Grand Hyatt Wailea Resort and Spa on Maui cost $600 million, about $800,000 per room, to build. Daily operating expenses average $135 a room if occupied and $80 a room if unoccupied (much of the labor cost of running a hotel is fixed). At an average room rate of $500 a night, a marginal tax rate of 40%, and a cost of capital of 11%, what year-round occupancy rate do the Japanese investors who financed the Grand Hyatt Wailea require to break even in economic terms on their investment over its estimated 40-year life? What is the likelihood that this investment will have a positive NPV? Assume that the $450 million expense of building the hotel can be written off straight line over a 30-year period (the other $150 million is for the land which is not depreciable) and that the present value of the hotel's terminal value will be $200 million.

4. Conduct a sensitivity analysis for a project with the following characteristics. Each parameter can take on any of three different values but once a parameter value is selected, that value remains constant for the 10-year period. The discount rate is 10% and the project life is 10 years. Ignore taxes and depreciation.

	Low	Mean	High
(1) Sales (units)	160	500	960
(2) Price (per unit)	$3,000	$3,750	$4,000
(3) Variable cost (per unit)	3,000	3,000	3,000
(4) Fixed cost	100,000	200,000	4,000
(5) Initial investment	1,000,000	2,000,000	4,000,000

5. American Fruit Co. is considering constructing a new plant to process frozen fruit juices. One plant would be capital intensive, the other much more labor intensive. Although the final decision would hinge on the relative cost of capital versus labor in the northern

California area, management is curious about the behavior of the plants' return on assets during a typical business cycle.

a. Given the following information, calculate the break-even point in units of production for the two plants.

b. The economics department has prepared sales projections for three business scenarios: recession, normal, and recovery. Sales under each scenario are expected to be as follows: recession, 300,000 units; normal, 500,000 units; and recovery, 800,000 units. Calculate the return on assets for the two plants under these three scenarios.

c. If the three scenarios are all equally likely, what will be the variance of the return on assets for plant 1? For plant 2? What would you advise American Fruit?

	Plant 1	Plant 2
Fixed cost	$200,000	$600,000
Variable cost (per unit)	1.50	.50
Price (per unit)	2.00	2.00
Investment	1,000,000	1,000,000

6. For the following project, the chief financial officer has prepared a set of certainty-equivalent factors to adjust the cash flows for the estimated risk. The economics department has also prepared a set of risk-adjusted interest rates at which to discount the project's cash flow. The project's initial investment is $150,000 and the Treasury security rate is 8%.

a. What is the NPV of the project from the finance department's estimates?

b. What is the NPV from the economics department's estimates?

c. What would you advise the company to do?

Year	1	2	3
Cash flows ($000)	$50	$75	$130
Certainty equivalents (finance department)	0.982	0.964	0.947
Risk-adjusted rates (economics department)	10%	12%	14%

7. A gold mine is considering replacement of some machinery. The new conveyor belt will cost $5 million and lower the cost of removing ore from the mine by $4 per ton. The old belt can be scrapped for $500,000. The following table shows that the life of the new machine is uncertain, as is the annual amount of ore that will be moved:

	Low	Mean	High
Tons per year	200,000	250,000	350,000
Life of new machine	6 years	9 years	13 years

Conduct a sensitivity analysis of the NPV of the replacement project assuming a discount rate of 10%. Ignore taxes.

8. Teletech Co. wants to use a decision tree in evaluating a venture capital investment in cable TV. The projected investment has a life of three years, and the associated after-tax cash flows ($000) and probabilities are as follows:

Year 1	Year 2	Year 3
Cash flow: $100 $P = 0.50$ $200 $P = 0.50$	If cash flow in year 1 = $100 Year 2 cash flow = $120 $P = 0.60 = 9 $P = 0.40$ If cash flow in year 1 = $200 Year 2 cash flow = $250 $P = 0.50$ = $210 $P = 0.50$	If cash flow in year 2 = $120, can sell the investment for either $350 $(P = 0.70)$ or $250. If cash flow in year 2 = $95, can sell the investment for either $125 $(P = 0.60)$ or $75. If cash flow in year 2 = $250, can sell the investment for either $475 $(P = 0.80)$ or $275. If cash flow in year 2 = $210, can sell the investment for either $140 $(P = 0.50)$ or $110.

The initial investment for the firm is $500,000 after tax. The firm uses a cost of capital of 10%.

a. Construct a decision tree with the expected NPV of each alternative.
b. What is the expected NPV of the best possible outcome? What is its probability?
c. What is the expected NPV of the worst possible outcome? What is its probability?
d. Should Teletech make the investment? Why or why not?

9. Refer to the Starship project in Section 5.2.

a. What would the break-even quantity be initially if the cost of capital for the project were estimated at 14% rather than 10%?
b. What would the break-even quantity be if the Starship could be sold for only $2,000,000 each (assume a cost of capital of 10%)?
c. What would the break-even quantity be if cost overruns increased the initial investment from $130,000,000 to $230,000,000?

10. The following exhibit contains Beech's estimates of demand, price, and fixed and variable costs for the Starship under three alternative economic forecasts.

Variable (per year)	Pessimistic	Normal	Optimistic
Demand	50	75	125
Price*	2	2.7	3.2
Fixed cost*	22	15	7
Variable cost*	1.75	1.50	1.0

*Dollars in millions

a. If all other variables are assumed to be at their expected value (normal forecast), how sensitive is the project's NPV to changes in fixed cost? Use a cost of capital of 10%, tax rate of 35%, and project life of 10 years.
b. How sensitive is the project's NPV to changes in price?
c. How sensitive is the project's NPV to changes in variable cost?
d. Which factor seems most important to the success of the plane?
e. Is the Starship a risky project? Explain.

Estimating the Project Cost of Capital

If a man will begin with certainties, he shall end in doubts; but if he will be content to begin with doubts, he shall end in certainties.

—FRANCIS BACON

The net present value or worth of a project is dependent on both its expected cash flows and the rate at which those future cash flows are discounted. Chapter 3 showed how to estimate project cash flows, and Chapter 5 presented various techniques for assessing the riskiness of those cash flows. When performing a present value analysis using these data, we implicitly assumed that the discount rate was known. In this chapter, we relax that assumption and show how to calculate the discount rate, also known as the project's **cost of capital**. The issue of the cost of capital for new projects is one of the most complex in corporate finance. Yet it is an issue that must be addressed because the investment decision cannot be made properly without knowledge of the appropriate cost of capital.

The cost of capital for a project is the minimum risk-adjusted return required by shareholders of the firm for undertaking that project. As such, it is the basic measure of financial performance. Unless the investment generates sufficient funds to repay suppliers of capital, the firm's value will suffer. This return requirement can be met only if the NPV of future project cash flows, using the project's cost of capital as the discount rate, is positive. Thus, the emphasis here is on estimating the required rate of return for a specific project rather than for the firm as a whole.

This rate must take account of both the time value of money, measured by the risk-free rate of return, and the riskiness of the project's cash flows. As we will see, the key to measuring project risk is the capital asset pricing model (CAPM) and its focus on systematic or beta risk. In particular, for projects whose systematic risk is the same as the systematic risk of the firm, the firm's cost of capital is the correct discount rate to use. When systematic risk is similar for projects within each division but is different across divisions, a divisional cost of capital is appropriate. A project whose risk characteristics differ from the corporate or divisional norm will have its own unique cost of capital.

Section 6.1 begins by discussing the relationship between a project's riskiness and its cost of capital. Section 6.2 shows how to calculate a firm's overall cost of capital for the special case in which the project risk and firm risk are identical. Section 6.3 deals with the concept and calculation of a divisional cost of capital. Appendix 6A discusses some international dimensions to cost of capital estimation.

6.1 Risk and the Cost of Capital for a Project

Each project has its own required return, reflecting three basic elements: (1) the *real* or inflation-adjusted risk-free interest rate, (2) an inflation premium approximately equal to the amount of expected inflation, and (3) a premium for risk. The first two cost elements are shared by all projects and reflect the time value of money, whereas the third component varies according to the risks borne by investors in the different projects. For a project to be acceptable to the firm's shareholders, its return must be sufficient to compensate them for all three cost components. This minimum or *required* return is the *project's cost of capital* and is sometimes referred to as a **hurdle rate**. In discussing how to calculate the project's cost of capital, we begin by assuming the firm is all-equity financed and later relax that assumption.

The preceding paragraph bears a crucial message: *The cost of capital for a project depends on the riskiness of the assets being financed, not on the identity of the firm undertaking the project.* The risk-required return trade-off is set in the financial marketplace and is based on the yields available to investors on other investments with similar risk characteristics. Consequently, the required return on a project (the project's cost of capital) is an opportunity cost, which depends on the alternative market investments that investors must forgo. The upshot of this is that the required rates of return on corporate investments are not set by management. Rather, they are set in the financial marketplace on the basis of a complex interaction among three principal factors: (1) the volume and risk-expected return characteristics of productive investments in the economy, (2) the supply of capital available to take advantage of these investment opportunities, and (3) the risk preferences of the investors providing the capital.

BOX 6.1

APPLICATION: COST OF CAPITAL FOR NONPROFITS

One argument often advanced in favor of nonprofit organizations such as hospitals, correctional facilities, and schools is that because they do not have to earn a profit, nonprofits have lower costs and therefore can charge lower prices than for-profit organizations need to. This argument ignores the huge amounts of capital tied up in nonprofits and the fact that this capital has a cost to society—the return foregone on

---

alternative investments. Society pays for any lower prices charged by nonprofits in the form of the goods and service that could be made available to all by investing this capital elsewhere. This does not mean that nonprofits harm society. What it does mean is that to evaluate any project properly, one must recognize that all capital has a cost and that that cost can be measured, albeit imperfectly, by reference to the returns required by the capital markets. The bottom line is that society benefits when resources are invested in the projects that earn better returns, whether the projects are undertaken by for-profit or by nonprofit organizations.

THE CAPITAL ASSET PRICING MODEL

One way to estimate the cost of capital for a project is to take the nominal riskless interest rate—as measured by the return on Treasury securities—and add to it a risk premium. Note that by beginning with the required return on Treasury securities, the real risk-free interest rate and the inflation premium are incorporated already because they are embedded in Treasury yields. Because the project is likely to last for many years, we need a risk-free return that reflects a long-term inflation forecast. One approach, which is the one recommended here, is to use the rate on a long-term Treasury bond of the same maturity as the project.[1] Once this has been done, the problem is reduced to estimating the risk premium on the project.

This can be done with the aid of modern capital market theory. This theory posits an equilibrium relationship between an asset's required return and its associated risk, which can be represented by the capital asset pricing model (CAPM) or the arbitrage pricing theory(APT). According to both models, intelligent, risk-averse investors will seek to diversify their risks. Consequently, the only risk that will be rewarded with a risk premium will be the asset's systematic or *unavoidable* risk (or risks in the case of the APT), as measured by the asset's "beta" coefficient(s).

Despite doubts concerning the CAPM, it is still the most widely used risk-based cost of capital model. For example, Graham and Harvey found that 73.5% of respondents surveyed always or almost always used the CAPM to estimate the cost of equity capital.[2] Hence, the remainder of this chapter will illustrate how to estimate a project's cost of capital using the CAPM.

The CAPM asserts that the risk premium for any asset, including a corporate project, equals the asset's beta multiplied by the market risk premium or

$$\text{Asset risk premium (\%)} = \text{Asset beta} \times \text{Market risk premium}$$
$$= \beta_i(r_m - r_f)$$

---

[1]Although the 90-day Treasury bill rate is often used to measure the risk-free rate, it seems appropriate to use the rate on long-term Treasury bonds when estimating the long-term cost of capital.

[2]Graham, J., and Harvey, C. "How Do CFOs Make Capital Budgeting and Capital Structure Decisions?" *Journal of Applied Corporate Finance*, Spring 2002, pp. 8–23.

where

β_i = asset i's beta coefficient, measured as σ_{im}/σ_m^2, where σ_{im} stands for the covariance between returns on asset i and returns on the market, and σ_m^2 is the variance of returns on the market portfolio

r_m = required return on the market portfolio, which consists of all risky assets

r_f = risk-free interest rate, usually measured as the yield to maturity on a U.S. Treasury bond

Therefore, to use the CAPM to calculate the cost of capital (required return) for a project, which is an asset, three numbers are necessary — the risk-free interest rate, the project's beta coefficient, and the market risk premium.

Substituting the risk premium in the CAPM, we have

$$\begin{array}{ccc} \text{Cost of capital} & \text{Risk-free} & \text{Project risk} \\ \text{for project } i & = \text{interest rate} + \text{premium} \end{array}$$

$$r_i = r_f + \beta_i(r_m - r_f) \tag{6.1}$$

where

$$r_i = \text{cost of capital for project } i$$

$$\beta_i(r_m - r_f) = \text{risk premium on project } i$$

For example, suppose that the long-term Treasury bond rate is 5.5% and the differential between the required return on the market and the risk-free Treasury bond rate is believed to be 7.0%, the same as its historical differential. Then if the estimated beta for the project is 1.15, slightly higher than the market portfolio's beta of 1.0 (why does the market portfolio's beta equal 1.0?),[3] the CAPM-calculated required return on the project will be 13.6%:

$$\begin{array}{ccc} \text{Project cost} & \text{Risk-free} & \text{Project risk} \\ \text{of capital} & = \text{interest rate} + \text{premium} \end{array}$$

$$= 5.5\% + 1.15 \times 7.0\%$$

$$= 13.6\%$$

Estimating the Market Risk Premium

In actual applications, as indicated above, the market risk premium, also known as the equity risk premium, is ordinarily assumed to equal the average historical difference between the return on the stock market and the average return on long-term Treasury bonds. The return on the market is usually taken to be the return on a well-diversified portfolio of stocks, such as the New York Stock Exchange (NYSE) index or

---

[3]Because the market moves perfectly in phase with itself, its beta is 1.0.

Standard & Poor's 500 index (the S&P 500). Drawing on data compiled by Ibbotson Associates, over the 77-year period from 1926 through 2002, the difference in returns between the S&P 500 and long-term U.S. Treasury bonds was 7.0%. This figure is one measure of the market risk premium relative to long-term Treasury bonds. However, a number of researchers and practitioners argue that the historical equity risk premium does not measure the forward-looking equity risk premium, that is, the risk premium that equity investors expect to realize on stocks bought today.

One argument against the use of the historical equity risk premium is that it does not allow for changes in investors' perceptions of the relative risks of holding stocks versus bonds. Over time, the volatility of stocks has fallen whereas the volatility of bonds has risen.[4] As such, one would expect the equity risk premium demanded by investors to have declined over time. Similarly, the liquidity of stocks have increased over time relative to that of bonds, a result that one would expect to have reduced the equity risk premium as well.

For these and other reasons, many academics, consultants, and Wall Street practitioners use a forward-looking equity risk premium that is below its historical average. Typically, those who reject the use of the historical equity risk premium of 7% use an expected equity risk premium on the order of 4 to 6%. For example, Ibbotson and Chen estimate the expected long-term equity risk premium (relative to the long-term Treasury bond yield) of 6%.[5] Others argue for an equity risk premium closer to 4%. In an extensive analysis of historical performance data compiled by Dimson, Marsh, and Staunton, the authors examined the historical equity risk premium for 16 countries over 1900 to 2001, a period of 102 years. They used these data to estimate a set of forward-looking equity risk premia for the United States, the United Kingdom, and the world that falls within the range of 3.5 to 5.3%.[6] Another approach, by Welch, surveyed the opinions of 519 financial economists as to the 30-year average equity risk premium. As of August 2001, he found that the median and mean consensus long-term equity risk premium forecasts were 5 and 5.5%, respectively.[7] In a related approach, Graham and Harvey conducted quarterly surveys of chief financial officers (CFOs) of U.S. corporations from the second quarter of 2000 through the second quarter of 2003. They found that the 10-year expected equity risk premium (relative to the 10-year Treasury bond yield) is stable and equal to approximately 3.8%.[8]

---

[4]For evidence that stocks have become less risky over time while bonds have become more risky, see Asness, C.S. "Stocks versus Bonds: Explaining the Equity Risk Premium." *Financial Analysts Journal*, 56(2), 2000, pp. 96–113.

[5]Ibbotson, R.G., and Chen, P. "Long-Run Stock Returns: Participating in the Real Economy." *Financial Analysts Journal*, 59(1), 2003.

[6]Dimson, E., Marsh, P., and Staunton, M. *Triumph of the Optimists: 101 Years of Global Investments Returns*. Princeton University Press: Princeton, 2002; "New Evidence Puts Risk Premium in Context." *Corporate Finance*, March 2003, pp. 8–10. The 16 countries are the United States, United Kingdom, Italy, Japan, Germany, Italy, Spain, Belgium, France, Denmark, Switzerland, Ireland, Netherlands, South Africa, Sweden, and Australia.

[7]Welch, I. "The Equity Premium Consensus Forecast Revisited." Cowles Foundation Discussion Paper No. 1325, Yale University, September 2001.

[8]Graham, J.R., and Harvey, C.R. "Expectations of Equity Risk Premia, Volatility and Asymmetry." Duke University Working Paper, July 7, 2003.

On the basis of this and other evidence, an expected equity risk premium of 4 to 6% appears reasonable. In contrast, the historical equity risk premium of 7% appears to be too high for current conditions.

Estimating the Project Beta

Unfortunately, the type of information that we need to estimate project betas directly—a history of past project returns or future project returns relative to predicted market returns—does not exist. About the only practical way to get around this problem is to find a firm—or, preferably, a portfolio of firms—that shares similar risk characteristics and use the firm's beta to proxy for the project beta. For example, if a steel company decides to enter the petroleum refining business, it will estimate the average beta for a portfolio of firms already in the industry and substitute this value for beta in Equation 6.1.

Although coming up with reasonable estimates of these stock betas is easier said than done, a number of services provide estimated betas for a broad range of companies. Some popular sources of stock betas include the *Value Line Investment Survey*, Barra, Bloomberg, and Yahoo. All have Internet sites and some (e.g., Bloomberg and Yahoo) are free (others, like *Value Line* and Barra, are restricted to subscribers). Despite the seeming precision of the estimated betas from these sources, problems remain. One such problem is that, like all estimates based on a limited data sample, there is the possibility of substantial estimation error.

Estimation error can be reduced by computing the average stock beta for a portfolio of similar firms instead of basing the project beta estimate on a one-firm sample. If the stock beta estimates are independent, the standard deviation of the estimated portfolio beta will decline in proportion to the square root of the number of stocks in the portfolio. For example, the standard error of a project beta computed as the average of nine stock betas of similar firms will be about one third the size of the average standard error of the individual beta estimates.

The catch is the word *similar*. Even if the firms are in the same industry and share similar business risk, their financial risks will differ if they use differing amounts of debt financing. As we will see in the Section 6.2, the more the firm borrows, the higher its stock's beta will be. It would be inappropriate, therefore, to average the betas of Exxon Mobil, which uses relatively little debt financing, and Kerr-McGee, which uses much more debt financing.

FINANCIAL STRUCTURE AND APPROPRIATE DISCOUNT RATES

In our discussion of how to calculate project betas, we implicitly assumed that firms finance their investments on an all-equity basis. As a result, the risks faced by equity investors reflect only the business risks borne by the firm's investments. In this case, the beta for a firm's common stock, its **equity beta**, will equal the beta for the firm's existing assets, its **asset beta**. This justifies substituting the equity beta derived from a portfolio of comparable firms for the project beta in Equation 6.1.

Most firms, however, finance their investments with both debt and equity. This means that the returns on corporate projects must be split among the debtholders and equityholders. Because debtholders have first claim on the firm's cash flows, the riskiness of the residual flows to equityholders is magnified. Thus, shareholders bear both the business risk of the company's real assets and the financial risk associated with the use of debt financing. Consequently, the firm's equity beta will exceed its asset beta.

This complicates matters when we are trying to measure indirectly the cost of capital for a new project by using a proxy company whose existing assets face similar business risks. To perform this calculation, we need to know the proxy firm's asset beta, β_a; what we have instead is the company's equity beta, β_e. To transform the equity beta into the asset beta, we must separate out the effects of debt financing. This is known as **unlevering**, converting a levered equity beta to its unlevered, or **all-equity**, value. Unlevering can be accomplished by recognizing that—ignoring the tax deductibility of interest payments for the moment—the returns to an investor who owned 100% of the firm's debt and 100% of its equity would be the same as the returns the firm would generate if it were all-equity financed. Thus, in the absence of taxes, the beta of the combined debt and equity portfolio would equal the firm's asset beta, β_a.

The beta of this portfolio is just a weighted average of the common stock or equity beta, β_e, and the debt beta, β_d, or

$$\beta_a = \beta_d \frac{D}{D + E} + \beta_e \frac{E}{D + E} \tag{6.2}$$

where

D = market value of debt

E = market value of equity.

If the debt is relatively risk free, a common assumption for many large firms, then β_d will be approximately zero. Using this approximation, we see that Equation 6.2 becomes

$$\beta_a = \frac{\beta_e}{1 + D/E} \tag{6.3}$$

For example, if β_e is 1.4 and D/E equals 0.8, then $\beta_a = 0.78$.

Alternatively, the equity beta for a project or a company with a debt-equity ratio of D/E and an asset beta of β_a can be found by multiplying both sides of Equation 6.3 by $(1 + D/E)$:

$$\beta_e = \beta_a \left(1 + \frac{D}{E}\right) \tag{6.4}$$

The tax deductibility of interest payments reduces the after-tax cost of debt financing and changes the relationship between the asset and equity betas. In particular, if t is the firm's marginal tax rate, then Equations 6.3 and 6.4 become Equations 6.5 and 6.6, respectively:

$$\beta_a = \frac{\beta_e}{1 + (1 - t)D/E} \tag{6.5}$$

and

$$\beta_e = \beta_a \left[1 + (1 - t)\frac{D}{E} \right] \tag{6.6}$$

We will use Equations 6.5 and 6.6 in all subsequent conversions between equity betas and asset betas. Their effect, assuming a marginal corporate tax rate of 35%, is to increase the estimated asset beta in the previous example from 0.78 to a tax-adjusted value of 0.92 (1.4/[1 + 0.8(1 − 0.35)]). Exhibit 6.1 shows the relationship between the asset and equity betas for different debt-to-equity ratios, assuming a 35% marginal corporate tax rate.

The required rate of return derived from the asset beta is known as the "all-equity" rate $k*$. According to the CAPM, the all-equity cost of capital is computed as:

$$k* = r_f + \beta_a (r_m - r_f) \tag{6.7}$$

and is the rate that would apply directly if the project were financed entirely by equity; that is, it is the rate used to discount the project's cash flows ignoring any financing costs. These are the same cash flows that are discounted using the **weighted average cost of capital (WACC)**, a concept that will be introduced in Section 6.2. Conversely, the cost of capital estimated using the equity beta should be used to discount only the cash flows to equity; that is, project cash flows *net* of any debt financing charges.

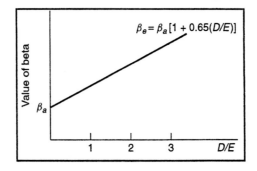

EXHIBIT 6.1 Relationship between Asset and Equity Betas for Different Debt-to-Equity Ratios (assumes a 35% corporate tax rate)

BOX 6.2

APPLICATION: ESTIMATING CARBORUNDUM'S COST OF CAPITAL

In November 1977, Kennecott Copper Corporation was considering the acquisition of the Carborundum Company. What discount rate should Kennecott have used to evaluate this potential acquisition? Here are some facts:[9]

1. Carborundum's equity beta was estimated at 1.16.

2. The long-term Treasury bond rate at this time was 7.6%.

3. The historical spread (1926 through 1974) between returns on the S&P 500 index and on long-term Treasury bonds was 7.5%.

4. The market value of Carborundum's equity was $271 million, and its market value of debt was $86.2 million.

5. If Kennecott decided to go ahead with the acquisition, it would be financed in part by having Carborundum issue an additional $100 million in debt followed immediately by payment of a $140 million dividend to Kennecott.

6. The cash flows being discounted by Kennecott were those it would receive from Carborundum, net of financing costs.

On the basis of this information, we can calculate Carborundum's preacquisition cost of equity capital as 16.3% (0.076 + 1.16 × 0.075). This discount rate is suitable for evaluating Carborundum's cash flows to equity under its current capital structure. But because the cash flows being discounted are the net flows to Kennecott, the appropriate discount rate is Carborundum's cost of equity capital under its new capital structure. This discount rate can be found by first unlevering Carborundum's equity beta under its current capital structure and then relevering it to reflect the projected capital structure.

Using Equation 6.5 and assuming a marginal corporate tax rate at the time of 50%, Carborundum's unlevered or asset beta can be estimated as

$$\frac{1.16}{[1 + (1 - 0.5)86.2/271]} = 1.00$$

Under Kennecott's planned financial restructuring, Carborundum's debt:equity ratio would rise from 0.32 to 1.42 [(86.2 + 100)/(271 − 140)]. According to Equation 6.6, this increase in leverage would result in an equity beta for the recapitalized company equal to

$$1.00(1 + 0.5 \times 1.42) = 1.71$$

Substituting a beta of 1.71 in Equation 6.1 yields an estimate of Carborundum's cost of equity capital under its postacquisition capital structure equal to 20.4% (0.076 + 1.71 × 0.075).

---

[9]The numbers and the issues raised come from "Valuing an Acquisition Candidate: Kennecott Copper Corporation," in Keith Butters, J. et al. *Case Problems in Finance*, 8th ed. Richard D. Irwin: Homewood, Ill., 1981.

6.2 The Cost of Capital for the Firm

Suppose a new project entails an across-the-board expansion of the investing firm's current operations or otherwise is an average-risk project. Then the corporatewide cost of capital will serve as a reasonable proxy for the required return on the project. One approach to calculating this required return was presented in the previous section and involved estimating the all-equity rate. An alternative approach, presented here, takes explicit account of the different financing sources employed by the firm and their costs.

This approach is based on the notion that for a project to be acceptable to the firm's shareholders, it must generate a stream of returns sufficient to compensate the suppliers of capital in proportion to the amount and cost of the capital supplied by each. This minimum return is the *cost of capital for the firm*.

In this section, we will see how the costs of equity capital, debt, and preferred stock can be calculated individually and then combined into an overall cost of capital for the firm. The relevance of this number, known as the **weighted average cost of capital**, is that it equals the required return on average-risk projects—those whose risk is similar to that for the firm as a whole. As mentioned earlier, the WACC is used to discount the project's cash flows ignoring financing charges such as interest and dividend payments.

THE COST OF EQUITY CAPITAL

By definition, the cost of equity capital for a firm is the minimum rate of return necessary to induce investors to buy or hold the firm's stock. This required return equals a basic yield covering the time value of money plus a premium for risk. Because owners of common stock have only a residual claim on corporate income, their risk is the greatest and therefore so are the returns they demand.

Alternatively, the cost of equity capital is the rate used by shareholders to capitalize their portion of corporate cash flows. As such, it is just the weighted average of the required rates of return on the firm's individual activities. From this perspective, the corporation is a mutual fund or portfolio of specific projects selling a compound security to capital markets. According to the *principle of value additivity*, introduced in Chapter 2, the value of this compound security equals the sum of the individual values of the projects.

Although both definitions are equivalent, the latter view is preferred from a conceptual standpoint because it focuses attention on the most important feature of the cost of equity capital, namely, that this cost is not an attribute of the firm per se but is a function of the riskiness of the activities in which it engages. Thus, the cost of equity capital for the firm as a whole can be used to value the stream of future equity cash flows (i.e., to set a price on equity shares in the firm). It *cannot* be used as a measure of the required return on equity investments in future projects *unless* these projects are similar to the average of those already being undertaken by the firm.

An alternative means of estimating the cost of equity capital is provided by the dividend growth model and is presented in Appendix 6B. We must emphasize that the resulting estimate of the cost of equity capital, regardless of the method used to calculate it, applies only at the corporate level or to investments with financial characteristics typical of the "pool" of projects represented by the corporation. The estimated cost of equity capital for the firm is useless in calculating project-specific, required returns on equity when the characteristics of the project diverge from the corporate norm.

THE COST OF DEBT CAPITAL

The cost of debt capital is fairly straightforward to estimate because interest rates are readily observable. Because the firm is trying to calculate its required return on new investments, the appropriate interest rate is the rate on the *new* securities that the firm would issue to finance these investments. The interest rate on previously issued debt is irrelevant; what matters is the marginal cost of additional debt. In calculating this cost, it is assumed that the new debt is issued at its face value F so that the interest yield C/F, where C is the interest coupon, equals the yield to maturity or internal rate of return. When the price of the bond differs from its face value, then the cost of debt is based on its actual yield.

The interest rate on debt equals the nominal risk-free rate plus a risk premium sufficient to compensate debtholders for the possibility of default; the higher the probability of default is, the greater the risk premium will be. The risk-free rate already incorporates both the real interest rate and the inflation premium.

The cost of debt capital must be adjusted for taxes to reflect the firm's actual out-of-pocket or cash costs. Because interest is tax deductible, the true cost of debt to the firm is the after-tax interest rate. Suppose, for example, that a firm with a marginal tax rate of 35% is able to borrow additional funds at 15%. Then the firm's after-tax cost of debt will equal the before-tax rate of 15% multiplied by one minus the tax rate or 9.8% $[0.15 \times (1 - 0.35)]$.

In general, the cost of debt capital equals $k_d(1 - t)$, where k_d is the interest rate on new debt sold at par and t is the firm's marginal tax rate. According to this formulation, two firms with the same before-tax costs of debt will have different after-tax costs of debt if their corporate tax rates differ. For example, many airlines have a relatively high cost of debt because their years of large losses, which can be carried forward for five years to offset future taxable income, have put them in a zero-tax situation for the foreseeable future. This means that their after-tax cost of debt is the same as their before-tax cost. On the other hand, for profitable firms like Coca-Cola and Merck, the after-tax cost of debt is two-thirds of its before-tax cost.

THE COST OF PREFERRED STOCK

Preferred stock is a hybrid of debt and equity. Like debt, preferred shares carry a fixed commitment by the firm to make periodic payments. The claims of preferred shareholders also take precedence over those of common shareholders in the event of bankruptcy. Unlike the nonpayment of interest on bonds, however, the failure to pay preferred dividends cannot precipitate an event of bankruptcy. In this respect, preferred stock acts more like common equity. Similarly, preferred dividends, like common stock dividends, are not tax deductible; they must be paid out of after-tax income.

If the preferred stock has no maturity date, and assuming the dividend is fixed, it can be treated as a perpetuity with a resulting cost (or required return) equal to its dividend yield, or

$$k_p = \frac{PD}{P_s} \tag{6.8}$$

where PD is the preferred dividend and P_s is the price per share of preferred stock.

For example, if *PD* is $8 per share and P_s is $47, the firm's cost of preferred stock will be 17.02%. Note that this cost is not tax adjusted because preferred dividends are not tax deductible.

CALCULATING THE WEIGHTED AVERAGE COST OF CAPITAL

Once the different component costs of capital have been calculated, they can be combined into an overall WACC for the firm. The weights are based on the proportion of the firm's capital structure accounted for by each source of capital using market, not book, values.

To illustrate, suppose a company is financed with 60% common stock, 35% debt, and 5% preferred stock, all on a market value basis. Assume, furthermore, that the respective before-tax costs of these different financing sources are 20%, 14%, and 16%. The firm is assumed to face a 40% marginal tax rate, giving it an after-tax cost of debt equal to 8.4% $[0.14 \times (1 - 0.40)]$. The after-tax costs of equity and preferred stock are the same as their before-tax costs. Exhibit 6.2 summarizes these assumptions.

On the basis of the financing proportions and the after-tax costs of the various capital components, the WACC for this firm is calculated in Exhibit 6.3 as 15.74%.

An obvious question that immediately arises in this example is why not reduce the WACC by substituting debt at 8.4% for equity at 20% or preferred at 16%? The answer is that the component costs of capital vary with the firm's capital structure. Specifically, as the fraction of debt in the capital structure goes up, the returns to the different sources of capital become riskier. This increase in risk causes the cost of each capital component to rise, offsetting the benefit of cheaper debt. For example, Equation 6.6 shows how the equity beta, and thus the cost of equity capital, rises with the amount of debt financing.

If a new project is relatively small, the company may well be able to finance it with borrowed money bearing an after-tax cost of around 8.4%. But this is because the

EXHIBIT 6.2 Capital Structure and Capital Costs (%)

	Proportion	Before-Tax Cost	After-Tax Cost
Equity	60	20	20
Debt	35	14	8.4
Preferred stock	5	16	16

EXHIBIT 6.3 The Weighted Average Cost of Capital (%)

	Proportion × (1)	After-Tax Cost (2)	=	Weighted Cost (3)
Equity	0.60	20		12.00
Debt	0.35	8.4		2.94
Preferred stock	0.05	16		0.80
		WACC	=	15.74

lenders will look to the parent and its equity capital for repayment. If instead the company tried to finance the project with just borrowed money on a *stand-alone* basis, with no recourse to itself (that is, the lenders could look only to the project for repayment), it would find that it could not do so. The parent would have to put in equity as well; the less equity it put in, the higher the interest rate charged.

It is generally accepted today that an optimal capital structure exists, particularly when taxes and bankruptcy costs are considered. Debt should be substituted for equity until the point at which the advantages of debt are just offset by the effect of increasing risk. An indication of the likely acceptable proportions of each type of security in the optimal capital structure can be determined by analyzing well-run firms in the industry, talking with security analysts familiar with the industry, and analyzing the firm's ability to service debt under various possible future scenarios (i.e., its debt capacity).

In general, the WACC k_0 is calculated as

$$k_0 = w_e k_e + w_d k_d (1 - t) + w_p k_p \tag{6.9}$$

where

w_e = proportion of equity in the firm's target capital structure

w_d = proportion of debt in the firm's target capital structure

w_p = proportion of preferred stock in the firm's target capital structure.

As before, k_e is the cost of equity capital, $k_d(1 - t)$ is the after-tax cost of debt, and k_p is the cost of preferred stock.

Note that the weights in Equation 6.9 are based on the firm's target capital structure, not the actual capital structure. What does this mean? And how do the flotation costs associated with issuing new securities enter into the calculations? Here are some answers.

Marginal Weights

The WACC is supposed to represent the marginal cost of raising new capital to finance new investments. This means that in calculating the WACC the firm's historical debt-equity mix is not relevant. Rather, the weights must be marginal weights that reflect the **target capital structure**, that is, the proportions of debt and equity the firm plans to use in the future. These proportions should be selected so as to maximize shareholder wealth. Thus, the target capital structure and the optimal capital structure should be one and the same. In addition, the component cost of financing for each source of capital must equal the required return on new capital, not the past cost of raising capital from that source.

If the firm's current capital structure is considered to be optimal, then the weights should be based on it. But as noted earlier, in calculating these weights, the market values of debt and equity, not their book values, should be used.

A typical assumption is that as the firm raises additional capital in any time period, its cost rises[10]; that is, the firm has a rising marginal cost of capital or weighted average

---

[10]A rising marginal cost of capital is most likely to appear when flotation costs are included in this figure. The definition and effects of flotation costs will be discussed very shortly.

EXHIBIT 6.4 Deriving the Optimal Capital Budget

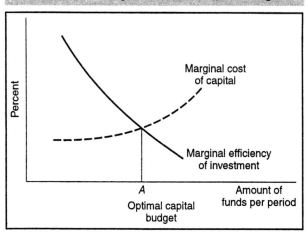

cost of capital. This is depicted in Exhibit 6.4. The firm's optimal capital budget occurs at point A, where the marginal cost of capital curve just intersects the marginal efficiency of investment schedule. The **marginal efficiency of investment** schedule shows the internal rate of return on the last dollar spent in each capital budget. The size of the capital budget—the dollars of investment per year—appears on the horizontal axis. Exhibit 6.4 implicitly assumes that all projects have the same risk, and so the same marginal cost of capital schedule is relevant for all projects. The effect of relaxing this assumption is discussed later.

BOX 6.3

APPLICATION: ESTIMATING GALAXY'S WACC

Galaxy Corporation faces the following schedule for the marginal cost of additional capital:

Debt	$0 to 7,000,000	10%
	7,000,001 to 10,500,000	11%
	over 10,500,000	14%
Preferred	$0 to 250,000	18%
	250,001 to 375,000	24%
	over 375,000	28%
Common	$0 to 2,000,000	28%
	2,000,001 to 5,000,000	32%
	over 5,000,000	40%

Assuming that Galaxy will maintain a capital structure of 70% debt, 10% preferred, and 20% common, calculate its weighted average cost of capital (marginal) schedule.

SOLUTION

The following table sets out the amounts and costs of debt, preferred stock, and common stock that will be issued for each range of capital raised. For example, the first $2,500,000 raised consists of $1,750,000 in debt, $250,000 in preferred stock, and $500,000 in common stock with respective costs in this range of 10%, 18%, and 28%. Once Galaxy raises capital in excess of $2,500,000, it must pay 24% on the additional preferred that it issues (because this amount now exceeds $250,000).

Additional Capital	Cost of:		
Range (%)	Debt (%)	Preferred (%)	Common (%)
0–2,500,000	10	18	28
2,500,001–3,750,000	10	24	28
3,750,001–10,000,000	10	28	28
10,000,001–1,000,000	11	28	32
15,000,001–25,000,000	14	28	32
25,000,001–and up	14	28	40

Given this schedule and weights of 70% debt, 10% preferred, and 20% common, we calculate WACC for each range:

Range ($)	WACC
0–2,500,000	0.144
2,500,001–3,750,000	0.150
3,750,001–10,000,000	0.154
10,000,001–15,000,000	0.169
15,000,001–25,000,000	0.190
25,000,001–and up	0.206

For example, the WACC for the first $2,500,000 raised is

$$k_0 = 0.7 \times 0.10 + 0.1 \times 0.18 + 0.2 \times 0.28 = 14.4\%$$

Flotation Costs

So far, we have ignored the costs of selling new common stock, preferred stock, and debt. These **flotation costs** include all legal, accounting, printing, marketing, and other expenses associated with the new security issue. Flotation costs, which can range from less than 1% to over 15%, affect the profitability of new investments. For example, suppose a firm wishes to finance a $10,000,000 investment by issuing stock. If flotation costs are 6% of gross proceeds, then the firm must sell $10,638,000 of stock to obtain the $10,000,000 it needs ($10,638,000 \times 0.94 = $10,000,000).

One way to incorporate the effect of flotation costs is to raise the cost of capital. In our example, if the cost of equity capital in the absence of flotation costs were 12%, then the cost of equity capital factoring in flotation costs would rise by 6.38% in order to reflect the fact that the company must issue $1.0638 in stock to net $1.00. Hence, the cost of external equity capital becomes 12.77% (1.0638 × 12%). Because flotation costs on internal funds are nonexistent, these funds are usually considered to be less expensive than external funds.

Alternatively, the $638,000 difference between gross and net proceeds can be accounted for by adding it to the initial outlay of $10,000,000. This reduces the project's NPV by the amount of flotation costs. So, for example, if the project's NPV in the absence of flotation costs comes to $1,530,000, then its adjusted NPV will be $892,000 ($1,530,000 − $638,000). One argument for using this procedure to deal with flotation costs is that it is more transparent and therefore easier to understand and apply.

Misusing the WACC

It is worthwhile to repeat the admonition at the beginning of this chapter: *The required return or cost of capital for a project depends on the assets being financed, not on the identity of the company that undertakes the project.* This is because the required return on an asset depends on the risk of the cash flows produced by that asset. Therefore, the WACC can be used only to value assets the firm already owns or new assets of similar risk. Conversely, the required return on an investment with a different risk complexion will not equal the company's WACC. Thus, the WACC can be used on an across-the-board basis only if the firm's projects are of similar risk.

For example, we saw previously that when estimating Carborundum's value before acquiring it in 1977, Kennecott should have used Carborundum's cost of equity capital to discount the projected cash flows from the acquisition. Instead, Kennecott used its own WACC, estimated to be 10.5%, about half our 20.4% estimate of Carborundum's cost of equity capital.[11] As a result, even using its own optimistic cash flow figures, Kennecott overvalued Carborundum by more than $100 million. Not surprisingly, Kennecott's stock price dropped when management announced that it intended to acquire Carborundum at the inflated price.

6.3 The Cost of Capital for a Division

In multiproduct firms, the requirement that projects be of similar risk is more likely to be met for divisions than for the company as a whole. This suggests that the use of a divisional cost of capital may be valid in some cases in which the use of a companywide cost of capital would be inappropriate. Conglomerate firms that compete in a variety of different product markets, such as AOL Time Warner and Occidental Petroleum, often estimate separate divisional costs of capital that reflect both the differential risks and the differential debt capacity of each division.

The estimation of these divisional costs of capital is tricky. All that the firm observes is its overall cost of capital, which is a weighted average of its divisional costs of capital. It is impossible to decompose this overall cost into its divisional components without additional information. Fortunately, this information—in the form of return data for publicly traded companies operating in similar lines of business as the different divisions—is often available.

Estimating the cost of capital for a division, therefore, is a three-stage process. The first stage is identifying corporate proxies whose business closely parallels the

---

[11]See Butters et al. *Case Problems in Finance.*

division's operations. Usually, the matchups are only approximate because no *pure-plays* (proxies operating only in that business segment) exist. Consequently, the more proxy firms selected, the more confidence the company can have in its final estimate.

In the second stage, the cost of capital must be estimated for each of the proxy firms. This means estimating the equity beta for each firm and then unlevering the beta to obtain the asset beta.[12] The third stage is just averaging the resulting estimates of the individual asset betas. Assuming the company was careful in selecting its proxy firms, this average should yield an unbiased estimate of the division's required return.[13]

BOX 6.4

APPLICATION: ESTIMATING VULCAN MATERIALS' DIVISIONAL COSTS OF CAPITAL

Vulcan Materials Company has decided to determine the hurdle rate(s) — cost(s) of capital — it should use in evaluating projects. Because Vulcan is a multi-industry company — with positions in construction materials, chemicals, metals, and oil and gas — it decided to use different hurdle rates for each business segment to reflect the fact that project risk is likely to vary by industry.

Vulcan proceeds as follows: For each business segment, it collects data on five or six firms whose activities the management decided were most similar to Vulcan's activities in that industry. The data gathered include the stock beta for each firm (collected from *Value Line*), the market value of its equity, and the book value of debt in its capital structure. Stock betas are then converted into asset betas using Equation 6.5 and assuming a 50% marginal tax rate. To apply Equation 6.5, however, it is necessary to use market values of debt, not book values. The market value of debt is set equal to 110% of its book value to reflect the fact that a decade-long decline in interest rates had increased the market value of book liabilities by about 10%, on average.

Finally, the asset beta for each business segment is estimated as the asset beta for the equally weighted portfolio of firms in that business; that is, the asset beta for a business segment is set equal to the average of the asset betas of the companies in that industry. The following table shows the companies, the data used in performing these calculations, and their results.

---

[12]When no pure-plays exist because all possible proxies are nontraded divisions of larger multidivisional companies, a different procedure is required. One suggested approach in this case is to use mathematical programming to determine the beta of an industry segment. See Boquist, J.A., and Moore, W.T. "Estimating the Systematic Risk of an Industry Segment: A Mathematical Programming Approach." *Financial Management*, Winter 1983, pp. 11–24.

[13]In calculating the divisional cost of capital, the betas for proxy firms can be averaged on an equally weighted or value-weighted basis. I recommend equally weighted averaging because there is no reason to believe that estimation errors are correlated with size.

Calculating Asset Betas for Vulcan Materials' Business Segments

Company	Market Value of Equity	Market Value of Debt	Stock Beta	Asset Beta
Construction Materials				
Gifford Hill	$114.7	$222.7	0.95	0.48
Ideal	242.5	347.1	1.10	0.64
Kaiser	155.0	157.7	1.10	0.73
Lone Star	280.2	369.4	1.05	0.63
Texas Industries	203.6	139.5	1.00	0.74
			Average	0.64
Chemicals				
Allied	1,303.4	771.3	1.20	0.95
Diamond Shamrock	1,433.6	769.2	1.20	0.95
Dow Chemical	4,597.6	3,580.2	1.25	0.90
Du Pont	8,718.5	6,597.0	1.15	0.83
Stauffer	1,004.1	375.6	0.90	0.76
Penwalt	252.6	152.0	0.85	0.65
			Average	0.84
Metals				
Nucor	342.4	75.4	1.30	1.17
N.W. Steel	153.5	–	0.65	0.65
Proler	44.0	9.0	1.00	0.91
Kaiser Aluminum	613.7	817.3	1.05	0.63
Reynolds Metals	469.9	801.0	1.10	0.58
			Average	0.79
Oil and Gas				
Patrick Petroleum	131.3	152.0	1.50	0.95
Louisiana Land	995.2	299.9	1.20	1.04
Mesa	1,202.4	762.4	1.45	1.10
Superior Oil	3,879.6	1,030.4	1.45	1.28
Wainoco	138.7	113.0	1.30	0.92
Woods Petroleum	260.1	13.5	1.35	1.32
			Average	1.10

On the basis of a current long-term Treasury bond rate of 6.3% and a 5% estimated risk premium relative to the long-term Treasury bond rate, we can estimate the cost of capital for each business segment, as follows:

Cost of Capital by Business Segment	
Construction materials:	$0.063 + 0.64 \times 0.05 = 0.095$ or 9.5%
Chemicals:	$0.063 + 0.84 \times 0.05 = 0.105$ or 10.5%
Metals:	$0.063 + 0.79 \times 0.05 = 0.103$ or 10.3%
Oil and gas:	$0.063 + 1.10 \times 0.05 = 0.118$ or 10.8%.

Thus, on the basis of these data, the hurdle rates for Vulcan's various business segments range from 9.5 to 10.8%. A caveat: *These numbers, although looking precise and scientific, are only estimates of the costs of capital for Vulcan's different lines of business.* But they do provide us with objective data based on a scientific theory.

Calculating the WACC Using the CAPM: Some Common Errors

There are a number of common errors in using the CAPM for calculating the risk-adjusted cost of capital for either a division or an individual project. We have alluded to some of these earlier; here is a more complete list:

1. Computing the betas of individual divisions by beginning with the equity beta for the company overall and then unlevering and relevering this equity beta on the basis of the individual divisions' capital structures. Instead, the divisional betas should be based on the pure-plays.
2. Using different capital structure assumptions in computing the cost of equity than are used in calculating the WACC. No mixing and matching.
3. Using a risk-free rate of one maturity in the CAPM but then estimating the market risk premium on the basis of a risk-free rate having a different maturity. You must match the risk premium with the maturity of the security used to compute the risk-free rate.
4. Using a market risk premium on the basis of the most recent returns, rather than using a long time series. Using a long time series will reduce the standard deviation of your estimate.
5. Using a negative market risk premium. The market risk premium, that is, the difference between the expected return on the market portfolio and the expected risk-free rate, is always positive. If you get a negative premium, you have made a mistake somewhere.
6. Using the historical average Treasury bond or Treasury bill return as the risk-free rate in the CAPM instead of using the actual (current) rate. You must use the current risk-free rate as the risk-free rate.
7. Using the unlevered beta in the computation of the cost of equity capital for individual divisions and then using this cost of equity capital to compute the WACC for the individual divisions based on their target debt ratios. You must relever the asset beta to come up with a new equity beta that matches the target capital structure of the individual divisions.

8. Using only one or two comparables to estimate the unlevered betas for the individual divisions. Unless you come up with a perfect comparable, you will want a bigger sample to reduce the error involved in any such estimation.
9. Failing to include the effect of taxes when levering and unlevering beta.
10. Using the historical market return as the market risk premium instead of measuring it as the difference between the historical market return and the corresponding risk-free rate.
11. Computing the average asset beta of comparables by taking the average equity beta and delevering it using the average D/E ratio for the comparables instead of unlevering the beta for each individual comparable.

These errors are easy to avoid. Doing so will not guarantee a correct cost-of-capital estimate but failing to avoid them will guarantee an incorrect one.

ASSESSING THE WEIGHTED AVERAGE COST OF CAPITAL

The WACC is simple in concept and easy to apply. A single rate is appropriate, however, only if the financial structures and commercial risks are similar for all investments undertaken. Projects with different risks are likely to possess differing debt capacities with each project, therefore necessitating a separate financial structure. Moreover, the financial packages for certain investments, especially foreign ventures, often include project-specific loans at concessionary rates, leading to different component costs of capital.

The weighted cost of capital figure can, of course, be modified to reflect these deviations from the firm's typical investment. But doing that destroys one of the principal advantages of the WACC, its simplicity. More importantly, for some companies, such as those in extractive industries, there is no norm. Project risks and financial structure vary by country, raw material, production stage, and position in the life cycle of the project. On balance, therefore, the advantages of using the WACC in analyzing new projects appear to be outweighed by its disadvantages.

ADJUSTED PRESENT VALUE

An alternative and more flexible procedure, suggested earlier, is to discount cash flows at a rate that reflects only the business risks of the project and abstracts from the effects of financing. This rate, introduced earlier as the *all-equity rate*, k^*, would apply directly if the project were financed entirely by equity.

It should be emphasized that the all-equity cost of capital equals the required rate of return on a specific project (i.e., the risk-free rate plus an appropriate risk premium based on the project's particular risk). Thus, k^* varies by project as project risks vary.

Financing Side Effects

The all-equity rate can be used in capital budgeting by viewing the value of a project as being equal to the sum of the present value of project cash flows after tax but before financing costs, discounted at k^*; the present value of the tax shield provided by debt financing; plus the present value of any savings on interest costs associated with project-specific financing. This latter term would generally result from government regulations and/or subsidies that caused interest rates on restricted funds to diverge from the interest rate on unsubsidized, arm's length borrowing. Examples include industrial development bonds that are tax exempt — thereby bearing lower interest rates — and that can be issued by firms under certain circumstances, and low-cost export financing provided by governments worldwide to stimulate their exports.

The net present value using this approach, often referred to as the **adjusted present value**, or APV, is defined as:

$$APV = \begin{array}{c} NPV \text{ of project if} \\ \text{all-equity financed} \end{array} + \begin{array}{c} NPV \text{ of financing side effects} \\ \text{caused by project acceptance} \end{array}$$

$$(6.10)$$

$$APV = -I_0 + \sum_{i=1}^{n} \frac{CF_i}{(1 + k^*)^i} + \sum_{i=1}^{n} \frac{T_i}{(1 + k_d)^i} + \sum_{i=1}^{n} \frac{S_i}{(1 + k_d)^i}$$

where

T_i = tax savings in period i resulting from the specific financing package

S_i = before-tax dollar value of interest subsidies in period i resulting from project-specific financing

k_d = before-tax cost of unsubsidized debt.

The latter two terms in Equation 6.10 are discounted at the before-tax cost of debt to reflect the relatively certain value of the cash flows resulting from interest tax shields and interest savings. The tax savings in period i, T_i, equals tk_dD_i, where t is the corporate tax rate and D_i is the incremental debt supported by the project in period i.

Calculating the Value of Arranging Low-Cost Financing

Many governments offer a variety of investment incentives designed to achieve goals other than economic efficiency. The value of arranging such low-cost financing can be illustrated by examining the case of Xebec, a California manufacturer of disk-drive controllers. Suppose that one of the inducements provided by Taiwan to woo Xebec into setting up a local production facility is a 10-year, $12.5 million loan at 8% interest. The principal is to be repaid at the end of the tenth year. The market interest rate on such a loan is about 15%. With a marginal tax rate of 40%, how much is this loan worth to Xebec? That is, what is its net present value?

At 8% interest, Xebec must pay $1 million in interest annually for the next 10 years and then repay the $12.5 million principal at the end of 10 years. In return, Xebec receives $12.5 million today. Given these cash inflows and outflows, we can calculate the loan's NPV just as we would for any project analysis. Note, however, that, unlike the typical capital-budgeting problem we looked at, the cash inflow occurs immediately, and the cash outflows later. But the principle is the same.

Given a marginal tax rate of 40%, the annual after-tax interest payments on the loan will be $600,000 (0.6 × 0.08 × $12,500,000). Now we can calculate the NPV of

Xebec's financing bargain:

$$NPV = \$12,500,000 - \sum_{i=1}^{10} \frac{\$600,000}{(1.15)^i} - \frac{\$12,500,000}{(1.15)^{10}}$$

$$= \$12,500,000 - \$6,101,070$$

$$= \$6,398,930$$

You do not need a degree in financial economics to realize that borrowing money at 8% when the market rate is 15% is a good deal. But what the NPV calculations tell you is just how much a particular below-market financing option is worth. Note that this analysis captures both the tax benefits *and* the interest subsidies.

The annual interest subsidy alone, ignoring tax effects, equals $875,000, the difference between the interest payment of $1,875,000 required on a 15% loan and the interest payment of $1 million on the 8% loan. The present value of this interest subsidy is

$$PV(\text{interest subsidy}) = \sum_{i=1}^{10} \frac{\$875,000}{(1.15)^i} = \$4,391,523$$

Similarly, the annual tax benefit associated with this loan is $0.4 \times 0.08 \times \$12,500,000 = \$400,000$, the annual tax write-off associated with the interest payment. The present value of this tax benefit is

$$PV(\text{tax benefit}) = \sum_{i=1}^{10} \frac{\$400,000}{(1.15)^i} = \$2,007,507$$

Adding these two figures yields a total benefit of $6,398,930, the same as the NPV for the loan that we calculated previously.

LEVERED EQUITY METHOD

A third capital-budgeting approach is the **levered equity** (LE) method. This approach discounts the levered cash flows—that is, the project's cash flows net of debt payments—at the levered cost of equity capital, k_e. This cost of equity capital with leverage is estimated using the levered equity beta, β_e, and is the same one that appears in the weighted average cost of capital. Ignoring preferred stock financing, which is rarely used by companies, there is a simple relation between the levered cost of equity capital and the all-equity cost of capital. Without proof, and using the same notation as before, this relation is as follows:

$$k_e = k^* + \frac{D}{E}(1-t)(k^*-k_d) \tag{6.11}$$

The cash flows discounted with the LE method are those that flow to the shareholders of the company sponsoring the project. These cash flows are the unlevered cash flows used in the WACC and APV methods less the after-tax debt charges associated with the project's financing. To be consistent, the initial investment used in the LE method is the equity portion of the initial out-of-pocket investment expenses; that is, it equals I_0 less the amount borrowed to finance the project.

COMPARING THE WACC, APV, AND LE METHODS

Exhibit 6.5 summarizes the three different approaches to capital budgeting and cost of capital. This summary includes only debt and equity financing; it ignores preferred stock financing. As shown, the cash flows discounted and the discount rates vary depending on the method selected. The following simplified example illustrates the application of these alternative methods.

Giant Manufacturing Company has an opportunity to invest $30 million in a new solar power source. Once completed, the new solar energy project is expected to yield annual free cash flows of $4,880,000 in perpetuity. Assuming that k^* equals 16%, then this project has a NPV of $550,000:

$$NPV = -\$30,000,000 + \frac{\$4,888,000}{0.16} = \$550,000$$

EXHIBIT 6.5 Discount Rates and Cash Flows Used in Three Capital-Budgeting Methods

---

Weighted Average Cost of Capital (WACC) Method

$$\text{WACC formula: } NPV = -I_0 + \sum_{i=1}^{n} \frac{CF_i}{(1 + k_0)^i}$$

where

WACC discount rate: $k_0 = k_e \dfrac{E}{D + E} + k_d (1 - t) \dfrac{D}{D + E}$

WACC cash flows: CF_i = project cash flows ignoring financing effects

Adjusted Present Value (APV) Method

$$\text{APV formula: } APV = -I_0 + \sum_{i=1}^{n} \frac{CF_i}{(1 + k*)^i} + \begin{array}{c}\text{financing}\\\text{side effects}\end{array}$$

where

APV discount rate: k^* = all-equity cost of capital

Levered Equity (LE) Method

$$\text{LE formula: } NPV = -(I_0 - D) + \sum_{i=1}^{n} \frac{LCF_i}{(1 + k_e)^i}$$

where

LE discount rate: $k_e = k^* + \dfrac{D}{E}(1 - t)(k^* - k_d)$

LE cash flows: $LCF_i = CF_i$ − debt servicing charges

LE initial investment = I_0 − the amount borrowed to finance the project (D)

Given the initial investment, this investment is just marginally profitable. However, suppose the project can support a permanent addition to debt equal to $6.5 million. If the interest rate on this debt is 10% and the company's marginal tax rate is 30%, we can calculate the value of the project using the three different approaches.

APV Method

According to the APV method (see Equation 6.10),

$$APV = \begin{array}{c} NPV \text{ of project if} \\ \text{all-equity financed} \end{array} + \begin{array}{c} NPV \text{ of financing side effects} \\ \text{caused by project acceptance} \end{array}$$

In this case, the only financing side effect is the tax savings provided by the tax deductibility of interest payments. As we saw previously, the annual tax savings equals the tax rate times the annual interest expense. For Giant, this works out to $195,000 ($0.30 \times 0.10 \times $6,500,000$). On the basis of this interest tax shield, the APV of the solar energy project is $2.5 million:

$$APV = \$550,000 + \frac{\$195,000}{0.10} = \$2,500,000$$

The tax benefits of debt financing have turned this project from being marginally acceptable to one that is reasonably profitable.

Using market values, the debt ratio for this project is 6.5/32.5, or 20%. That is, the amount of debt selected for this project has been set equal to 20% of the project's $32.5 million present value.

WACC Method

With a debt ratio of 0.20, we can now calculate the weighted average cost of capital. To begin, we use Equation 6.11 to estimate the project's levered cost of equity capital:

$$k_e = k^* + \frac{D}{E}(1 - t)(k^* - k_d) = 0.16 + \frac{6.5}{26}(1 - 0.30)(0.16 - 0.10) = 0.1705$$

With a 17.05% cost of equity capital, the project's WACC equals 15.04%:

$$k_0 = 0.80 \times 0.1705 + 0.20 \times 0.10(1 - 0.30) = 0.1504$$

At this discount rate, the NPV of Giant's project is $2.5 million; the same result we got using the APV method:

$$NPV = -\$30,000,000 + \frac{\$4,888,000}{0.1504} = \$2,500,000$$

LE Method

To employ this method, we need to combine the levered cost of equity, which we have already calculated to be 17.05%, with the cash flows to equity. With permanent debt of $6.5 million, the annual after-tax interest expense is $0.7 \times 0.1 \times 6.5 million = $455,000.

Subtracting this figure from the $4.888 million in free cash flow yields an annual cash flow to equity of $4,433,000. Lastly, Giant's initial equity investment in the project is $23.5 million ($30 million − $6.5 million). Using these figures, together with the LE method, we can now estimate the NPV value of Giant's project:

$$NPV = -\$23,500,000 + \frac{\$4,433,000}{0.1705} = \$2,500,000$$

We see that under this set of simplified assumptions all three capital-budgeting methods give the same answer. Although these assumptions are commonly violated — after all, when do you see a project yielding a perpetuity and financed with an amount of debt that stays level over its lifetime? — the formulas usually give answers that are off by only a few percent from the true present value.[14]

6.4 Summary and Conclusions

The development of appropriate cost-of-capital measures for a firm is closely bound up with how those measures will be used. Because they are to be used as discount rates to aid in the global resource allocation process, the rates must reflect the value to the firm's shareholders of engaging in specific activities. More specifically, because investors put up the money, they — not the firm undertaking the project — decide what return they require. Thus, the emphasis in this chapter is on the cost of capital or required rate of return for a specific project rather than for the firm as a whole.

This rate reflects three elements: (1) the real or inflation-adjusted rate of interest, (2) an inflation premium approximately equal to the expected rate of inflation, and (3) a premium for risk. The risk premium depends on the riskiness of the cash flows produced by the project's assets: The riskier the cash flows are, the larger the risk premium will be. According to the capital asset pricing model, this risk premium equals the project's beta coefficient, which measures its degree of systematic or unavoidable risk times the market risk premium, as measured by the difference between the return on the market and the risk-free rate of interest.

For projects whose systematic risk is identical to the firm's systematic risk, the firm's cost of capital is the correct discount rate to use. This discount rate can be estimated by calculating separately the firm's costs of equity, debt, and preferred stock and then combining them into an overall cost of capital for the firm. This number is known as the *weighted average cost of capital* and equals the required return on average-risk projects.

When systematic risk is the same within divisions but differs across divisions, a divisional cost of capital is appropriate. A project whose degree of systematic risk differs from the corporate or divisional norm will have its own unique cost of capital. The key to estimating any of these costs of capital is to find proxy firms that have comparable business risks and are publicly traded. Estimates of their costs of capital can be used as a basis for calculating the project's cost of capital. We saw how the different

---

[14]For a further discussion, see Myers, S.C. "Interactions of Corporate Financing and Investment Decisions — Implications for Capital Budgeting." *Journal of Finance*, March 1974, pp. 1–25.

financial risks borne by firms with similar business risks can be removed from their estimated beta coefficients to yield the pure, all-equity cost of capital. This is the appropriate number to use in estimating the cost of capital for the project.

Finally, we examined some international aspects of the cost of capital. In the case of the required return for foreign projects, we concluded that the systematic risk for such projects is likely to be less than the systematic risk for comparable domestic projects. Therefore, using the same cost of capital figure for foreign projects as the one used to evaluate comparable domestic projects will likely provide a conservative estimate of the worth of foreign projects.

REFERENCES

Fama, E.F. "Risk-Adjusted Discount Rates and Capital Budgeting Under Uncertainty." *Journal of Financial Economics*, August 1977, pp. 3–24.

Kester, W.C. and Luehrman, T.A. "The Myth of Japan's Low-Cost Capital." *Harvard Business Review*, May–June 1992, pp. 130–138.

Rubinstein, M.E. "A Mean-Variance Synthesis of Corporate Financial Theory." *Journal of Finance*, March 1973, pp. 167–182.

SAMPLE PROBLEMS

1. A company is deciding whether to issue stock to raise money for an investment project that has a beta of 1.0 and an expected return of 20%. Suppose the risk-free rate is 10%, the company's stock price beta is 2.5, and the expected return on the market is 15%. Should the company go ahead with the project? Explain.

   Answer: With a project beta of 1.0, the project's required return is just equal to the expected return on the market, or 15%. Since the 20% expected return on the project exceeds the project's cost of capital, the company should make the investment. The data also allow us to calculate the cost of equity capital for the company. With a stock price beta of 2.5 and a market risk premium of 5%, the company's cost of equity capital is 22.5% $(0.10 + 2.5 \times 5)$. Although this figure exceeds the expected return on the project, it has no bearing on the project selection decision. What matters for that decision is the project cost of capital, not the company's cost of capital.

2. Multi-Foods has four divisions: pet foods, canned goods, frozen entrees, and instant foods. These contribute 10%, 25%, 50%, and 15%, respectively, to the firm's value. Multi-Foods has found what it feels are good proxies for its divisions in the following competitors:

Company	Beta	D/TA*
Pet Products	0.50	0.33
Candlelight	1.50	0.50
Freezies	1.75	0.20
RedyEeet	2.25	0.25

   *D/TA = debt/total assets

   a. Assuming the firms are accurate proxies, estimate the asset betas for Multi-Foods divisions. (Assume the debt betas are zero.) Ignore taxes.

Answer: We begin by transforming the debt/total assets ratio into a debt/equity ratio using the formula $D/E = D/(TA - D)$. Pet Products, for example, has a $D/TA = 1/3$, giving it a $D/E = 1/(3 - 1) = 0.50$. Then applying Equation 6.3,

$$\beta_a = \frac{\beta_e}{1 + D/E}$$

we can estimate the asset beta for Pet Products as $\beta_a = 0.5/(1 + 0.5) = 0.33$. Using the same approach, we can estimate D/E and β_a for the other divisions as well. These estimates are presented below.

b. With a risk-free rate of 8% and an average market rate of return of 16%, what is the cost of capital for each of the divisions?
Answer: The data in the problem tell us that $r_f = 0.08$ and $r_m = 0.16$. Using these data along with the CAPM, we can estimate the cost of capital for Pet Products, k_{pp}, as follows:

$$k_{pp} = r_f + \beta_a (r_m - r_f) = 0.08 + 0.33(0.16 - 0.08) = 10.64\%$$

The other cost of capital estimates can be calculated similarly. The results that are presented below are rounded to the nearest hundred.

Company	D/E	Asset Beta	Cost of Capital (%)
Pet Products	0.50	0.33	10.64
Candlelight	1.00	0.75	14.00
Freezies	0.25	1.40	19.20
RedyEeet	0.33	1.69	21.52

c. With a D/TA of 0.50, what is Multi-Foods' equity beta?
Answer: Multi-Foods' asset beta is the weighted average of the figures above: $0.10 \times 0.33 + 0.25 \times 0.75 + 0.50 \times 1.40 + 0.15 \times 1.69 = 1.174$. With a D/TA of 0.50, Multi-Foods has a D/E of $1/(2 - 1) = 1$. Assuming the debt has no systematic risk, Multi-Foods' equity beta is $1.174 \times (1 + D/E) = 1.174 \times 2 = 2.348$.

d. If the debt of each division also had a beta equal to 0.50, what would be the cost of capital for each division? For Multi-Foods?
Answer: Here, we use Equation 6.2, $\beta_a = (D/TA)\beta_d + (E/TA)\beta_e$, to convert from an equity beta to an asset beta. The resulting estimates of the cost of capital for each division and for Multi-Foods is as follows:

Company	Asset Beta	Cost of Capital (%)
Pet Products	0.50	12.0
Candlelight	1.00	16.0
Freezies	1.50	20.0
RedyEeet	1.81	22.5

The weighted average asset beta is 1.32. This yields a CAPM-estimated cost of capital for Multi-Foods equal to 18.58% ($0.08 + 1.32 \times 0.8$).

QUESTIONS

1. Show how the following events change the discount rate applicable to an expansion of an existing restaurant chain.

   a. The covariance between restaurant sales and the market rate of return increases.
   b. The riskless rate decreases.
   c. Several other companies are planning to expand their chains.

2. A large manufacturer is evaluating the purchase of a smaller firm. The firm has the same required return as the manufacturer, estimated at 10%; yet its actual rate of return is about 8%. Although the project appears to have a negative NPV, company executives have considered the low cost of debt financing. Because the manufacturer has no existing debt outstanding, it may borrow at only 7%. Furthermore, interest deductibility and a tax rate of 50% lower the effective cost of debt to 3.5%. Because the cost of financing the acquisition with debt is much lower than the 8% expected return, the executives are considering going ahead with the acquisition. Comment.

3. Which of the following companies is likely to have a higher beta, and thus a higher cost of capital?

   a. An auto manufacturer who runs an assembly line with union workers.
   b. A "high-tech" auto manufacturer with a fully automated line requiring only a handful of nonunion workers.

4. What impact will each of the following events have on a firm's weighted average cost of capital?

   a. The corporate tax rate is lowered.
   b. The firm increases its leverage.
   c. The firm's stock price falls dramatically.
   d. New York City imposes a stamp tax on share issues floated there.
   e. The government allows private investors to exclude up to $1,000 in dividends from taxable income.
   f. The firm sells a division and replaces it with a less risky project.

5. Suppose a new investment opportunity offers a 14% rate of return. Is this an attractive project to an ongoing firm if the firm can finance the project with 100% debt at an 11% interest rate?

6. A corporation has the following balance sheet (liabilities side):

Current liabilities	$2,000
Long-term debt	5,000
Preferred stock	2,000
Common stock	8,000
Retained earnings	3,000
	$20,000

   Currently, the riskless interest rate is 8%; the corporate tax rate is 50%; the current price of a share of common stock is $20; and dividends have been level at $1 per share per year for many years.

   Recently, company executives have considered expanding the existing business by acquiring a competitor. To do so, they must calculate the WACC of the firm and estimate the NPV of the acquisition. Because the acquisition is of the same risk as the firm, the WACC (unlevered equity cost) can be used.

A financial executive has used the following procedure to calculate the WACC. Debt and preferred stock are fixed claims offering a fairly secure constant return, and so their before-tax cost is assumed to equal the riskless rate. The dividend yield has held constant at about 5%; so this is used as the cost of new and retained equity. Finally, the balance sheet shows the firm to be composed of 25% debt, 10% preferred, 55% equity (common plus retained), and 10% current liabilities. Current liabilities are assumed to be costless; therefore the WACC is 4.55%. Comment on this procedure.

7. "Our conglomerate recognizes that foreign investments have a very low covariance with our domestic operations and thus are a good source of diversification. We do not 'penalize' potential foreign investments with a high discount rate but, rather, use a discount rate just 3% above the prevailing riskless rate." Comment.

8. A large food processor and distributor is considering expansion into a chain of privately owned sports shoe outlets. The food company wishes to estimate the risky discount rate for such investments so as to negotiate a fair price for the acquisition. Unfortunately, there are no stock exchange-listed sports shoe companies with a price history with which a "sports shoe outlet beta" can be estimated. However, executives are considering using the price history of another company to estimate the beta. Which of the following companies would be the most appropriate? Explain.

   a. Another large food company.
   b. A holding company for a football team.
   c. A company that manufactures shoes.
   d. A chain of swimwear and surfboard stores in California.

9. When Gamma Company computes its cost of capital, it uses zero as the cost of retained earnings.

   a. Comment on this procedure.
   b. How is this procedure likely to affect its investment decisions?

10. Which investment is likely to have a higher degree of systematic risk, a copper mining project in Chile or an investment in a Brazilian auto plant whose output would be sold locally? Explain.

PROBLEMS

1. Ampex common stock has a beta of 1.4. If the risk-free rate is 8%, the expected market return is 16%, and Ampex has $20 million of 8% debt, with a yield to maturity of 12% and a marginal tax rate of 50%, what is the WACC for Ampex?

2. Calvin Inc. earned $2.00 per share during the past year and has just paid a dividend of $0.40 per share. Investors forecast that Calvin will continue to retain 80% of its earnings for the next four years and that earnings will grow at 25% per year through year 5. The dividend payout ratio is expected to be raised in year 5 to 50%, reducing the dividend growth rate to 8% thereafter. If Calvin's equity beta is 0.9, the risk-free rate is 8.5%, and the market risk premium is 8%, what should its price be today?

3. As a financial analyst for National Engineering, you are required to estimate the cost of capital the firm should use in evaluating its heavy construction projects. The firm's balance sheet data and other information are listed below. Assume the corporate tax rate is 35%.

   a. What is your estimate? What assumptions must you make to calculate this estimate?
   b. What qualifications to this estimate should you mention in your report when National applies this rate to its various projects?

Selected Balance Sheet Items		Market Data		
			Market Value	Yield (bonds)
Bonds	(see market data)	Bonds		
Preferred stock	$400,000	8%, 10-year	$250,000	12%
Common stock	$800,000	12%, 15-year	$1,000,000	15%
Retained earnings	$2,000,000	21%, 1-year	$250,000	11%
		Common stock:		
		Average dividend growth (5 years) = 10%		
		Current dividend yield = 7%		
		Price = $47.25		
		Shares = 100,000		
		Preferred stock:		
		$4.50 preferred dividend		
		Price = $22.50		
		Shares = 20,000		

4. A corporation's securities have the following betas and market values:

	Beta	Market Value ($)
Debt	0.1	100,000
Preferred	0.4	200,000
Common	1.5	100,000

Calculate the following figures given a riskless interest rate of 10% and market risk premium of 5%:

a. Discount rates for each security.
b. The asset beta for the corporation.
c. The weighted average cost of capital.
d. The discount rate for the unlevered assets.

5. As part of its efforts at diversification, the Sherbert theater organization, producer of Broadway plays, is considering acquiring a movie theater chain. A prime acquisition candidate is Consolidated Cinemas, currently owned by a conglomerate, Tryon. Although Tryon has given Sherbert what it feels is an accurate forecast of expected cash flows from the cinema chain, Sherbert would like to have its own estimate of the required rate of return to apply to these cash flows. The chief financial officer has acquired the following information on independently owned movie house chains:

Movie House	Beta	D/TA*
NCO Theater, Inc.	1.70	0.40
Worldwide/Global	0.50	0.10
Screen Rocks	2.50	0.50
Ultimate Theater	−0.10	0.75

*D/TA = debt/total assets

a. Using a risk-free rate of 7.5% and a market risk premium of 8.5%, what is your estimate of the cost of equity capital for Consolidated?

b. What qualifications would you include with your estimate?

6. Westcon is considering building a facility to tap thermal energy using wind power. Part of the project's cost, $750,000, can be financed with a loan from the Federal Energy Commission at the below-market rate of 5%. The remainder, $250,000, can be financed with an industrial revenue bond at 10%. Current debt rates for Westcon are 15%. The project should generate pre-tax net profit of $425,000 a year for 10 years. Westcon has a 40% tax rate, and the *D/E* ratio is 0.50. Westcon estimates that the project beta is 1.50 and forecasts a risk-free rate of 10% for the life of the project. The market rate is estimated to be 20%.

a. Should Westcon undertake the project?

b. Assuming the project is of the same risk as Westcon itself, would the project be acceptable *without* the subsidies? Explain.

7. In analyzing the possible placement of their first fast-food fish restaurant overseas, the Gill Corp. has the following data:

Correlation of rate of return on common stock indexes, last 10 years	United States with
0.44	France
0.75	Canada
0.75	Japan
0.61	United Kingdom
0.27	Italy

The CFO for Gill reasons that the beneficial effect of foreign diversification should be included in the financial analysis, by multiplying the risk of equity capital by this correlation. With a U.S. beta of 1.15, what would the project's beta be under this system? Is this a defensible procedure to use?

8. Tom Swift Company has a target capital structure of 40% debt and 60% equity. Its estimated beta is 0.9. Tom Swift is evaluating a new project that is unrelated to its existing lines of business. However, it has identified three proxy firms exclusively engaged in this line of business. The average beta for these firms is 1.2, and their debt ratios average 50%. Tom Swift's new project has a projected return of 11.9%. The risk-free return is 10% and the market risk premium is 5%. All firms have a marginal tax rate of 40%. Tom Swift's before-tax cost of debt is 13%.

a. What is the unlevered project beta?

b. What is the beta of the project if undertaken by Tom Swift, assuming the company maintains its target capital structure?

c. Should Tom Swift accept the project?

9. The following are the beta estimates from Value-Line for several computer firms as well as the *D/TA* for the firms. Suppose the risk-free rate of return is 8%, the expected market return is 17%, and the tax rate is 35%.

a. What risk premium must these companies pay as a result of leverage?

b. What proportion of their total equity cost is a result of financing?

Company	Beta	D/TA
Apple	1.70	0
Amdahl	1.55	0.31
Burroughs	1.00	0.24
Commodore	1.50	0.14
Cray	1.45	0.05
Sperry	1.25	0.23
Tandem	1.60	0.03

10. In late 1984, Sonat, the Birmingham, Alabama-based, energy and energy services company, ordered six drilling rigs that can be partly submerged from Daewoo Shipbuilding, a South Korean shipyard. Daewoo agreed to finance the $425 million purchase price with an 8.5-year loan, at an annual interest rate of 9% paid semiannually. The loan principal is repayable in 17 equal semiannual installments ($25 million every six months). At the time the loan was arranged, the market interest rate on such a loan would have been about 16%. If Sonat's marginal tax rate (federal plus state corporate taxes) was 50% at the time, how much would this loan be worth to Sonat?

Appendix 6A

International Dimensions of the Cost of Capital

Up to now, we have implicitly assumed that the projects under consideration are located in the United States, but this is becoming less true all the time. According to the U.S. Department of Commerce, total U.S. direct foreign investment—the acquisition abroad of physical assets such as plant and equipment—exceeded $6 trillion at the end of 2001. The enormity of this stake and the fact that many U.S. corporations that are household names—such as IBM, General Electric, and Ford—earn over 40% of their profits abroad means that for many of these multinational corporations (MNCs) there is no turning back; foreign operations and successful foreign investments are crucial to their success. This appendix addresses some of the issues surrounding the cost of capital for foreign projects.

APPENDIX 6A.1

THE COST OF CAPITAL FOR FOREIGN PROJECTS

As the multinational corporation becomes the norm rather than the exception, the issue of cost of capital for foreign projects is being raised more frequently. A central question that must be addressed by the MNC is whether the required rate of return on foreign projects should be higher, lower, or the same as that for comparable domestic projects. Although a definitive answer is not possible, both the CAPM and APT supply some useful insights.

The importance of the CAPM and APT for the MNC is that the relevant component of risk in pricing a firm's stock is its systematic risk as measured by its beta coefficient. Much of the systematic or general market risk affecting a company, at least as measured using a domestic stock index such as the S&P 500 or the NYSE index, is caused by the cyclical nature of the national economy in which the company is operating. For this reason, it is highly possible that multinationals, by having operations in a number of countries whose economic cycles are not perfectly in phase, may be reducing the variability of their earnings through international diversification.

A number of studies suggest that this is in fact the case.[15] Such studies find little correlation among the earnings of the various national components of MNCs. Thus, to the extent that foreign cash flows are not perfectly correlated with those of domestic investments, the total risk associated with variations in cash flows appears to be *reduced*, not increased, by international investment. Of greater importance, most of the economic and political risks faced by the multinational corporation appear to be unsystematic and can, therefore, be eliminated by shareholder diversification.[16]

---

[15]See, for example, Cohen, B.I. *Multinational Firms and Asian Exports*. Yale University Press: New Haven, Conn., 1975; and Rugman, A. "Risk Reduction by International Diversification." *Journal of International Business Studies*, Fall 1976, pp. 75–80.

[16]As noted in Chapter 3, however, even though the unsystematic component of risk should not affect the required discount rate, it will likely reduce the expected cash flow of the firm undertaking the project.

Paradoxically, it is the less-developed countries (LDCs), where political risks are greatest, that are likely to provide the largest diversification benefits. This is because the economies of LDCs are less closely tied to the economy of the United States or that of any other Western nation. By contrast, the correlation among the economic cycles of developed countries is considerably stronger; so the diversification benefits from investing in industrialized countries, from the standpoint of a Western investor, are proportionately less.

Yet, the systematic risk of projects even in relatively isolated LDCs is unlikely to be far below the average for all projects because these countries are still tied to the world economy. The important point about projects in LDCs, then, is that their ratio of systematic to total risk generally is quite low; their systematic risk, though perhaps slightly lower, is probably not significantly less than that of similar projects located in industrialized countries (and could be somewhat more if their risk were sufficiently high to offset the effects of a low correlation with market returns).

Even if a nation's economy is not closely linked to the world economy, the systematic risk of a project located in that country might still be rather large. For example, a foreign copper-mining venture probably will face systematic risk very similar to that faced by an identical extractive project in the United States, whether the foreign project is located in Canada, Chile, or Zaire. The reason is that the major element of systematic risk in any extractive project is related to variations in the price of the mineral being extracted, which is set in a world market. The world market price, in turn, depends on worldwide demand, which itself is systematically related to the state of the world economy. By contrast, a market-oriented project in an LDC, whose risk depends largely on the evolution of the domestic market in that country, is likely to have a systematic risk that is small in both relative and absolute terms.

An example of the latter type of project would be a Ford plant in Brazil whose profitability is closely linked to the state of the Brazilian economy. The systematic risk of the project, therefore, largely depends on the correlation between the Brazilian economy and the U.S. economy. Although positive, this correlation is much less than 1.

Thus, **corporate international diversification** should prove beneficial to shareholders, particularly where there are barriers to **international portfolio diversification**. To the extent that multinational firms are uniquely able to supply low-cost international diversification, investors may be willing to accept a lower rate of return on shares of MNCs than on shares of single-country firms. By extension, the risk premium applied to foreign projects may be lower than the risk premium for domestic ones; that is, the required return on foreign projects may be less than the required return on comparable domestic projects. The net effect may be to enable MNCs to undertake overseas projects that would otherwise be unattractive.

However, if international portfolio diversification can be accomplished as easily and as cheaply by individual investors, then, although required rates of return on MNC securities would be lower to reflect the reduced covariability of MNC returns caused by international diversification, the discount rate would not be reduced further to reflect investors' willingness to pay a premium for the indirect diversification provided by the shares of MNCs. In fact, American investors actually undertake very little foreign portfolio investment. The lack of widespread international portfolio diversification has an important implication for estimating the beta coefficient.

EVIDENCE FROM THE STOCK MARKET

Ali Fatemi has produced a useful study of the effects of foreign operations on the cost of equity capital.[17] This study compared the performance of two carefully constructed stock portfolios: a portfolio of 84 MNCs, each with at least 25% of its annual sales generated from international operations; and a portfolio of 52 purely domestic firms. Monthly performance comparisons were made over the five-year period, January 1976 to December 1980.

Although the validity of the study is limited by the relatively short time period involved, the difficulty in properly matching MNCs with their purely domestic counterparts (most firms do business in more than one industry), and the difficulty in calculating the degree of sales from abroad (consider the transfer pricing problem, for example), its conclusions are nonetheless of interest.

1. The rates of return on the two portfolios are statistically identical. Ignoring risk, MNCs and uninational (purely domestic) corporations (UNCs) provide shareholders the same returns.
2. Consistent with our expectations, the rates of return on the MNC portfolio fluctuate less than those on the UNC portfolio. Thus, corporate international diversification seems to reduce shareholder total risk and may do the same for the firm's total risk.
3. The betas of the multinational portfolio are significantly lower and more stable than the betas of the purely domestic portfolio, indicating that corporate international diversification reduces the degree of systematic risk, at least, if systematic risk is calculated relative to the domestic portfolio. It was also found that the higher the degree of international involvement, the lower the beta.

APPENDIX 6A.2

KEY ISSUES IN ESTIMATING FOREIGN PROJECT DISCOUNT RATES

Although the CAPM is the model of choice for estimating the cost of capital for foreign projects, the type of information that is needed to estimate foreign subsidiary betas directly—a history of past subsidiary returns or future subsidiary returns relative to predicted market returns—does not exist. About the only practical way to get around this problem is to find publicly traded firms that share similar risk characteristics and use the average beta for the portfolio of corporate surrogates to proxy for the subsidiary's beta. This approach, however, introduces four additional questions for a U.S. multinational:

1. *Should the corporate proxies be U.S. or local (i.e., foreign) companies?* Although local companies should provide a better indication of risk, such companies may not exist. By contrast, selecting U.S. proxies ensures that such proxies and their data exist, but their circumstances—and hence their betas—may be quite different from those facing the foreign subsidiaries. In addition, it is important to differentiate

---

[17]Fatemi, A.M. "Shareholder Benefits from Corporate International Diversification." *Journal of Finance,* December 1984, pp. 1325–1344.

between the unsystematic risks faced by a foreign project—which individual investors can eliminate through diversification—and the systematic risks affecting that project, which may be small relative to the project's total risk.

2. *Is the relevant base portfolio against which the proxy betas are estimated the U.S. market portfolio, the local portfolio, or the world market portfolio?* Selecting the appropriate portfolio matters because a risk that is systematic in the context of the local market portfolio may well be diversifiable in the context of the United States or the world portfolio. If this is the case, using the local market portfolio to calculate beta will result in a higher required return—and a less desirable project—than if beta were calculated using the United States or the world market portfolio.

3. *Should the market risk premium be based on the U.S. market or the local market?* One argument in favor of using the local market risk premium is that this is the risk premium demanded by investors on investments in that market. On the other hand, estimates of the local-market risk premium may be subject to a good deal of statistical error. Moreover, such estimates may be irrelevant to the extent that an MNC's investors are not the same as the investors in the local market and the two sets of investors measure risk differently.

4. *How, if at all, should country risk be incorporated in the cost of capital estimates?* One approach to incorporate country risk that has been widely adopted in recent years is to add a country risk premium to the discount rate estimated using the CAPM. These premiums are often computed from the yield spread on dollar-denominated local government bonds versus U.S. Treasury bonds. However, such an approach may involve double counting of risks and be inconsistent with the theoretical foundations of the CAPM.

Let us now address these four questions and their related issues. As in any application of a theoretical model, the suggested answers are not precisely right but are instead based on a mix of theory, empirical evidence, and judgment.

PROXY COMPANIES

Three alternatives for estimating proxy betas are proposed here. These alternatives are presented in the order of their desirability. Other approaches are also mentioned[18].

Local Companies. As much as possible, the corporate proxies should be local companies. The returns on an MNC's local operations are likely to depend, in large measure, on the evolution of the local economy. Inevitably, therefore, the timing and magnitude of these returns will differ from those of the returns generated by comparable U.S. companies. This means that the degree of systematic risk for a foreign project, at least as measured from the perspective of an American investor, may well be lower than the systematic risk of comparable U.S. companies. Put differently, using U.S. companies and their returns to proxy for the returns of a foreign project will likely lead to an upward-biased estimate of the risk premium demanded by the MNC's investors.

Some indication of the upward bias in the estimate of beta imparted by using U.S. proxy companies to estimate the betas for foreign projects is provided by presenting the foreign market betas relative to the U.S. index for some foreign countries. The betas for the foreign markets from a U.S. perspective are calculated in the same way

---

[18]This section has benefited from a discussion with Rene Stulz.

that individual asset betas are calculated:

Foreign market beta

$$= \frac{\begin{array}{c}\text{Correlation with}\\\text{U.S. market}\end{array} \times \begin{array}{c}\text{Standard deviation}\\\text{of foreign market}\end{array}}{\text{Standard deviation of U.S. market}}$$

$$\text{(6A.1)}$$

According to Equation 6A.1, in conjunction with data from the 31-year period 1970 to 2000, the beta for the Australian market relative to the U.S. market was 0.76 (0.47 × 0.8635/0.5320). The corresponding betas for Hong Kong and Singapore were 0.85 and 0.94 respectively:

Country	Correlation with U.S. Market	Standard Deviation of Returns (%)	Beta from U.S. Perspective
Australia	0.47	86.35	0.76
Hong Kong	0.33	135.55	0.85
Singapore	0.47	106.09	0.94
United States	1.00	53.20	1.00

It may be that some U.S. companies operating overseas would have betas in the foreign markets in excess of 1.0, thereby raising their betas relative to the estimated foreign market betas. Nonetheless, this evidence does suggest the possibility that the average beta of U.S. proxy companies overstates the betas for foreign subsidiaries from a U.S. perspective.

Notice also that despite investment risks associated with the Hong Kong and Singapore markets (standard deviations of 135.55 and 106.09% respectively), risks that are about twice that of the U.S. market (a standard deviation of 53.20%), both markets had betas that were substantially lower than the U.S. market beta of 1.0. The reason is that much of the risk associated with markets in individual countries is unsystematic and so can be eliminated by diversification, as indicated by the relatively low betas of these markets.

Proxy Industry. If foreign proxies are not directly available, a second alternative is to find a proxy industry in the local market, that is, one whose U.S. industry beta is similar to that of the project's U.S. industry beta. One way to analyze the empirical validity of this approach is to check whether the betas of the two industries (the project's and the proxy's) are also similar in other national markets that contain both industries (e.g., Britain, Germany, and Japan).

Adjusted U.S. Industry Beta. The third alternative is to estimate the foreign project's beta by computing the U.S. industry beta for the project, $\beta_{USPROXY}$, and multiplying it by the foreign market beta relative to the U.S. index. Specifically, suppose that β_{AUS} is the beta for the Australian market relative to U.S. market. Then, under this proposed methodology, the beta for the Australian project, β_{AUSSUB}, would be estimated as:

$$\beta_{AUSSUB} = \beta_{USPROXY} \times \beta_{AUS} \quad \text{(6A.2)}$$

This approach is the least preferred of the three alternatives because implicit in it are two questionable assumptions:

1. *The beta for an industry in the United States will have the same relative beta in each foreign market.* In other words, the project has the same risk relative to the risk of the local market as a comparable project would have in the U.S. market. That is a large assumption considering that national markets have different industries and different weightings of industries in their indices.
2. *The only correlation with the U.S. market of a foreign company in the project's industry comes through its correlation with the local market and the local market's correlation with the U.S. market.* However, it is conceivable that, say, an oil firm could have a low correlation with the local market but a high correlation with the U.S. market.

That being said, to the extent that returns for a foreign project depend largely on the evolution of the local economy in which it operates, then these two assumptions are likely to be satisfied. In that case, this approach would be an appropriate compromise.

Although these approaches to estimating foreign subsidiary betas involve a variety of assumptions, these assumptions appear to be no less plausible than the assumption that foreign operations are inherently riskier than comparable domestic operations and should be assessed an added risk premium.

THE RELEVANT BASE PORTFOLIO

In employing the CAPM, the base portfolio against which the proxy betas are estimated can be the home portfolio, or the global market portfolio. The resulting implementation of the CAPM depends on which base portfolio is selected. For a U.S. MNC evaluating a foreign investment opportunity, the use of its home market portfolio would result in the following version of the CAPM:

$$r_i = r_f + \beta_{ius}(r_{us} - r_f) \quad (6A.3)$$

where β_{ius} refers to the project beta when measured relative to the U.S. market (which is its home market) and r_{us} is the expected return on the U.S. market.

The **global capital asset pricing model** can be represented as

$$r_i = r_f + \beta_{ig}(r_g - r_f) \quad (6A.4)$$

where β_{ig} refers to the project beta when measured relative to the global market and r_g is the expected return on the global market portfolio (which is measured by something like the Morgan Stanley Capital International, or MSCI, World Index). The foreign project beta using the global CAPM is computed as follows:

$$\beta_{ig} = \frac{\text{Correlation with} \atop \text{global market} \times \text{Standard deviation} \atop \text{of foreign project}}{\text{Standard deviation of global market}}$$
$$(6A.5)$$

The appropriate market portfolio to use in measuring a foreign project's beta depends on one's view of world capital markets. More precisely, it depends on whether or not capital markets are globally integrated. If they are, then the world portfolio is the correct choice; if they are not, the correct choice is the home or domestic portfolio. The test of capital market integration depends on whether these assets are priced in a common context; that is, capital markets are integrated to the extent that security prices offer all investors worldwide the same trade-off between systematic risk and real expected return. Conversely, if capital markets are segmented from each other, then risk is priced in a domestic context.

The truth probably lies somewhere in between. Capital markets now are integrated to a great extent, and they can be expected to become ever more so with time. However, because of various government regulations and other market imperfections, this integration is not complete. Unfortunately, it is not currently within our power, if indeed it ever will be, to empirically determine the relevant market portfolio and, hence, the correct beta to use in project evaluation. (The problem of determining the appropriate market portfolio to use in estimating beta arises domestically as well as internationally.)

The Impact of Globalization on the Cost of Capital. To the extent that a global CAPM is the appropriate model to use, it has important implications for companies. First, risk that is systematic in the context of the domestic economy may well be unsystematic in the context of the world economy. As long as the domestic economy is less than perfectly correlated with the world economy, the beta for a project that depends on the state of the local market will be less when measured against the global portfolio than when measured against the domestic portfolio. Other things being equal, the use of a global CAPM means a lower cost of capital for this company.

Another benefit of globally integrated markets is that investors are able to reduce some of the risk that they would otherwise have to bear in a segmented market. In particular, by diversifying across nations whose economic cycles are not perfectly in phase, a globally diversified portfolio will be less risky than a purely domestic portfolio. The reason is that risk, which is systematic in the context of the U.S. economy, may be unsystematic in the context of the global economy. For example, an oil price shock that hurts the U.S. economy helps the economies of oil-exporting nations, and vice versa. Thus, just as movements in different stocks partially offset one another in an all-U.S. portfolio, so also do movements in the United States and non-U.S. stock portfolios cancel each other out somewhat.

The lower risk of a globally diversified portfolio translates into a lower risk premium if markets are globally integrated. To understand this result, consider a segmented national market in which domestic securities can only be held by local investors and local investors cannot buy foreign assets. These investors will bear more risk than if they were free to invest internationally. Hence, they will demand a higher rate of return for holding domestic securities than would a globally diversified investor who can diversify away the country-specific risk. Once the domestic market is integrated into a global market, the purely domestic risk on local stocks will be diversified away in the global portfolio. With investors holding domestic stocks now bearing less risk, they will demand a lower risk premium.

The lower risk premium can be seen by recognizing that if the global CAPM holds, the market risk premium for the domestic market portfolio will equal the domestic market beta relative to the global market portfolio, β_d, multiplied by the global market risk premium. Given that β_d will usually be less than 1 and that the global market risk premium will be less than the domestic risk premium, the product of the two will also be smaller.

Illustration: How Globalization Affected Nestlé's Cost of Capital. A striking example of the impact of globalization on the cost of capital is provided by the November 1988 decision of Nestlé, the giant Swiss foods conglomerate, to eliminate restrictions on foreign ownership of its shares.[19] Until that point, Nestlé had two classes of shares that differed only in who could own them. *Bearer* shares were available to both Swiss and foreign investors, whereas *registered* shares could be owned only by Swiss investors. Despite the fact that these shares had identical voting and dividend rights, registered shares were worth only about half as much as bearer shares. Once the restrictions on foreign ownership of registered shares were lifted, the price of registered shares rose by over 36%, while the price of bearer shares fell by about 25%. Overall, the market value of Nestlé's equity rose by 10%. The explanations for these changes are straightforward.

Once the restrictions on registered shares were lifted, the Swiss could sell some of these shares to foreigners. As the Swiss better diversify their portfolios, they demand a lower risk premium for holding the remaining registered shares. The price of these shares will rise as their future cash flows are less heavily discounted.

With respect to bearer shares, the lifting of restrictions on registered shares meant that the supply of Nestlé shares available to foreign investors rose. With the supply of Nestlé

---

[19]This example and the data come from an exceptional article written by Stulz, R. "Globalization of Capital Markets and the Cost of Capital: The Case of Nestlé" *Journal of Applied Corporate Finance*, Fall 1995, pp. 30–38.

shares exceeding the demand for these shares at the then existing price, the price of bearer shares fell.

Finally, the jump in the total value of Nestlé's equity is consistent with a decline in its cost of equity capital. We can illustrate this using some numbers provided by René Stulz.[20] The estimated Swiss beta for Nestlé was 0.90. The fact that Nestlé's home beta is close to 1.0 is not surprising given that it comprises a large portion of the Swiss stock market.

The Swiss market risk premium is estimated at 5.2% based on the difference between the Swiss stock market's historical average return of 9.8% and the 4.6% historical return to Swiss government bonds. With a 4.5% risk-free rate, the home version of the CAPM yields an estimated cost of capital for Nestlé equal to 9.2%:

$$k_e(\text{Nestlé}) = r_f + \beta_{\text{Nestlé(s)}}(r_s - r_f)$$
$$= 4.5\% + 0.90 \times 5.2\% = 9.2\%$$

where $\beta_{\text{Nestlé(s)}}$ is Nestlé's beta relative to the Swiss market and r_s is the expected return on the Swiss market.

Once Swiss shares are readily available to foreign investors, we might expect the global version of the CAPM to more accurately describe the pricing of risk for Nestlé and hence, its cost of equity capital. The beta for Nestle relative to a global index of stocks is about 0.60. With an estimated world market risk premium of about 6%, Nestlé's estimated cost of capital using the global CAPM will be 8.1%, 110 basis points below its previously estimated cost of capital:

$$k_e(\text{Nestlé}) = r_f + \beta_{\text{Nestlé(g)}}(r_g - r_f)$$
$$= 4.5\% + 0.60 \times 6.0\% = 8.1\%$$

where $\beta_{\text{Nestlé(g)}}$ is Nestlé's beta relative to the global market and r_g is the expected return on the global market portfolio. If we accept that an updated world risk premium would be on the order of 4% and that closer integration of the world stock markets would increase Nestlé's global beta to 0.70, then the global CAPM would yield an estimated cost of capital for Nestlé of 7.3% ($4.5\% + 0.70 \times 4\%$), 190 basis points below the estimate using the local CAPM.

The impact of the lower cost of capital on the value of Nestlé's shares can be seen with the aid of the dividend growth model. According to this model, if a company's dividend is expected to grow at a constant rate g per annum, the price of that company's stock is determined as follows:

$$P_0 = \frac{DIV_1}{k_e - g} \tag{6A.6}$$

where k_e is the cost of equity capital and DIV_1 is the expected dividend for the upcoming year. Suppose the dividend is set equal to SFr 1 and g is equal to 3%. According to

[20]See Stulz, R. "Globalization of Capital Markets and the Cost of Capital: The Case of Nestlé." *Journal of Applied Corporate Finance*, Fall 1995, pp. 30–38.

Equation 6A.6, the value of Nestlé's stock based on the home version of the CAPM will be 1/(0.092 – 0.03), or SFr 16.13. Using the global version of the CAPM and an 8.1% cost of capital yields a value for Nestlé shares of SFr 19.61 (1/(0.081 – 0.03)), or 22% higher than the previously calculated estimate (19.61/16.13 = 1.22). With a 7.3% cost of equity capital, Nestlé's price will jump by 44%, to SFr 23.26 (1/(0.073 – 0.03). Thus, seemingly small changes in the cost of capital brought about by increased globalization can have large impacts on value.

Empirical Evidence. The evidence on asset pricing models is mixed, largely because of the statistical difficulty of testing any such model. For example, a substantial literature exists on the **home bias** — the tendency to hold domestic assets in one's investment portfolio — exhibited by investors.[21] This evidence shows that domestic residents hold a disproportionate share of the nation's stock market wealth. Such home bias leads to capital market segmentation and results in a preference for using the domestic or local version of the CAPM rather than the global CAPM.[22] If the domestic CAPM is the appropriate model to use, the cost of capital for a foreign project is likely to be lower than the cost of capital for the same project undertaken in the home market, assuming that the total risks of the projects are the same.

A different stream of research supports the use of the global CAPM. In the most widely cited study on the use of a global CAPM, Campbell Harvey examined the historical returns of markets in 17 countries over the period February 1970 to May 1989.[23] He found that the main prediction of the global CAPM (that the domestic market risk premium will equal the product of the domestic market beta computed relative to the global portfolio times the global market risk premium) held for 14 of the 17 countries studied. Other tests of the global CAPM are also supportive.[24]

A Recommendation. Despite the evidence in favor of the global CAPM, a pragmatic recommendation is for U.S. MNCs to measure the betas of international operations against the U.S. market portfolio. This recommendation is based on the following two reasons:

1. It ensures comparability of foreign with domestic investments, which are evaluated using betas that are calculated relative to a U.S. market index.
2. The relatively minor amount of international diversification attempted (as yet) by American investors suggests

---

[21]The home bias has been documented by French, K.R., and Poterba, J.M. "Investor Diversification and International Equity Markets." *American Economic Review, Papers and Proceedings*, 1991, pp. 222–226; Cooper, I., and Kaplanis, E. "What Explains the Home Bias in Portfolio Investment." *Review of Financial Studies*, 7, 1994, pp. 45–60; Tesar, L., and Werner, I.M. "Home Bias and High Turnover." *Journal of International Money and Finance*, 14, 1995, pp. 467–493.

[22]The use of the local version of the CAPM is recommended, for example, by Cooper, I., and Kaplanis, E. "Home Bias in Equity Portfolios and the Cost of Capital for Multinational Companies." *Journal of Applied Corporate Finance*, Fall 1995, pp. 95–102.

[23]Harvey, C.R. "The World Price of Covariance Risk." *Journal of Finance*, 1991, pp. 111–158.

[24]See, for example, Chan, K.C., Andrew Karolyi, G., and Stulz, R.M. "Global Financial Markets and the Risk Premium on U.S. Equity." *Journal of Financial Economics*, October 1992, pp. 137–167; DeSantis, G., and Gerard, B. "International Asset Pricing and Portfolio Diversification with Time-Varying Risk." *Journal of Finance*, 52, 1997, pp. 1881–1913.

that the relevant portfolio from their standpoint is the U.S. market portfolio.

This reasoning suggests that the required return on a foreign project may well be lower, and is unlikely to be higher, than the required return on a comparable domestic project. Thus, applying the same discount rate to an overseas project as to a similar domestic project probably will yield a conservative estimate of the relative systematic riskiness of the project.

Using the domestic cost of capital to evaluate overseas investments also is likely to understate the benefits that stem from the ability of foreign activities to reduce the firm's total risk. As we saw in Chapter 5, reducing total risk can increase a firm's cash flows. By confining itself to its domestic market, a firm will be sensitive to periodic downturns associated with the domestic business cycle and other industry-specific factors. By operating in a number of countries, the MNC can trade off negative swings in some countries against positive ones in others. This option is especially valuable for non-U.S. firms whose local markets are small relative to the efficient scale of operation.

Despite the apparent benefits of corporate international diversification for shareholders, research by Bertrand Jacquillat and Bruno Solnik concluded that, although multinational firms do provide some diversification for investors, they are poor substitutes for international portfolio diversification.[25] Their results indicate that an internationally diversified portfolio leads to a much greater reduction in variance than does one comprising firms with internationally diversified activities. Thus, the advantages of international portfolio diversification remain.

For non-U.S. companies, especially those from smaller countries whose markets are open to foreign investors, it would probably make more sense to use the global CAPM. This model should be used for both domestic and foreign investments to ensure comparability across projects.

THE RELEVANT MARKET RISK PREMIUM

In line with the basic premise that multinationals should use a methodology that is as consistent as possible with the methodology used to calculate the cost of capital for U.S. investments, the recommended market risk premium to be used is the U.S. market risk premium. This is the appropriate market risk premium to use for several reasons. First, the U.S. market risk premium is the one likely to be demanded by a U.S. company's mostly American investors. A second reason for preferring the U.S. market risk premium is the earlier recommendation that the betas of foreign subsidiaries be estimated relative to the U.S. market. Using the U.S. market risk premium will ensure consistency between the measure of systematic risk and price per unit of this systematic risk. Finally, the quality, quantity, and length of U.S. capital market data are by far the best in the world, increasing the statistical validity of the estimated market risk premium.

Conversely, no other country has a stock market data series of the same length and quality as that of the United States. In addition, virtually all foreign countries have undergone dramatic economic and political changes since the end of World War II — changes that inevitably will affect the required risk premium for those markets. To

---

[25]Jacquillat, B. and Solnik, B.H. "Multinationals Are Poor Tools for Diversification." *Journal of Portfolio Management*, Winter 1978, pp. 8–12.

the extent that such regime changes have altered the market risk premium in foreign countries, estimates of these risk premiums based on historical data are less useful as forecasts of required risk premiums going forward.

The bottom line is that U.S. capital markets have the best data available on the required return that investors demand per unit of risk. Moreover, as national capital markets become increasingly integrated globally, the market price of risk becomes the same worldwide. Add to these points the fact that shareholders of U.S. firms are mostly American, and a strong case can be made that the U.S. market risk premium is the appropriate price of risk for a foreign project.[26]

APPENDIX 6A.3

RECOMMENDATIONS

In summary, the recommended approach to estimating the cost of equity capital for the foreign subsidiary of a U.S. multinational is to find a proxy portfolio in the country in which that subsidiary operates and calculate its beta relative to the U.S. market. That beta should then be multiplied by the risk premium for the U.S. market. This estimated equity risk premium for the foreign subsidiary would then be added to the U.S. (home country) risk-free rate to compute a dollar (home currency) cost of equity capital.

An alternative, but problematic, approach used by many investment bankers these days is to estimate a **sovereign risk premium** for the foreign country (by taking the difference between the interest rate on U.S. dollar-denominated debt issued by the foreign government and the rate on U.S. government debt of the same maturity) and to add that figure to the estimated U.S. cost of equity capital. In particular, to the extent that the estimated sovereign risk premium measures risk (it may measure a liquidity premium), it is not systematic risk but rather default (or rescheduling) risk that is being measured. And default risk does not enter into the cost of equity capital. Of course, default risk is likely to be closely linked to political risk, but adjusting the cost of capital is not necessarily the best way to factor political risk into a foreign investment analysis. As recommended in Appendix 3C, a better approach for dealing with political risk is to first identify its likely cash-flow consequences and then adjust projected cash flows to incorporate those consequences.

---

[26]Stulz, R.M. Globalization, Corporate Finance, and the Cost of Capital." *Journal of Applied Corporate Finance,* Fall 1999, pp. 8–25 argues for the use of the global market risk premium, which he estimates at about two-thirds of the historical U.S. market risk premium based on the assumption that the standard deviation of an internationally diversified portfolio is about 20% lower than that of a diversified portfolio invested only in U.S. stocks.

Appendix B

Using the Dividend Growth Model As a Check on the CAPM

Section 6.1 showed how to measure the cost of equity capital by using the CAPM (represented by Equation 6.1). One check on the CAPM-derived estimate is to compare it with the cost of equity capital obtained from the dividend valuation model previously presented as Equation 6A.6. Solving Equation 6A.6 for the cost of equity capital yields the following formula:

$$\text{Estimated cost of equity capital} = \text{Dividend yield} + \text{Expected dividend growth rate}$$

$$k_e = \frac{DIV_1}{P_0} + g$$

(6B.1)

where

DIV_1 = expected dividend in year 1

P_0 = current stock price

g = average expected annual dividend growth rate

The dividend growth rate, g, in Equation 6B.1 can be estimated using either historical data or, if the past is not considered a reliable indicator of future performance, expectations of future earnings and resulting dividends.

The dividend growth model has its own potentially troubling aspects. Most importantly, it assumes that the firm's dividends will grow at the constant rate g forever. This means it cannot be applied to firms that pay no dividends, firms whose dividend growth rate is highly unstable, or firms whose historical dividend growth rate is clearly unsustainable. It is applicable primarily to firms with slow but steady dividend growth. Even for these firms, however, the potential for substantial measurement error exists. By contrast, the CAPM is applicable to a broader class of firms, and there is less subjectivity in estimating its parameters.

The main difference between the two methods for estimating the cost of equity capital is that the dividend growth model infers the cost of equity capital from the current expected dividend yield and expected dividend growth rate. The underlying theory is that the value of an asset equals the present value of its future cash flows. The CAPM, by contrast, infers the cost of equity capital by relating the historical pattern of returns on the stock to the historical pattern of returns on the markets. Underlying the CAPM is a theory of how risk is priced in the marketplace. If the assumptions underlying both models are correct (to within a close approximation) in a specific instance, then both models should lead to the same estimated cost of equity capital.[27]

---

[27]Harris, R.S., and Marston, F.C. "Estimating Shareholder Risk Premia Using Analysts' Growth Forecasts." *Financial Management*, Summer 1992, pp. 63–70 find that both methods yield reasonably comparable estimates of the cost of equity capital.

BOX 6.5

APPLICATION: ESTIMATING HEWLETT-PACKARD'S COST OF EQUITY CAPITAL

We can use the CAPM to find Hewlett-Packard's cost of equity capital as of October 2003. With an estimated risk-free rate of 4.29% (the long-term Treasury bond yield in that month), a market risk premium of 5%, and a beta of 1.35 (from Value Line), the CAPM-based estimate of the required return on HP stock is calculated as 11.04%:

$$k_{HP} = 0.0429 + 1.35 \times 0.05 = 11.04\%$$

To apply the dividend growth model, we need some additional information about Hewlett-Packard. Its stock price in October 2003 was about $20.25, and its dividend for the coming year was estimated by Value Line—one of the leading Wall Street providers of such data—at $0.36. This gives a dividend yield of

$$\frac{D_1}{P_0} = \frac{0.36}{20.25} = 1.78\%$$

Estimating the dividend growth rate is a bit trickier because forecasts are unavailable. The approach taken here is to use a five-year dividend forecast supplied by Value Line. According to Value Line, Hewlett-Packard's dividend should grow from $0.32 in 2003 to $0.50 in 2008, a 9.34% compound annual growth rate over the next five years.

Substituting the values $DIV_1/P_0 = 1.78\%$ and $g = 9.34\%$ into the dividend growth model yields the following estimate of H-P's cost of equity capital

$$k_{HP} = \frac{DIV_1}{P_0} + g = 0.0178 + 0.0934 = 11.12\%$$

This figure is very close to the 11.04% cost of equity capital estimated above using the CAPM. Although any conclusions must be tempered by the potential for error associated with our estimating procedures, both the CAPM and the dividend growth model give consistent estimates of Hewlett-Packard's cost of equity capital.

CHAPTER 7

Corporate Strategy and the Capital-Budgeting Decision

Man is not the creature of circumstances. Circumstances are the creature of men.

—DISRAELI

Our future...depend(s) on the treasures of the human mind and spirit. The most fertile and rapidly growing sector of any economy is that part that exists right now only as a dream in someone's head or an inspiration in his heart.

—RONALD REAGAN

The 23-year period, 1980 through 2002, began with back-to-back recessions and ended in a lingering recession. Yet throughout these years of economic turmoil, companies like Abbott Laboratories, Nalco Chemical, and Wal-Mart were money-making stars, earning an average return on shareholders' equity in excess of 20% return. To gain some perspective, a dollar invested in 1980 at a compound annual return of 20% would have grown to $66.25 by the end of 2002, a healthy return even after allowing for the effects of inflation.[1]

The demonstrated ability of these firms to consistently earn such extraordinary returns on invested capital must be due to something more than luck or its proficiency at applying sophisticated techniques of investment analysis. That something is the knack for creating positive net present value projects, projects with rates of return in excess of the required return. The scarcity of this skill is attested to by the fact that for every Wal-Mart earning a return on equity (ROE) in excess of 20%, there appears to be a Sears, Roebuck earning less than a 10% ROE.

---

[1]Inflation causes income to be overstated and the value of assets to be understated. Thus, these return-on-equity figures are overstated in nominal terms because of the effects of inflation.

Moreover, even companies like IBM, which used to earn consistently high ROEs, can stumble and see their ROEs and stock prices fall.

Despite this evidence, it is usually taken for granted that positive NPV projects exist and can be uncovered using fairly straightforward techniques. Consequently, the emphasis in most capital-budgeting analyses is on estimating and discounting future project cash flows. Projects with positive NPVs are accepted; those that fail this test are rejected.

Yet, selecting positive NPV projects in this way is equivalent to picking undervalued securities on the basis of fundamental analysis. The latter can be done with confidence only if financial market imperfections exist that do not allow asset prices to reflect their equilibrium values. Similarly, the existence of **economic rents**—excess returns that lead to positive net present values—are the result of monopolistic control over product or factor supplies (a real market imperfection).

The difficulty in earning such economic rents is attested to by the problems that once dominant firms, such as IBM, General Motors (GM), and Sears, have faced over the past decade in trying to regain some of their past luster. If uncovering positive NPV projects were that simple, these companies would surely have avoided the pain and suffering they are currently undergoing.

It is the thesis of this chapter that generating projects likely to yield positive excess returns is at least as important as doing the conventional quantitative investment analysis. This is the essence of corporate strategy—creating and then taking advantage of imperfections in product and factor markets (known collectively as *real markets*). Thus, an understanding of the strategies followed by successful firms in defending and exploiting those **barriers to entry** created by product and factor market imperfections is crucial to any systematic evaluation of investment opportunities. For one thing, it suggests those projects that are most likely ex-ante to have positive net present values. This ranking is useful because constraints of time and money limit the investment alternatives that a firm is likely to consider.

More important, a good understanding of corporate strategy should help uncover new and potentially profitable projects; only in theory is a firm fortunate enough to be presented, at no effort or expense on its part, with every available investment opportunity. Perhaps the best way to gain this understanding is to study a medley of firms, spanning a number of industries and nations, which have managed to develop and implement a variety of value-creating investment strategies. This is the basic approach taken here.

Section 7.1 discusses what happens to economic rents—and thus to opportunities for positive NPV projects—in a competitive industry over time. Section 7.2 then studies in more detail the nature of market imperfections that give rise to economic rents and how one can design investments to exploit those imperfections. Section 7.3 introduces a normative approach to strategic planning and investment analysis. The fourth section deals with the evolution of domestic firms into multinational corporations (MNCs), including a discussion of the rationale and means whereby MNCs transfer abroad their competitive strengths.

7.1 Competitive Markets and Excess Returns

A perfectly competitive industry is one characterized by costless entry and exit, undifferentiated products, and increasing marginal costs of production. These undifferentiated products, also known as *commodities*, are sold exclusively on the basis of price.

In such an industry, as every student of microeconomics knows, each firm produces at the point at which price equals marginal cost. Long-run equilibrium exists when price also equals average cost. At this point, total revenue equals total cost for each firm taken individually and for the industry as a whole. This cost includes the required return on the capital used by each firm. Thus, in the long run, the actual return on capital in a competitive industry must equal the required return.

Any excess return quickly attracts new entrants to the market. Their additional capacity and attempts to gain market share lead to a reduction in the industry price and a lowering of returns for all market participants. In the early 1980s, for example, the high returns available in the video-game market, combined with the ease of entry into the business, attracted a host of competitors. This led to a red ink bath for the industry, followed by the exit of a number of firms from the industry. Alternatively, should the actual return for the industry be below the required return, the opposite happens. The weakest competitors exit the industry, resulting in an increase in the industry's price and a boost in the overall return on capital for its remaining members. This process, which is now taking place in the airline industry, continues until the actual return once again equals the required return.

The message is clear: The run-of-the-mill firm operating in a highly competitive, commodity-type industry is doomed from the start in its search for positive NPV projects. Only firms that can bring to bear on new projects competitive advantages that are difficult to replicate have any assurance of earning excess returns in the long run. These advantages take the form of either being the low-cost producer in the industry or being able to add value to the product—value for which customers are willing to pay a high (relative to cost) price. The latter type of advantage requires the ability to convert a commodity business into one characterized by products that are differentiated on the basis of service and/or quality. By creating such advantages, a firm can impose barriers to entry by potential competitors, resulting in a less than perfect competitive market and the possibility of positive NPV projects.

BOX 7.1

APPLICATION: IBM AND THE COMMODITIZATION OF COMPUTERS

Historically, IBM and other mainframe makers have enjoyed gross margins of 70% or so on their machines. However, the advent of the personal computer and the microprocessor has changed all that. The painful fact is that computers are becoming commodities that customers buy as cheaply as possible. And these small computers, with their razor-thin profit margins, are encroaching on turf once reserved for mainframes.

The personal computer has become a commodity because Intel, which makes its microprocessors, and Microsoft, which makes the operating system software, sell their technologies to practically all comers. The companies that assemble PCs from those components press suppliers of all other parts—screens, power supplies, disk drives, and memory chips—to slash prices and push technology. At the same time, Sun Microsystems and others have developed powerful, commodity-like workstations using interchangeable software that target users of minicomputers and even mainframes.

Loss of product differentiation has had the inevitable impact on profits. Profitability of every sector of the industry is under pressure or becoming nonexistent. And with the companies constantly leapfrogging each other with machines that run the same software, the industry is condemned to ceaseless innovation, price-cutting, and short product cycles. Instead of having twice the profit margin on sales of average industrial companies, as they did in 1984, by 1991, computer companies had margins 20% lower than average. Over the five-year period 1987 to 1991, profit margins (net income divided by sales) for the 11 largest U.S. computer companies averaged just 6.5%; in the previous five years, they averaged 11.5%. Companies such as IBM, Digital Equipment Corporation (DEC), and Unisys, long accustomed to double-digit sales growth and profit margins, began reporting shrinking computer revenue and paper-thin profits—and huge restructuring charges ($11.4 billion in such charges for IBM alone in 1992). By the end of 1992, IBM had reduced its workforce by over 100,000 people, from a peak of 406,000 in 1985.

In the meantime, Microsoft and Intel—the two near-monopoly suppliers of the basic PC technology—reaped huge profits. Exhibit 7.1 on page 193 shows the diverging paths of the ROEs for IBM, Microsoft, and Intel from 1980 on. It also includes the ROE for the S&P 500. You can see how IBM's ROE was substantially in excess of the S&P 500's ROE until 1985, when the gap began to narrow in line with the erosion in IBM's competitive advantage. By 1988, that spread had turned negative. As Exhibit 7.2 on page 194 shows, the change in the ROE spread had predictable consequences for IBM's cumulative stock market return relative to that of the S&P 500. The two series track each other well until 1985, when computing power unexpectedly became a commodity product. The resulting dramatic decline in IBM's returns relative to the market's returns is consistent with the narrowing and then reversal of the ROE spread. From a peak of $106 billion in 1987, IBM had lost $76 billion in market value by the end of 1992.

In response, IBM and other computer manufacturers transformed themselves into sellers of business systems solutions rather than hardware. IBM has been the most successful of the hardware makers at restructuring their companies to minimize the commodity end of the computer business and differentiate their offerings. The payoff has been IBM's ability to earn large excess returns once again.

7.2 Barriers to Entry and Positive Net Present Value Projects

We have just seen that the ability to discourage new entrants to the market by erecting barriers to entry is the key to earning rates of return on capital that consistently exceed capital costs. If these barriers did not exist, new competitors would enter the market and drive down the rate of return to the required return. High barriers to entry and the threat of a strong reaction from entrenched competitors will reduce the risk of entry and so prolong the opportunity to earn excess returns.

This analysis suggests that successful investments (those with positive NPVs) share a common characteristic: They are investments that create, preserve, enhance, and/or capitalize on competitive advantages, which serve as barriers to entry. A common characteristic of successful companies is that they are able to define their strengths—marketing,

EXHIBIT 7.1 Return on Equity for IBM, Intel, Microsoft, and the S&P 500: 1980–1994

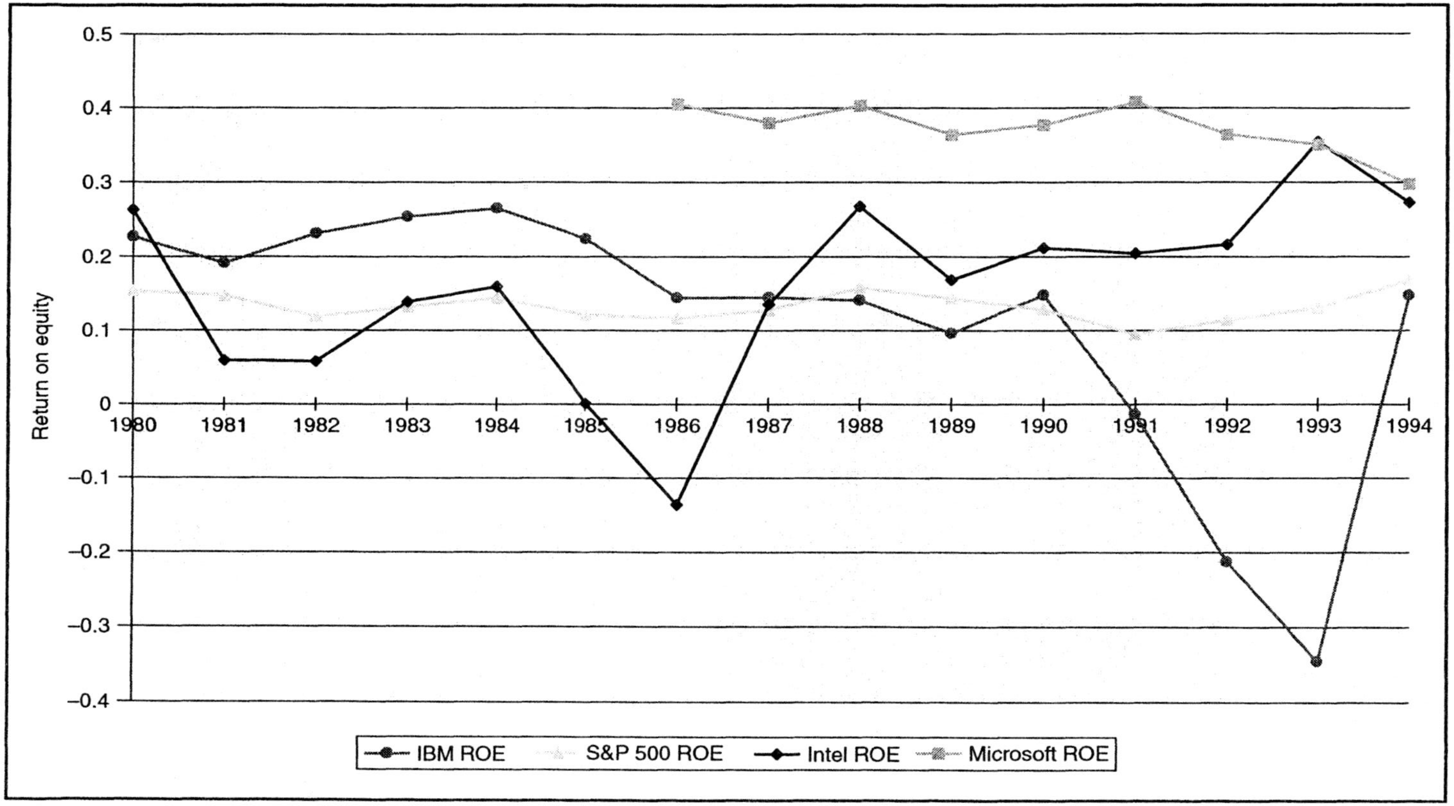

EXHIBIT 7.2 Return on Equity and Cumulative Stock Returns: IBM versus S&P 500 (1972–1994)

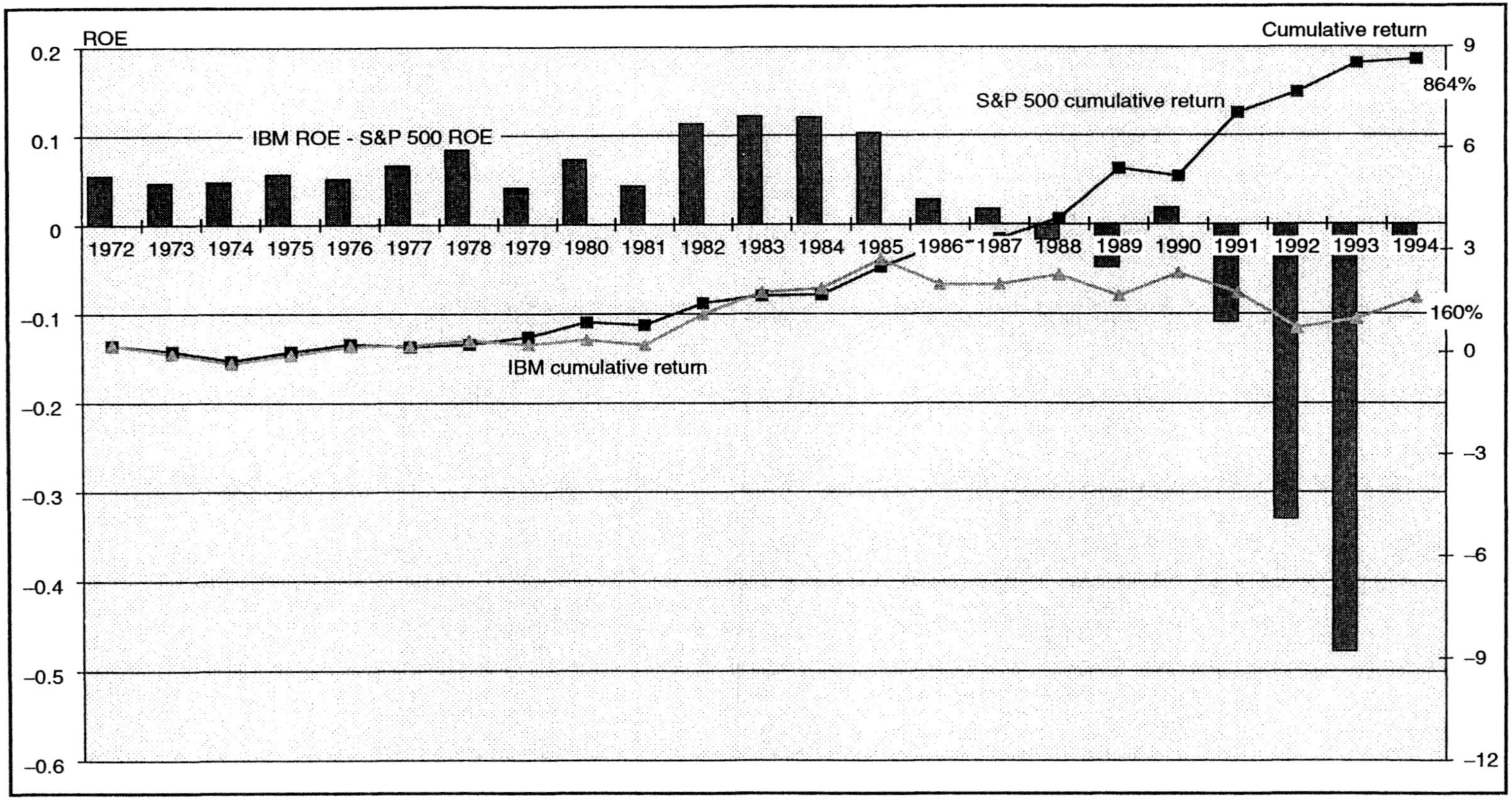

customer contact, new product innovation, low-cost manufacturing—and build on them. They have resisted the temptation to move into new businesses that look attractive but require the corporate skills that they lack.

A clearer understanding of the potential barriers to competitive entry can help identify potential value-creating investment opportunities. This section now examines the five major sources of entry barriers—economies of scale and scope, cost advantages, access to distribution channels, product differentiation, and government policy[2]—and suggests some lessons for successful investing.

ECONOMIES OF SCALE AND SCOPE

Economies of scale exist whenever a given increase in the scale of production, marketing, or distribution results in a less-than-proportional increase in cost. By contrast, **economies of scope** exist whenever the same investment can support multiple profitable activities less expensively in combination than separately.

Economies of Scale

The existence of scale economies means that there are *inherent cost advantages to being large.* The more significant these scale economies are, therefore, the greater will be the cost disadvantage faced by a new entrant to the market. For example, Intel's huge market share in microprocessors is a major deterrent to potential entrants. It can spend great sums on research and development, marketing, service, and new plants, since it can spread the costs over millions more chips than other chipmakers can. So Intel can invest more than its rivals and still undercut their prices. In natural resource industries, firms such as Alcan, the Canadian aluminum company, and Exxon fend off new market entrants by exploiting economies of scale in production and transportation.

High capital requirements go hand in hand with economies of scale. In order to take advantage of scale economies in production, marketing, or new product development, firms must often make enormous up-front investments in plant and equipment, research and development, and advertising. These capital requirements themselves serve as a barrier to entry; the more capital that is required, the higher will be the barrier to entry. This is particularly true in industries such as petroleum refining, mineral extraction, and mainframe computers. As scale economies become less important, however, as has happened in the computer industry, new entrants are attracted, and profitability shrinks.

A potential entrant to a market characterized by scale economies in production will be reluctant to enter unless the market has grown sufficiently to permit the construction and profitable utilization of an economically sized plant. Otherwise, the new entrant will have to cut price to gain market share, in the process destroying the possibility of abnormal profits. By expanding in line with growth in the market, therefore, entrenched competitors can preempt profitable market entry by new competitors.

Consider, for example, the economics of the cement industry. The low value-to-weight ratio of cement makes the cement business a very regional one; beyond a radius of about 150 to 200 miles from the cement plant, transportation costs become prohibitive unless cheap water or rail transportation is available. At the same time, the

---

[2]See, for example, Porter, M.E. "How Competitive Forces Shape Strategy." *Harvard Business Review,* March–April 1979, pp. 137–145 for a good summary and discussion of these barriers to entry and their implications for corporate strategy.

significant economies of scale available in cement production limit the number of plants that a given region can support. For instance, suppose that demand in a land-locked region is sufficient to support only one or two modern cement plants. By expanding production and adding substantial new capacity to that already available, a firm can significantly raise the price of market entry by new firms and make plant expansion or replacement by existing competitors look much less attractive. This type of move obviously requires a longer time frame and the willingness to incur potential losses until the market grows larger.

Scale economies, on both the individual store level and the citywide market level, are all-important to the grocery-retailing business as well. Whether a store has $100,000 or $10 million in annual sales, it still needs a manager. In addition, the cost of constructing and outfitting a supermarket does not increase in proportion to the number of square feet of selling space. Thus, the ratio of expenses to sales exhibits a significant decline as the volume of sales rises.

Similarly, whether it has 10 or 25% of a given market, a supermarket chain has to advertise and supply its stores from a warehouse. The greater the share of market is, the lower the advertising cost per customer will be, the faster the warehouse will turn over its inventory, and the more likely its delivery trucks will be used to capacity. These cost efficiencies translate directly into a higher return on capital.

The relationship between the market dominance of a supermarket chain in a given market and its profitability is evident in the relative returns for firms following contrasting expansion strategies. Chains such as Food Lion and Winn-Dixie, which have opted for deep market penetration in a limited geographic area (ranking number 1 or 2 in almost all their major markets), have realized returns on equity that far exceed their equity costs. On the other hand, chains such as A&P and National Tea that expanded nationally by gaining toehold positions in numerous (but scattered) markets, consistently earned less than their required returns.

Economies of Scope

The existence of economies of scope means that some efficiencies are wrought by variety, not volume. Examples abound in the cost advantages to producing and selling multiple products related by a common technology, set of production facilities, or distribution network. For example, 3M has taken its basic adhesives and coatin technology and applied it across a broad range of products and markets—bandages and dental restoratives in health care; Post-it notes and Scotch tape in the office supplies market; reflective highway signs; floppy disks and optical disks for personal computers; and videocassettes and audiocassettes in the consumer electronics market. Similarly, Honda has leveraged its investment in small engine technology in the automobile, motorcycle, lawn mower, marine engine, generator, and chain saw businesses.

Matsushita has leveraged its investment in advertising and distribution of Panasonic-brand products in a number of consumer and industrial markets, ranging from personal computers to plasma screens. Each dollar invested in the Panasonic brand name or distribution system aids sales of dozens of different products. Similarly, U.S. pharmaceutical companies typically have developed large sales forces to promote their products. The incremental cost of pushing one more drug through the distribution system represented by the sales force essentially consists of adding another page to the sales catalogue.

Production economies of scope are becoming more prevalent as flexible manufacturing systems allow the same equipment to produce a variety of products more cheaply in combination than separately. The ability to manufacture a wide variety of products with little cost penalty relative to the large-scale manufacture of a single product opens up new markets, customers, and channels of distribution, and, along with them, new routes to competitive advantage. For example, a plastics company, which manufactured the heavy garbage pails that it sold through wholesalers, found itself selling babies' bathtubs and diaper pails directly to boutiques when it acquired a new machine that greatly expanded the range of products it could make economically.

Lesson 1: Investments that are structured to exploit fully economies of scale or scope are more likely to be successful than are those that do not.

COST ADVANTAGES

Entrenched companies often have cost advantages that are unavailable to potential entrants, independent of economies of scale. Sony and Texas Instruments, for example, take advantage of the **learning curve** to reduce costs and drive out actual and potential competitors. This concept is based on the adage that you improve with practice. As production experience accumulates, costs can be expected to decrease because of the more efficient use of labor and capital, improved plant layout and production methods, product redesign and standardization, and the substitution of less expensive materials and practices. This cost decline creates a barrier to entry because new competitors, lacking experience, face higher unit costs than do established companies. By achieving market leadership, usually by price-cutting, and thereby accumulating experience faster, this entry barrier can be maximized.

Proprietary technology, protected by legally enforceable patents, provides another cost advantage to established companies. This is one of the avenues taken by many of the premier companies in the world, including 3M, Siemens (Germany), Hitachi (Japan), and L.M. Ericsson (Sweden).

Monopoly control of low-cost raw materials is another cost advantage open to entrenched firms. This was the advantage held for so many years by Aramco (Arabian-American Oil Company), the consortium of oil companies that until the early 1980s had exclusive access to low-cost Saudi Arabian oil.

McDonald's has developed yet another cost advantage vis-à-vis potential competitors—it has already acquired, at a relatively low cost, many of the best fast-food restaurant locations. *Favorable locations* are also important to supermarkets and department stores.

Sometimes, however, new entrants enjoy a cost advantage over existing competitors. This is especially true in industries undergoing deregulation, like airlines and trucking. In both these industries, regulation insulated firms from the rigors of competition and fare wars. Protected as they were, carriers had scant incentive to clamp down on costs. And still they made money. The excess returns provided by the regulatory barrier to entry were divided among the firms and their unionized employees.

Deregulation has exposed these firms to new competitors not saddled with outmoded work rules and high-cost employees. For example, new, low-cost competitors in the airlines industry, such as Southwest Airlines, have much lower wages and more flexible work rules (which permit flight attendants to serve at reservations phones).

Lesson 2: Investments aimed at achieving the lowest delivered cost position in the industry, coupled with a pricing policy to expand market share, are more likely to succeed, especially if the cost reductions are proprietary.

PRODUCT DIFFERENTIATION

Instead of a cost-based advantage, many companies invest in the capacity to differentiate their products. *Product differentiation* can stem from investments in advertising, R&D, or the development of a service- and quality-oriented organization. Regardless of the differentiation strategy pursued, the objective is the same—to reduce the total cost of use to the buyer and thereby enable management to price its product at a premium. In successful differentiation the higher price is more than offset by a reduction in the costs to the buyer. *The aim is not to be the low-cost producer but to be the low-cost provider.*

The buyer's costs include the costs of search and learning to use the product, uncertainty as to the product's characteristics, the costs of usage, and the costs of switching to another product or service if the initial purchase does not perform as expected. The latter two costs depend largely on the product's performance and durability. The buyer's problems are compounded because it is difficult and/or costly to determine the quality of many products before purchase and use.

BOX 7.2

APPLICATION: DEC'S BIG GAMBLE

In the late 1970s and early 1980s, DEC bet billions of dollars on developing an ambitious new generation of VAX minicomputers. Ranging from small desktop machines to computer clusters that can compete with mainframes, DEC's new VAXes use a common architecture, allowing them to run the same programs and share data over networks. This reduces customers' software costs and need for technical support. IBM itself stumbled badly by not recognizing quickly enough the emerging demand by its customers for linking computers into networks; it continued to proliferate products that were incompatible with one another, making them complex and expensive to integrate. Consequently, even though its machines often cost more than comparable IBM products do, DEC became the low-cost provider for many customers and took billions in business from the heart of IBM's market.

Manufacturers may try to signal the quality of their goods through price. But if consumers cannot measure that quality before use, they will hesitate to pay premium prices for what may turn out to be shoddy goods. The solution to this problem is *reputation.* A company's reputation for quality and integrity permits it to charge a premium price for a quality product or service. Reputation, therefore, is a valuable though intangible asset. Sometimes called **brand-name capital**, reputation is built up through time by performance—giving customers more than they expect—or through expensive advertising that creates a quality image in the minds of customers.

Whether the firm invests in reputation through advertising or by selling high-quality products at a relatively low price, the economic function of reputation is the same—to be a valuable asset that can be lost if the firm dishonors its promises to customers. It is this prospect for damage that makes a reputation credible. Businesses with strong reputations must behave well or suffer the loss of valuable intangible capital. Those without such reputations face a major barrier to entry.

There are numerous examples of product differentiation. Some companies, like Coca-Cola and Procter & Gamble, take advantage of *enormous advertising expenditures* and *highly developed marketing skills* to differentiate their products and keep out potential competitors wary of the high marketing costs and risks of new product introduction. Others sell expertise and high-quality products and service. For example, Nalco Chemical, a specialty chemical firm, is a counselor to its customers and problem solver, whereas Worthington Industries, which turns semifinished steel into finished steel, has a reputation for quality workmanship that allows it to charge premium prices. Both have been handsomely rewarded for their efforts, with average equity returns exceeding 20% during the 30-year period from 1973 to 2002.

BOX 7.3

APPLICATION: NALCO CHEMICAL MANAGES MOLECULES FROM CRADLE TO GRAVE

Faced with a proliferation of environmental laws, Nalco introduced a delivery and storage system for hazardous chemicals called Porta-Feed. It eliminates the use of 55-gallon metal drums, those unsightly vessels that often end up discarded in landfills, leaking dregs into the soil and exposing their owners to potentially huge liability under federal environmental law. Porta-Feed consists of a refillable 400-gallon stainless steel container installed at a customer's plant. When the tank is nearly empty, an electronic sensor hooked to a telephone sends a signal to Nalco saying, in effect, "Fill me!" Soon a Nalco delivery truck shows up to refill the tank. The empty transport container is returned to Nalco for cleaning. Nalco charges premium prices for the chemicals it delivers this way. But plant managers say Porta-Feed saves money by curbing pollution and simplifying the handling of dangerous chemicals.

Pharmaceutical companies have traditionally earned high returns by *developing unique products* protected from competition by patents, trademarks, and brand names. Three outstanding examples are Glaxo's Zantac for stomach ulcers, Merck's Vasotec for high blood pressure, Pfizer's cholesterol lowering drug Lipitor, and Hoffman-La Roche's tranquilizer, Valium. Although their price tags are high, these pharmaceuticals often substitute for far more expensive medical treatments involving hospitalization and surgery. For example, the cost of Zantac is $1,000, but the cost of ulcer surgery is $24,000. Similarly, Vasotec costs $1,000, compared with coronary bypass surgery at $40,000 per operation.

The *development of technologically innovative products* has led to high profits for firms like Xerox and Philips (Netherlands). But people do not pay for technology; they pay for the value added by technology. A fat R&D budget, therefore, is only part of the activity leading to commercially successful innovations. Firms that make technology pay off are those that closely link their R&D activities with market realities; unless the product lowers customer costs, it will not succeed. Even if these firms have strong technology, they do their marketing homework. This requires close contact with customers, as well as close coordination and communication between technical and business managers.

Failure to heed that message has led to Xerox's inability to replicate its earlier success in the photocopy business. In addition to its revolutionary copier technology, Xerox developed some of the computer industry's most important breakthroughs, including the first personal computer and the first network connecting office machines. But through lack of market support, it consistently failed to convert its research prowess in computer technology into successful products.

Service is clearly the key to extraordinary profitability for many firms. The ability to differentiate its computers from others through exceptional service has enabled Dell Computer to take on IBM and Compaq. Similarly, Caterpillar Tractor has combined dedication to *quality* with outstanding distribution and after-market support to differentiate its line of construction equipment and gain a commanding 35% share of the world market for earth-moving machinery. American firms, like the auto companies, that have been somewhat lax in the area of product quality have fallen prey to those Japanese firms for whom quality has become a religion.

What may not be obvious from these examples is that it is possible to differentiate anything, even commodity businesses like fast food, potato chips, theme parks, and candy bars. The answer—as companies like McDonald's, Disney, Frito-Lay, Mars, and Deluxe Check Printers have demonstrated—seems to be quality, service, and consistency. In combination, these attributes lower buyers' costs and risk. Cleanliness and consistency of service are the hallmarks of Disney and McDonald's, with both rating at the top of almost everyone's list as the best mass service providers in the world. Similarly, it is said that at Mars the plants are kept so clean you can "eat off the factory floor."

High-quality work and dependability have helped Deluxe Corp., the leading U.S. check printer, flourish in a world supposedly giving up checks. It fills more than 95% of orders in two days and ships 99% error free.

Frito-Lay's special edge is a highly motivated 10,000-person sales force dedicated to selling its chips. It guarantees urban supermarkets and rural mom and pop stores alike a 99.5% chance of a daily call. Although they get only a small weekly salary, the salespeople receive a 10% commission on all the Lay's, Doritos, and Tostitos they sell. So they hustle, setting up displays, helping the manager in any way possible, all the while angling for that extra foot of shelf space or preferred position that can mean additional sales and income.

Other firms have made their owners wealthy by understanding that they too are *selling solutions to their customers' problems*, not hardware or consumables. John Patterson, the founder of National Cash Register, used to tell salesmen: "Don't talk machines, talk the prospect's business." Thomas Watson, the founder of IBM, patterned his sales strategy on that admonition. Thus, while other companies were talking technical specifications, his salespeople were marketing solutions to understood problems, like making sure the payroll checks came out on time. Until IBM fell victim to the commoditization of computing power, it was the most profitable company in the world.

Lesson 3: Investments designed to create a position at the high end of anything, including the high end of the low end, differentiated by a quality or service edge, will generally be profitable.

ACCESS TO DISTRIBUTION CHANNELS

Gaining distribution and shelf space for their products is a major hurdle for newcomers to an industry. Most retailers of personal computers, for example, limit their inventory to around five lines. Currently, over 200 manufacturers are competing for this very limited amount of shelf space. Moreover, the concentration of retail outlets among chains means that new computer makers have even fewer avenues to the consumer. This presents new manufacturers with a Catch-22: You don't get shelf space until you are a proven winner, but you can't sell until you get shelf space.

Conversely, *well-developed, better yet unique, distribution channels* are a major source of competitive advantage for firms like Avon, Tupperware, Frito-Lay, and Dell Computer. Avon, for example, markets its products directly to the consumer on a house-to-house basis through an international network of 900,000 independent sales representatives. Using direct sales has enabled Avon to reduce both its advertising expenditures and the amount of working capital it has tied up in the business. Potential competitors face the daunting task of organizing, financing, and motivating an equivalent sales force. Thus, its independent representatives are the entry barrier that allows Avon to consistently earn exceptional profit margins in a highly competitive industry. Similarly, the sales forces of Frito-Lay, Procter & Gamble, and Dell help those firms distribute their products and raise the entry barrier in three very diverse businesses.

BOX 7.4

APPLICATION: DELL COMPUTER DIALS A WINNER

Dell Computer is primarily a direct marketer, selling its machines through the Internet, mail-order, telephone, and catalog channels. It has largely dispensed with brick-and-mortar retail outlets, having replaced them with toll-free telephone lines, a website, and the network of trucks supplied by shippers like United Parcel Service. In 1992, Dell's selling and administrative expenses ate up just 14% of its sales dollar, against 20 cents at Compaq, 24 cents at Apple, and 30 cents at IBM. (By 2002, Dell had cut SG&A expenses to less than 9% of sales.) Dell's cost savings continue further down the distribution channel. Even an efficient retailer, like CompUSA, selling Compaq or IBM PCs takes 13 cents on the sales dollar to cover rent and salaries. On a mail-order $3,000 computer, in contrast, Dell will bill its customer a shipping charge of only 2% or so. At the same time, Dell has managed to maintain a level of customer satisfaction at least equal to that of competitors who sell through stores. In the same way that McDonald's took the uncertainty out of short-order joints, Dell took the fears and uncertainty out of mail-order computers. Moreover, by selling directly to customers, Dell gains an instantaneous reading (gleaned from more than 5,000 sales calls a day) of the latest trends in a market that absorbs new models every six months. This market intelligence gives Dell an edge in designing computers that meet customer needs and allows it to respond quickly to the constantly changing personal computer business. In contrast, its Asian rivals, cut off from the U.S. market by thousands of miles and huge cultural gaps, have been overwhelmed by the rapid rate of change in the PC industry. Add in its minimal investment in plant and equipment (in 2002 Dell supported over $35 billion in sales with just $913 million in fixed assets), and Dell can deliver a return on equity that exceeds that of IBM in its prime—averaging over 36% for the 10 years ending 2002 and over 43% in 2002.

Conversely, their lack of a significant marketing presence in the United States is perhaps the greatest hindrance to Japanese drug makers attempting to expand their presence here. Marketing drugs in the United States requires considerable political skill in maneuvering through the U.S. regulatory process, as well as great rapport with U.S. researchers and doctors. This latter requirement means that pharmaceutical firms must develop extensive sales forces to maintain close contact with their customers. As noted earlier, there are economies of scope here; the cost of developing and maintaining such a sales force is the same, whether it sells one product or one hundred. Thus, only firms with extensive product lines can afford to invest in a large sales force, raising a major entry barrier to Japanese drug firms trying to go it alone in the United States.

One way the Japanese drug firms have found to get around this entry barrier is to form joint ventures with American drug firms, with the Japanese supplying the patents and the American firms supplying the distribution network. Such licensing arrangements are a common means of entering markets requiring the strong distribution capabilities that the firm lacks.

As an alternative to a large sales force, more companies are using the new information technologies to market and distribute products. For example, American Hospital Supply (AHS), which distributes products from 8,500 manufacturers to more than 100,000 health care providers, saw its market share and profits soar after it set up computer links to its customers and suppliers to speed up the order entry process. With lower ordering costs, hospitals are willing to place larger orders with AHS. The technology lets the company (now owned by Baxter International) cut inventories, improve customer service, and get better terms from suppliers for higher volumes. Even more important, it ties customers more closely to AHS by raising the costs of switching to a rival distributor.

Lesson 4: Investments devoted to gaining better product distribution often lead to higher profitability.

GOVERNMENT POLICY

We have already seen in the case of the airline, trucking, and pharmaceutical industries that government regulations can limit, or even foreclose, entry to potential competitors. Other government policies that raise partial or absolute barriers to entry include import restrictions, environmental controls, and licensing requirements. For example, American quotas on Japanese cars have limited the ability of companies such as Mitsubishi and Mazda to expand their sales in the United States, leading to a higher return on investment for American car companies. Similarly, environmental regulations that restrict the development of new quarries have greatly benefited those firms, like Vulcan Materials, that already had operating quarries.

A change in government regulations can greatly affect the value of current and prospective investments in an industry. For example, the Motor Carrier Act of 1935 set up a large barrier to entry into the business, as it allowed the Interstate Commerce Commission to reject applicants to the industry. The act also allowed the truckers themselves to determine their rates collectively, typically on the basis of average operating efficiency. Thus, carriers with below-average operating costs were able to sustain above-average levels of profitability. It is scarcely surprising, then, that the major trucking companies pulled out all the stops in lobbying against deregulation. As expected, the onset of trucking deregulation, which greatly reduced the entry barrier, has led to lower profits (and even losses) for trucking companies and a significant drop in their stock prices.

Lesson 5: Investments in projects protected from competition by government regulation can lead to extraordinary profitability. However, what the government gives, the government can take away.

BUILDING COMPETITIVE ADVANTAGE

The preceding discussion suggests that investment strategy should focus explicitly on building competitive advantages. This could be a strategy geared to building volume, when economies of scale are all-important, or broadening the product scope, when economies of scope are critical to success. Such a strategy is likely to encompass a sequence of tactical projects, several of which may yield low returns when considered in isolation, but when taken together either create valuable future investment opportunities or allow the firm to continue earning excess returns on existing investments. To evaluate a sequence of tactical projects designed to achieve competitive advantage, the projects must be analyzed collectively, rather than incrementally.

For example, if the key to competitive advantage is high volume, the initial entry into a market should be assessed on the basis of its ability to create future opportunities to build market share and the associated benefits thereof. Alternatively, market entry overseas may be judged according to its ability to deter a foreign competitor from launching a market share battle by posing a credible retaliatory threat to the competitor's profit base. By reducing the likelihood of a competitive intrusion, foreign market entry may lead to higher future profits in the home market. Conversely, firms with high domestic market share, and minimal sales overseas are especially vulnerable to the strategic dilemma illustrated by the example of Fiat.

BOX 7.5

APPLICATION: FIAT'S STRATEGIC DILEMMA

Suppose, Toyota, the Japanese auto company cuts price in order to gain market share in Italy. If Fiat, the dominant Italian producer with minimal foreign sales responds with its own price cuts, it will lose profit on most of its sales. In contrast, only a small fraction of Toyota's sales and profits are exposed. Fiat is effectively boxed in: If it responds to the competitive intrusion with a price cut of its own, the response will damage it more than Toyota.

The correct competitive response is for the local firm (Fiat) to cut price in the intruder's domestic market (Japan). Having such a capability will deter foreign competitors from using high home-country prices to subsidize marginal cost pricing overseas. But this necessitates investing in the domestic markets of potential competitors. The level of market share needed to pose a credible retaliatory threat depends on access to distribution networks and the criticality of the market to the competitor's profitability. The easier distribution access is and the more critical the market is to competitor profitability, the smaller the necessary market share.

As noted in Chapter 4, each project in a strategic investment program can be viewed as creating a sequence of growth options. Incidentally, the definition of an investment must be broadened to encompass any programs that add to competitive advantage. These include advertising to build brand awareness and add to the company's reputation, developing a sales force or a distribution system, and establishing employee training programs that add to service capabilities, a quality control program that increases product differentiation, and an intelligence system that tracks market and competitor trends. For example, a critical competitive advantage for Intel is its proprietary design tools. As the complexity of microprocessors climbed into the hundreds of thousands of transistors on a chip, making manual design unthinkable, Intel invested heavily in design automation software. In this way, Intel has been able to design successive chips, each with two or three times as many transistors while shrinking development time.

In designing and valuing a strategic investment program, one must be careful to consider the ways in which the investments interact. For example, where scale economies exist, investment in large-scale manufacturing facilities may be justified only if the firm has made supporting investments in foreign distribution and brand awareness. Investments in a global distribution system and a global brand franchise, in turn, are often economical only if the firm has a range of products (and facilities to supply them) that can exploit the same distribution system and brand name.

Developing a broad product line usually requires and facilitates (by enhancing economies of scope) investment in critical technologies that cut across products and businesses. Investments in R&D also yield a steady stream of new products that raises the return on the investment in distribution. At the same time, a global distribution capability may be critical to exploiting new technology.

The return to an investment in R&D is determined by the size of the market in which the firm can exploit its innovation and the durability of its technological advantage. As the technology imitation lag shortens, a company's ability to exploit fully a technological advantage may depend on its being able to quickly push products embodying that technology through distribution networks in each of the world's critical national markets.

Individually or in pairs, investments in large-scale production facilities, worldwide distribution, a global brand franchise, and new technology are likely to be negative NPV projects. Together, however, they may yield a highly positive NPV by forming a mutually supportive framework for achieving global competitive advantage.

By linking strategic planning and capital allocation, companies gain two major advantages. First, the true economics of investments can be assessed more accurately for strategies than for projects. Second, the quality of the capital-budgeting process typically improves greatly when capital expenditures are tied directly to the development and approval of business strategies designed to build or exploit competitive advantages.

BOX 7.6

APPLICATION: SOUTHWEST AIRLINES FLIES HIGH

In a virtually profitless industry, Southwest Airlines has been profitable in every year since 1973. In 1991 and again in 2002, it was the only major U.S. carrier to show a net profit based solely on operations—while offering the lowest fares in the industry.

Southwest's overall costs are the lowest of any major carrier (defined as one with more than $1 billion in annual revenue), yet its work force is among the industry's best paid. Southwest's ability to produce those kind of numbers is based on a coherent business strategy to which the airline has religiously clung. It is the nation's only high-frequency, short-haul (less than 500 miles), low-fare airline. Southwest has 83 flights a day between Dallas and Houston, for example. Prices are always rock bottom, usually about one-third what its competitors charge. The reason that Southwest flies such short distances and offers fares so much lower than other airlines is that the company views the automobile as its main competitor, not other airlines. Air traffic tends to double or triple when Southwest enters a market, as travelers are lured out of their cars and into the air by the low prices and frequent service.

To offer those remarkably low ticket prices, Southwest has geared its entire business strategy toward utilizing its assets to the fullest extent and at the lowest cost possible. It does so in a number of ways. First, its short-haul, frequent flights lend themselves to reliable, no-frills service. For example, Southwest flights do not make connections with others, do not transfer baggage, and do not serve meals. Boarding passes are reusable plastic cards and, to save boarding time, there is no assigned seating. Southwest does not subscribe to expensive computerized reservation system and does little business through commissioned travel agents.

Second, all of its aircraft are Boeing 737s. That standardization of service and product yields savings in fuel costs, training flight crews, maintenance, and inventory costs. Third, Southwest only services routes that can support many flights, allowing it to provide timely, frequent service. That gives customers a lot of options and spreads out fixed costs over more seats. For example, at Southwest, the average number of flights per gate each day is 10.5, more than twice the industry average of 4.5. The high frequency also yields critical mass. Customers come to see Southwest, omnipresent (and so affordable), as the airline of choice. Moreover, it does not fight big competitors toe-to-toe, but uses flanking tactics. In large cities, Southwest flies in and out of secondary airports—Love in Dallas, Hobby in Houston, Midway in Chicago, Burbank and Ontario in the Los Angeles basin, BWI in the Washington D.C. area, and Oakland in the San Francisco Bay area.

Finally, and most importantly, since a plane earns revenue only when it is in the air, Southwest focuses on getting its aircraft into and out of the gate faster than anyone else (it helps to avoid crowded, congested airports). While other airlines take upwards of an hour to unload passengers, clean and service planes, board passengers, and push back from the gate, Southwest has a turnaround time of 15 minutes or less. On a typical day, its planes are in the air 11 hours a day, versus an industry average of 8 hours. With such a high utilization of its costliest assets—planes—the airline need only achieve a load factor (that is, the number of paying passengers per total number of seats) of 55% to break even. And with its low prices and high-frequency service, Southwest exceeds that level easily.

The end result is a high return on equity for Southwest, relative to its industry and relative to the S&P 500. During the 23-year period 1972 through 1994, Southwest's ROE averaged 15.3% annually, in contrast to 13.8% for the S&P 500, 5.0% for American Airlines, and 4.3% for United Airlines. The payoff to Southwest's shareholders is graphically illustrated in Exhibit 7.3 on page 207. From 1973 through 1994, Southwest Airlines had a cumulative return of 21,989%, in contrast to 864% for the S&P 500, 175% for United, and only 40% for American. Overall, Southwest earned 21,949% in excess of the return for American. As other airlines tried to imitate Southwest's strategy, its relative performance fell but still far exceeds that of its competitors.

Lesson 6: A company's ability to exploit fully an investment in one area may require supporting investments in other areas. The corollary is that companies should make the business strategy, rather than the individual projects designed to further that strategy, the focal point of investment analysis.

7.3 Designing an Investment Strategy

To summarize the previous section, the companies that create value are those that develop business strategies geared toward achieving one or both of the following competitive positions within their respective industries and then single-mindedly tailoring their investments to attain these positions:

1. Become the lowest total delivered cost producer in the industry while maintaining an acceptable service/quality combination relative to competition.

EXHIBIT 7.3 Southwest Airlines versus American Airlines: 1972–1994

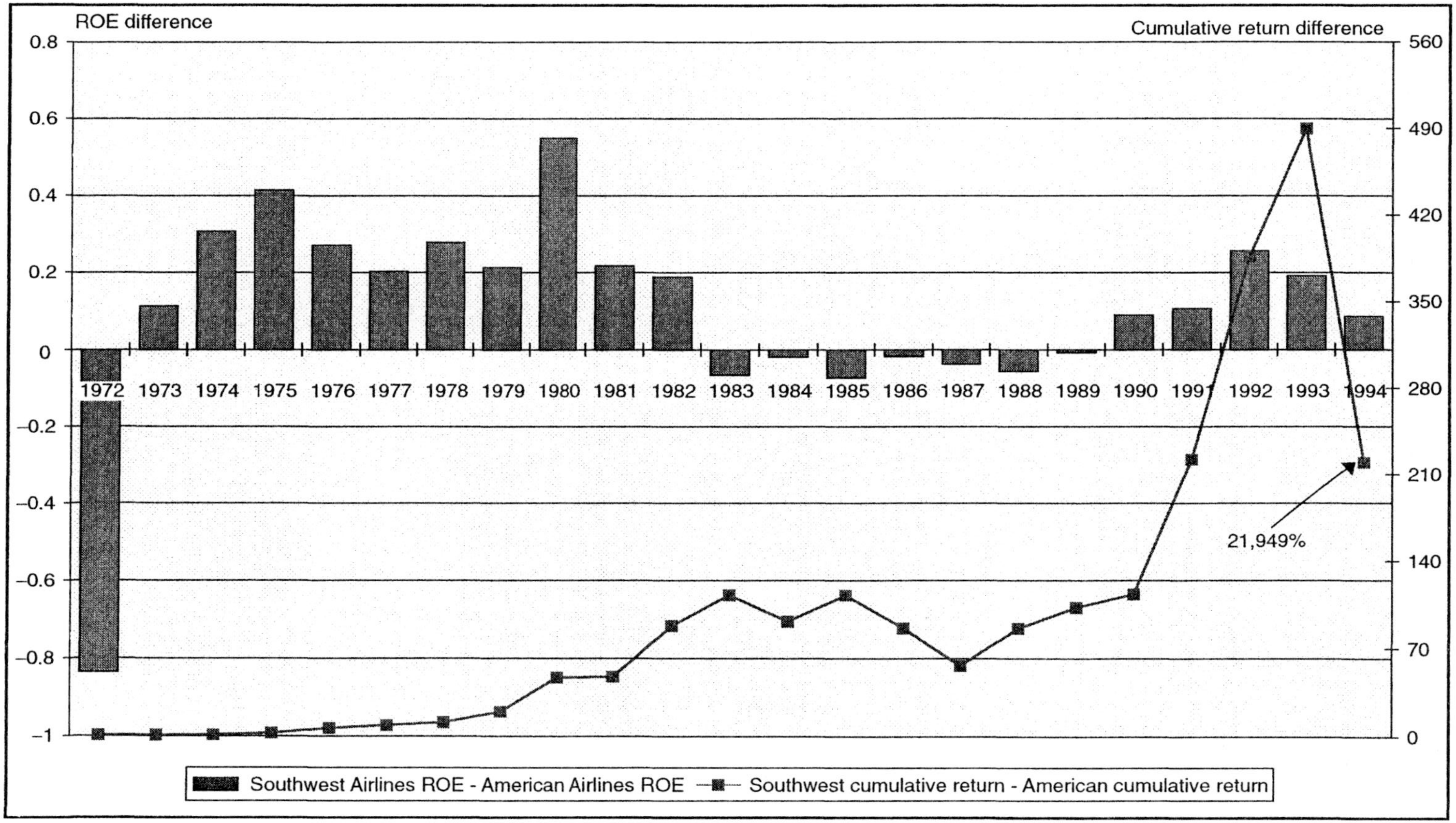

207

2. Develop the highest product/service/quality differentiated position within the industry, while maintaining an acceptable delivered cost structure.

Examples of the benefits of attaining the low-cost position in an industry or picking and exploiting specialized niches in the market abound. For instance, the low-cost route to creating positive NPV investments has been successfully pursued in, of all places, the American steel industry. The strategy, by companies such as Nucor and Chaparral Steel, has been to build minimills. Domestic minimills enjoy substantial cost advantages because unlike the major producers—which use a complicated, capital-intensive, time-consuming process to make steel from iron ore and coke—they make steel quickly from low-cost melted scrap with far less capital investment required. They also use nonunion labor and thereby avoid the costly restrictive work rules imposed by the United Steel Workers union.

Minimill wages are comparable to industry averages in the United States, but their labor cost per ton of steel is lower because they use people and machines more efficiently. For example, Chaparral Steel produces steel with a record low 1.6 hours of labor per ton. This compares with 4.9 hours per ton at integrated producers. By making more productive use of labor and capital, minimills like Nucor can now produce a ton of steel for almost one-third less than steel producers anywhere in the world, including South Korea and Taiwan.

Although their steelmaking capabilities are limited, in the product areas where minimills do compete—rod, bar, and small beams and shapes—big producers have all but surrendered. So, too, have foreign mills. In just two years, Nucor Corp.'s minimill in Plymouth, Utah, cut the Japanese share of California's rod and bar market from 50 to 10%. In all, the minimills have captured over 25% of the domestic steel market—against 18% for imports—by virtually taking over the production of small, lower quality goods. And now, with the introduction of newer technology, they can finally produce the premier products, such as high-quality sheet steel for the auto and appliance industries. This has been the major integrated steelmakers' largest, most profitable, and until now, untouchable, market.

Taking a different tack, Rubbermaid, a Wooster, Ohio, manufacturer of plastic and rubber goods, has specialized in simple, but perceptive innovations of everyday household items like dustpans, trash cans, and food storage containers. For example, its new mailbox is wide enough for magazines to lie flat, does not allow water to seep in when opened, does not rust, and puts up a yellow flag when mail has been delivered. And its new "litterless" lunchbox has capitalized on environmental concerns by including Rubbermaid food containers; so no disposable food wrappings are needed. Through product innovation (it churns out over 365 new products a year, more than one a day), and a reputation for good value and high quality, Rubbermaid manages to consistently grow sales by over 15% annually in seemingly mundane and saturated markets while generating an ROE in excess of 18%.

Some companies have combined elements of both strategies with spectacular success. Gillette has combined the lowest-cost manufacturing with highly differentiated products (e.g., its Sensor razor) and outstanding distribution to generate a return on equity in excess of 30% annually. Similarly, the cigarette division of Philip Morris (now Altria) has become the industry profit leader by combining the lowest-cost manufacturing facilities in the world with high-visibility brands, supported by high-cost promotion.

At the same time, it must be noted that gaining competitive advantage is not an end in itself; it must be tied to value creation. For many companies, the investment required to produce a sustainable competitive advantage may far exceed the gains. Yet managers persist in underestimating how efficient the forces of competition are at erasing the advantages their strategies are designed to create.

BOX 7.7

APPLICATION: PHILIP MORRIS LOSES A BUNDLE ON BEER

Philip Morris acquired Miller for about $200 million in 1970 and, by dint of clever market segmentation and heavy promotional spending, moved it from number 12 in the beer industry to number 2, behind Anheuser-Busch.[3] However, this marketing success cost Philip Morris's shareholders a bundle of money. Not only was its cash flow negative from 1970 to 1983, its return on investment was consistently below its weighted average cost of capital from 1970 through 1986. The net result was that Philip Morris's shareholders suffered a $250 million capital loss in 1970 dollars. In other words, the net present value in 1970 of Philip Morris's acquisition of Miller was –$250 million. For Philip Morris and its shareholders, the cost of gaining the differentiation advantage was clearly not worth it.

SIZE AND COMPETITIVE ADVANTAGE

The example of minimills successfully taking on the large steel producers makes another important point: Economies of scale brought about by size may well be oversold as the route to low-cost, profitable operations. Indeed, the newest technologies — flexible manufacturing, faster computers, and better telecommunications — have reduced the optimum size of many businesses, and will probably reduce it still more. The view that economies of scale are less important today will not surprise those who have seen General Motors with its legendary economies of scale, lose the lead in profitability not only to much smaller Japanese companies but to smaller U.S. companies like Ford and Chrysler as well. During the 1980s, GM invested over $80 billion to automate its U.S. factories. The net result of this investment was that by the end of the decade, GM was the high-cost producer in North America and had lost over 10% age points of market share, with each percentage point worth over $2 billion in annual revenue.

Exhibit 7.4, which shows sales and market value figures for General Motors and Microsoft, provides pointed evidence that the market does not value size, but rather profitability. GM's sales in 1992 were $135 billion, 48 times more than Microsoft's $2.8 billion in sales. Despite this huge difference in size, by the end of 1992, Microsoft had a market value in excess of GM's. Clearly, investors viewed Microsoft as better able to create sustainable competitive advantage in its industry and continue to capture the high returns that go along with that position.

---

[3]This example, and all the figures cited, are based on an analysis by Marakon Associates presented in McTaggart, J.M. "Business Strategy: Managing the ROI-Growth Tradeoff." *Commentary*, Fall 1986, pp. 12–20.

EXHIBIT 7.4 General Motors versus Microsoft: Sales Revenues and Market Values (1982–1994)

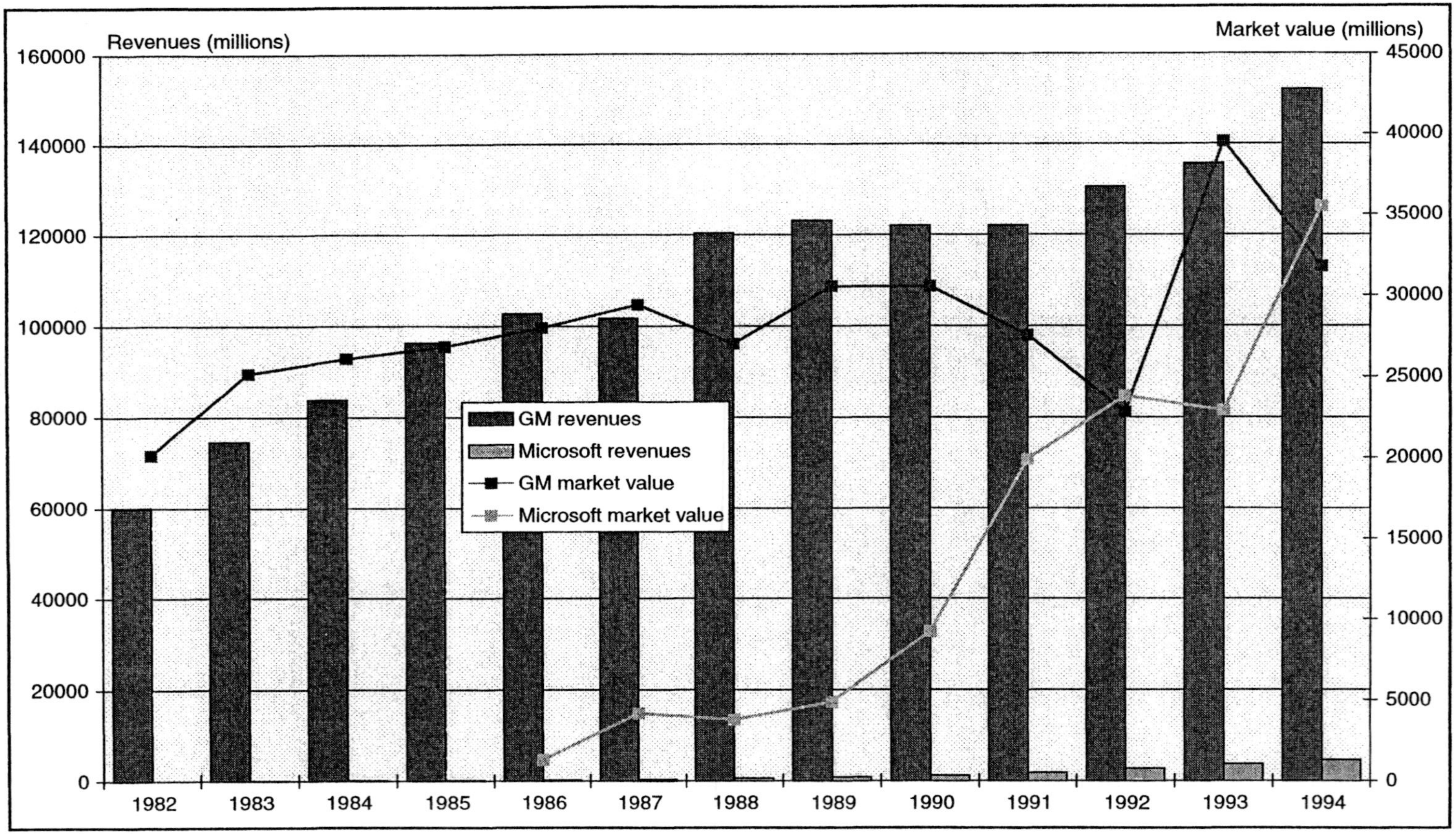

The apparent lack of correlation between size and economic profitability—in 1989 the biggest companies had the highest ROE in only 4 out of the 67 industries that appear in the *Business Week Top 1000*—is not to say that scale economies do not exist. For example, large production volumes of a variety of products may be necessary to justify the investment in new flexible manufacturing technologies. This evidence does, however, call into question the widespread belief that big is automatically better and cheaper.

Despite the view that size is necessary to compete against global rivals, the global marketplace requires attributes seldom associated with bigness: speed, agility, flexibility, and the ability to improvise and customize. In fact, the restructuring of corporate America during the 1980s indicates that many companies are too large—that bigness brings with it complexity, sluggish decision making, bureaucratic bloat, and inefficiency. In contrast, those companies that downsized and divested unrelated business activities were able to strip away superfluous management layers, reducing expenses, speeding decision making, and promoting initiative.

In such a world, the best strategy may be for firms to subject every part of their business to a test of "critical mass." Since each activity—R&D, purchasing, manufacturing, assembly, marketing, and distribution—has its own optimal size, promoting bigness across the board can be very inefficient. Rather, firms should focus on developing those areas where scale economies predominate. Lastly, companies that associate size with competitive advantage may well have it backwards: Firms become large because they are competitive, and not vice versa.

BOX 7.8

APPLICATION: COOPER TIRE ROLLS OVER ITS COMPETITION

The advantages of size have obviously been lost on Cooper Tire & Rubber of Findlay, Ohio. Cooper stands no better than ninth in its primary business—manufacturing tires—lagging far behind such behemoths as Goodyear, Michelin, and Bridgestone/Firestone. Yet Cooper is consistently the most profitable tire company in the world. In the words of its CEO, Ivan W. Gorr, "We have no designs on getting X share of the market. Our goal is return on equity and return on assets." In that Cooper has been successful, as is evident from Exhibit 7.5 on page 212, which compares ROEs from 1980 through 1994 for Cooper, Goodyear, and the S&P 500 companies. During this 15-year period, Cooper's ROE averaged 18.6% annually, in contrast to 11.7% for industry leader Goodyear, and 13.3% for the S&P 500.

Cooper prospers by intensely focusing on a single, but large, niche in its market. While the giants slug it out in the low-profit original-equipment market (OEM), Cooper concentrates on the replacement market, which is three times larger and growing faster. By foregoing OEM sales to automakers, Cooper can plan production more effectively—allowing it to operate its equipment at 100% capacity, versus the industry average of less than 80%. Cooper also saves on R&D since today's longer-lasting tires give it at least two years to see which of the new OEM tires are successful before producing its own version for the replacement market. Moreover, through an innovative incentive system that endows employees with significant stock ownership, Cooper has

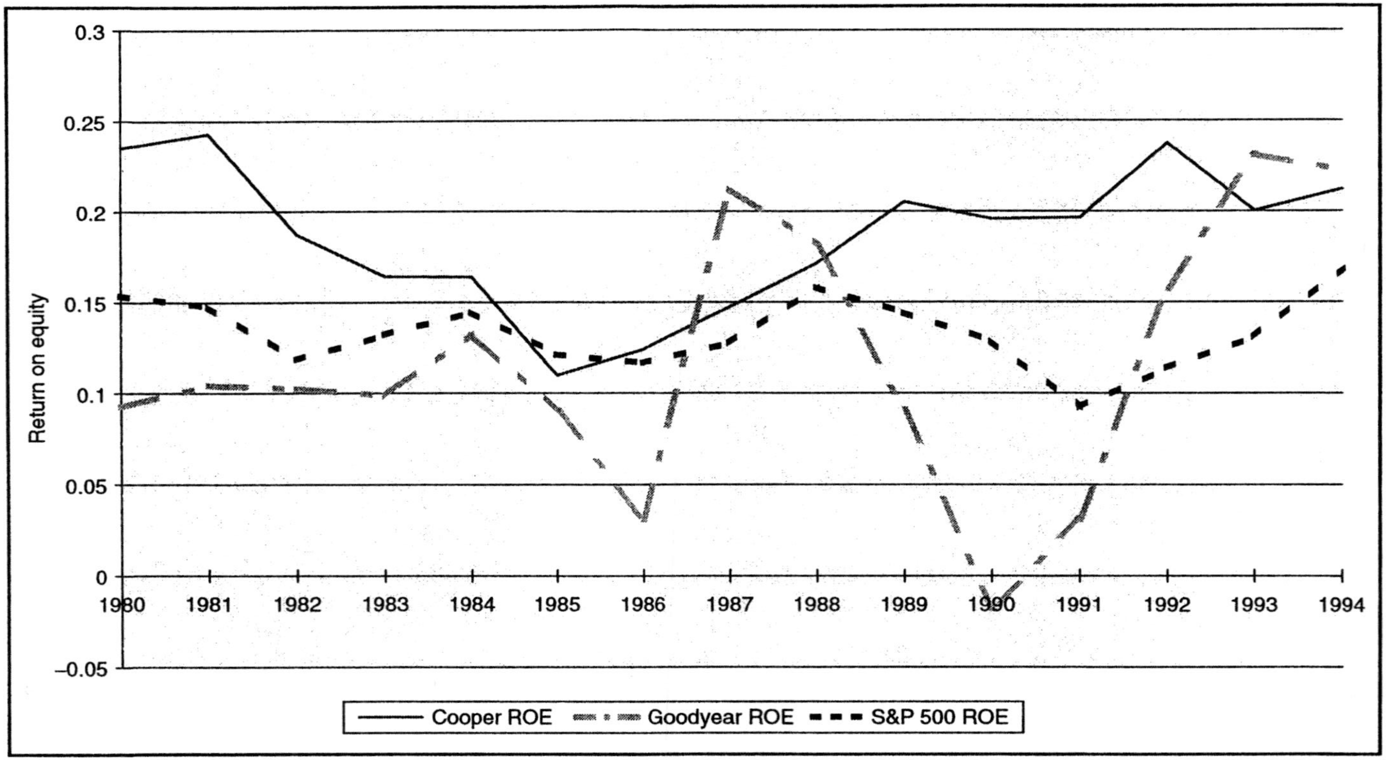

EXHIBIT 7.5 Return on Equity for Cooper Tire and Rubber, Goodyear, and the S&P 500: 1980-1994

significantly boosted its productivity year after year. Finally, rather than selling through its own retail outlets, like Goodyear and Bridgestone/Firestone, Cooper sells to independent dealers. These dealers appreciate Cooper because it does not compete with them and—as a low-cost producer—offers them very competitive prices. With Cooper's low prices yielding them the highest profit margins in the industry, dealers have a strong incentive to push Cooper tires rather than those of its competitors. Cooper thus saves on advertising, which allows it to cut costs and prices still further.

Cooper's high ROE has paid off for its shareholders. From 1980 through 1994, Cooper generated compound annual shareholder returns of 34.0% (in comparison to the S&P's 13.5% and Goodyear's 11.0%). Exhibit 7.6 on page 214 compares the returns and ROEs for Cooper relative to those of Goodyear.

THE DYNAMIC NATURE OF COMPETITIVE ADVANTAGE

Despite the inherent difficulties involved, we have seen that many companies do succeed in developing competitive advantages that create value. However, although a strong competitive edge in, say, technology or marketing skills may enable a firm to earn excess returns, these barriers to entry eventually erode, leaving the firm susceptible to increased competition. Existing firms are entering new industries, and there are growing numbers of firms from a greater variety of countries, leading to new, well-financed competitors that are able to meet the high marketing costs and enormous capital outlays necessary for entry. To stay on top, therefore, a firm's strategy must constantly evolve, seeking out new opportunities and fending off new competitors. The most successful companies work hard at finding process innovations—that drive down cost or investment—and product innovations—that enhance differentiation and provide the opportunity to either raise prices or gain market share at an equivalent price.

BOX 7.9

APPLICATION: CANON DOESN'T COPY XEROX

The tribulations of Xerox illustrate the problems associated with losing a competitive edge as well as the dynamic nature of competitive advantage.[4] For many years, Xerox was the king of the copier market, protected by its patents on xerography, with sales and earnings growing over 20% annually. The loss of its patent protection brought forth numerous, well-heeled competitors, including IBM, 3M, Kodak, and Canon. Its competitive strengths—a large direct sales force that constitutes a unique distribution channel, a national service network, a wide range of machines using custom-made components, and a large installed base of leased machines—defeated the attempts by IBM and Kodak to replicate its success by creating matching sales and service networks. In contrast, Canon sidestepped these barriers to entry by (1) creating low-end copiers that it sold through office-product dealers, thereby avoiding the need to set up a national sales force, (2) designing reliability and serviceability into its machines, so

---

[4]This example appears in Hamel, G., and Prahalad, C.K. "Strategic Intent." Harvard Business Review, May–June 1989, pp. 63–76.

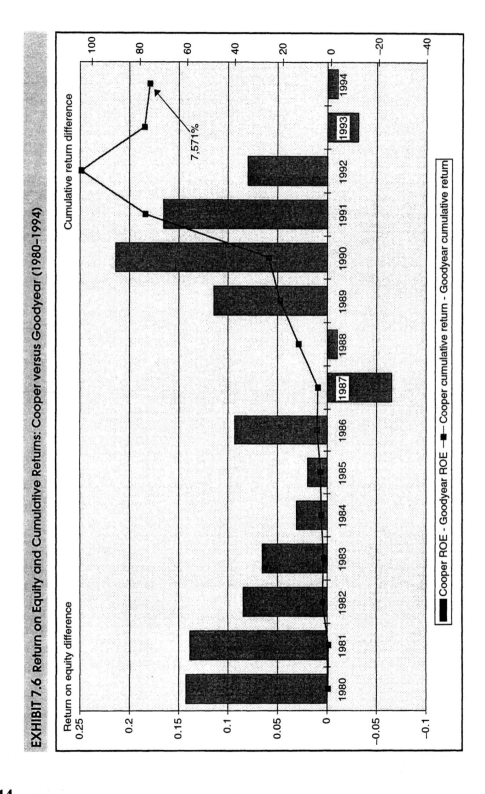

EXHIBIT 7.6 Return on Equity and Cumulative Returns: Cooper versus Goodyear (1980–1994)

users or nonspecialist dealers could service them, (3) using commodity components and standardizing its machines to lower costs and prices and boost sales volume, and (4) selling rather than leasing its copiers. By 1986, Canon and other Japanese firms had over 90% of copier sales worldwide. And having ceded the low end of the market to the Japanese, Xerox soon found those same competitors flooding into its stronghold sector in the middle and upper ends of the market.

Canon's strategy points out an important distinction between barriers to entry and barriers to imitation. Competitors like IBM that tried to imitate Xerox's strategy had to pay a matching entry fee. Through competitive innovation, Canon avoided these costs and, in fact, stymied Xerox's response. Xerox realized that the quicker it responded—by downsizing its copiers, improving reliability, and developing new distribution channels—the quicker it would erode the value of its leased machines and cannibalize its existing high-end product line and service revenues. Hence, what were barriers to entry for imitators became barriers to retaliation for Xerox.

Xerox's experience shows that even the most secure company is vulnerable to competitive innovation. And the absence of significant competitive pressure can increase that vulnerability by reinforcing the faith in accepted practice.

Common sense tells us that in order to achieve excess returns over time, the distinctive competitive advantage held by the firm must be difficult or costly to replicate. If it is easily replicated, it will not take long for actual or potential competitors to apply the same concept, process, or organizational structure to their operations. The competitive advantage of experience, for example, will evaporate unless a firm can keep the tangible benefits of its experience proprietary and force its competitors to go through the same learning process. Once a firm loses its competitive advantage, its profits will erode to a point that it no longer earns excess returns. For this reason, the firm's competitive advantage has to be constantly monitored and maintained so as to ensure the existence of an effective barrier to entry into the market. Should these barriers to entry break down, the firm must react quickly to either reconstruct them or build new ones.

One important source of extra profit is the quickness of management to recognize and use information about new, lower-cost production opportunities. The excess profits, however, are temporary, lasting only until competitors discover these opportunities for themselves. For example, purchasing the latest equipment will provide a temporary cost advantage, but this advantage will disappear as soon as competitors buy the equipment for their own plants. Only if the equipment is proprietary will the firm be able to maintain its cost advantage. Along the same line, many American electronics and textile firms shifted production facilities to Taiwan, Hong Kong, and other Asian locations to take advantage of lower labor costs. However, as more firms took advantage of this cost reduction opportunity, competition in the consumer electronics and textiles markets in the United States intensified, causing domestic prices to drop and excess profits to be dissipated. In fact, firms in competitive industries must continually seize new nonproprietary cost reduction opportunities, not to earn excess returns but to make normal profits and, thereby, survive.

Companies can also earn higher returns by being the first to market with a new product. Such products typically command a price premium based on their de facto monopoly status. At the same time, as product cycles shorten, speed to market is becoming an economic necessity, not a luxury. When core technologies become widely available and product life cycles are short, getting to market quickly is often the key determinant of economic profitability. Indeed, without those early new product price premiums, the company may not be able to recoup its development costs.

Similarly, market-oriented firms can earn excess returns by being among the first to recognize and exploit new marketing opportunities. For example, Crown Cork & Seal, the Philadelphia-based bottle-top maker and can maker, reacted to slowing growth in its U.S. business by expanding overseas. It set up subsidiaries in such countries as Thailand, Malaysia, Ethiopia, Zambia, Peru, Ecuador, Brazil, and Argentina, guessing correctly, as it turned out, that in those developing, urbanizing societies, people would eventually switch from homegrown produce to food in cans and drinks in bottles.

Profitable markets, however, have a habit of eventually attracting competition. Thus, to be assured of having a continued supply of value-creating investments on hand, the firm must institutionalize its strategy of cost reduction, product differentiation, and/or speed to market. Successful companies seem to do this by creating a corporate culture—a set of shared values, norms, and beliefs—that has as one of its elements an obsession with some facet of their performance in the marketplace. McDonald's has an obsessive concern for quality control, Dell for customer service, Southwest Airlines for asset utilization, 3M for innovation, and Canon for rapid commercialization of new technology. Forrest Mars set the tone for his company by going into a rage if he found one miswrapped candy bar leaving Mars. To maintain its low-cost position in the structural steel market, Chaparral Steel has teams of workers and foremen scour the world in search of the latest production machinery and methods.

Conversely, AT&T's manufacturing orientation—which focused on producing durable products with few options—was well suited to the regulated environment in which it operated throughout most of its existence. But such an inward-looking orientation has been a significant barrier to the company's ability to compete against the likes of IBM and other market-oriented, high-tech companies that react quickly to consumer demand.

The basic insight from all this is that sustained success in investing is not so much a matter of building new plants as of innovating the lower-cost production processes embodied in these plants, coming up with the right products for these plants to produce, adding the service and quality features that differentiate these products in the marketplace, and doing so quickly. In other words, it comes down to people and how they are organized and motivated. For example, 3M's ability to take advantage of economies of scope in R&D by leveraging a handful of proprietary technologies into a broad range of products largely derives from its well-organized system of technology transfer among its business units. Post-it notes, the most successful product in 3M's office supplies division, stems from a failed experiment in another unit.

Similarly, the most successful Japanese companies have focused on organizational forms that allow them to turn out better quality products faster and at lower cost. At companies like Honda and Canon, design engineers do not just hand off a product to manufacturing engineers with little regard for how easily it might be made or marketed; they develop it together, in teams that also include salespeople, financial analysts, customers, and suppliers so as to ensure that a high-quality, salable, and profitable product can be readily made at the lowest cost possible. More

American companies are now trying to emulate this "concurrent engineering" approach to product development.

The cost and difficulty of creating a corporate culture that adds value to capital investments — through product innovation, concurrent engineering, or high-quality service — is the ultimate barrier to entry; unlike the latest equipment, money alone cannot buy it. In the words of Maurice R. (Hank) Greenberg, president of American Insurance Group (AIG), a worldwide network of insurance companies that has enjoyed spectacular success by pioneering in territory relatively unpopulated by competitors:

> You can't imitate our global operation. It's just incapable of being reproduced. Domestically, we have some imitators for pieces of our business, but not the entire business. And in any event, you can only imitate what we've done. You can't imitate what we're thinking. You can't copy what we're going to do tomorrow.[5]

BOX 7.10

APPLICATION: NO TURBULENCE AT SOUTHWEST AIRLINES

A key factor in keeping costs low and asset utilization high at Southwest Airlines is the productivity of its employees. Although Southwest's workforce is 90% unionized, it owns 11% of the company — the highest percentage by far of any major airline. Because employees know they have a large stake in the efficient operation of the company, Southwest and its unions are able to write labor contracts devoid of overly restrictive language. Most of the time, Southwest uses one gate agent, not the standard three, to board an aircraft — and the employees may then work as flight attendants. Typically, ground crews of six, half the industry average, service the plane. And to speed up turnaround time, flight attendants and even pilots pick up the trash left behind on planes. At the same time, satisfied employees treat customers right, leading to extraordinary customer loyalty.

7.4 Corporate Strategy and Foreign Investment

Most of the firms we have examined are multinational corporations (MNCs) with worldwide operations. For many of these firms, becoming multinational was the end result of an apparently haphazard process of overseas expansion. But as international operations become a more important source of profit and as domestic and foreign competitors become more aggressive, it is apparent that domestic survival for many firms is increasingly dependent on their success overseas. To ensure this success, multinationals must develop global strategies that will enable them to maintain their competitive edge both at home and abroad.

---

[5]Robertson, W. "Nobody Top A.I.G. in Intricacy — Or Daring." *Fortune*, May 22, 1978.

OVERSEAS EXPANSION AND SURVIVAL

It is evident that if one's competitors gain access to lower-cost sources of production abroad, following them overseas may be a prerequisite for domestic survival. One strategy that is often followed by firms for which cost is the key consideration, like Chaparral Steel, is to develop a global scanning capability to seek out lower-cost production sites or production technologies worldwide. Similarly, companies supplying goods and services to multinationals have little choice but to follow their customers overseas. Otherwise, they risk the loss of not only their foreign but also their domestic business to a multinational competitor.

Economies of Scale

A somewhat less obvious factor motivating foreign investment is the effect of economies of scale. We have already seen that in a competitive market, prices will be forced close to marginal costs of production. Hence, firms in industries characterized by high fixed costs relative to variable costs must engage in volume selling just to break even. A firm that follows a domestic-only strategy may be unable to price competitively in the home market because it can no longer take full advantage of economies of scale and scope in R&D, production, brand awareness, and distribution.

A new term has arisen to describe the size necessary in certain industries to compete effectively in the global marketplace: *world-scale*. These large volumes may be forthcoming only if the firms expand overseas. For example, companies manufacturing products such as mainframe computers that require huge R&D expenditures often need a larger customer base than that provided by even a market as large as the United States to recapture their investment in knowledge. Similarly, firms in capital-intensive industries with significant economies of scale in production may also be forced to sell overseas to spread their overhead over a higher volume of sales.

To take an extreme case, L.M. Ericsson, the highly successful Swedish manufacturer of telecommunications equipment, is forced to think internationally when designing new products because its domestic market is too small to absorb the enormous R&D expenditures involved and to reap the full benefit of production scale economies. Thus, when Ericsson developed its revolutionary AXE digital switching system, it geared its design to achieve global market penetration.

As we saw in Section 7.2, investment in world-scale facilities or new technology may be unprofitable without supporting investments in global brand awareness and a worldwide distribution system. In addition, many firms have found that a local market presence is necessary in order to continue selling overseas. For example, a local presence has helped Data General adapt the design of its U.S. computers and software to the Japanese market, giving the company a competitive edge over other U.S. companies selling computers in Japan. Data General has also adopted some Japanese manufacturing techniques and quality control procedures that will improve its competitive position worldwide.

Knowledge Seeking

Some firms enter foreign markets for the purpose of gaining information and experience that is expected to prove useful elsewhere. For instance, Beecham, an English firm (now SmithKline Beecham), deliberately set out to learn from its U.S. operations how to be more competitive, first in the area of consumer products and, later, in pharmaceuticals. This knowledge proved highly valuable in competing with American and other firms in its European markets. Similarly, in late 1992, the South Korean conglomerate Hyundai moved its PC division to the United States in order to keep up with the rapidly evolving personal computer market, whose direction was set by the U.S. market. The flow of ideas is not all one way, however. As Americans have demanded better-built, better-handling, and more fuel-efficient small cars, Ford of Europe has become an important source of design and engineering ideas and management talent for its U.S. parent, including the hugely successful Taurus.

In industries characterized by rapid product innovation and technical break-throughs by foreign competitors, it is imperative to constantly track overseas developments. Japanese firms excel here, systematically and effectively collecting information on foreign innovation and disseminating it within their own research and development, marketing, and production groups. The analysis of new foreign products as soon as they reach the market is an especially long-lived Japanese technique. One of the jobs of Japanese researchers is to tear down a new foreign product and analyze how it works, as a base on which to develop a product of their own that will outperform the original. In a bit of a switch, as pointed out, Data General's Japanese operation is giving the company a close look at Japanese technology, enabling it to quickly pick up and transfer back to the United States new information on Japanese innovations in the areas of computer design and manufacturing.

Illustration: U.S. Chipmakers Produce in Japan. Many U.S. chipmakers have set up production facilities in Japan. One reason is that the chipmakers have discovered they cannot expect to increase Japanese sales from halfway around the world. It can take weeks for a company without testing facilities in Japan to respond to customer complaints. A customer must send a faulty chip back to the maker for analysis. That can take up to three weeks if the maker's facilities are in the United States. In the meantime, the customer will have to shut down its assembly line, or part of it. With testing facilities in Japan, however, the wait can be cut to a few days.

However, a testing operation alone would be inefficient; testing machines cost millions of dollars. Because an assembly plant needs the testing machines, a company usually moves in an entire assembly operation. Having the testing and assembly operations also reassures procurement officials about quality: They can touch, feel, and see tangible evidence of the company's commitment to service the market.

Tough competition in a foreign market is a valuable experience in itself. For many industries, a competitive home marketplace has proved to be as much of a competitive advantage as cheap raw materials or technical talent. Fierce domestic competition is one reason the U.S. telecommunications industry has not lost its lead in technology, R&D, design, software, quality, and cost. Japanese and European firms are at a disadvantage in this business because they do not have enough competition in their home markets. U.S. companies have been able to engineer a great leap forward because they saw firsthand what the competition could do. Thus, for telecommunications firms like Germany's Siemens, Japan's NEC, and France's Alcatel, a position in the U.S. market has become mandatory.

DESIGNING A GLOBAL EXPANSION STRATEGY

The ability to pursue systematically policies and investments congruent with world-wide survival and growth depends on four interrelated elements:

1. The first element, and the key to the development of a successful global strategy, is to understand and then capitalize on those factors that have led to success in the past. In order for domestic firms to become global competitors, therefore, the sources of their domestic advantage must be transferable abroad. A competitive advantage predicated on government regulation, like import restrictions, clearly does not fit in this category.

2. Second, this global approach to investment planning necessitates a systematic evaluation of individual entry strategies in foreign markets, a comparison of the alternatives, and the selection of the optimal mode of entry.

3. The third important element is a continual audit of the effectiveness of current entry modes. As knowledge about a foreign market increases, for example, or sales potential grows, the optimal market penetration strategy will likely change.

4. Fourth, top management must be committed to becoming or staying a multinational corporation. For example, Westinghouse demonstrated its commitment to international business by creating the position of president-international and endowing its occupant with a seat on the company's powerful management committee.

A truly globally oriented firm—one that asks, "Where in the world should we develop, produce, and sell our products and services?"—also requires an intelligence system capable of systematically scanning the world and understanding it, along with people who are experienced in international business and know how to use the information generated by the system.

Transfer of Competitive Advantages Abroad

Assuming that a firm does have the necessary resources to be successful internationally, it must carefully plan for the transfer of these resources overseas. For example, it must consider how it can best utilize its marketing expertise, innovative technology, or production skills to penetrate a specific foreign market. When a particular strategy calls for resources the firm lacks, like an overseas distribution network, management must first decide how and at what cost these resources can be acquired. It must then decide whether to acquire the resources (and how) or change its strategy.

7.5 Summary and Conclusions

We saw in this chapter that rates of return in competitive industries are driven down to their required returns. Excess profits quickly attract new entrants to the market, lowering returns until actual and required returns are again equal. Thus, the run-of-the-mill firm operating in a highly competitive market will be unable consistently to find positive net present value investments—projects that earn returns in excess of their required returns. The key to generating a continual flow of positive NPV projects, therefore, is to erect and maintain barriers to entry against competitors. This means either building defenses against potential competitors or finding positions in the industry where competition is the weakest.

The firm basically has two strategic options in its quest for competitive advantage: It can seek lower costs than its competitors, or it can differentiate its product in a number of ways, including high advertising expenditures, product innovation, high product quality, and first-rate service.

Each of these options necessitates a number of specific investment decisions—construction of efficient-scale facilities and vigorous pursuit of cost reduction through volume expansion and accumulated experience, in the case of cost leadership. If product differentiation is the main goal, the focus is on advertising, R&D, quality control, customer-service facilities, distribution networks, and the like. The more an investment widens a firm's competitive advantage and reduces the chances of successful replication by competitors, the greater will be the likelihood that the investment will be successful. Regardless of the strategy pursued, the company must aggressively monitor and motivate the people within its organization to make the strategy work.

Despite our understanding of the subject matter, it is difficult to offer a set of rules to follow in developing profitable investment strategies. Were it possible to do so, competitors would follow them and dissipate any excess returns. One must be creative and quick to recognize new opportunities. However, without dictating what should be done in every specific circumstance, the chapter points out some basic lessons we have learned from economic theory and the experiences of successful firms. These basic lessons include the following:

1. Invest in projects that take advantage of your competitive edge. The corollary is to stick to doing one or two things and doing them well; do not get involved in businesses with which you are unfamiliar.
2. Invest in developing, maintaining, and enhancing your competitive advantages. The corollary is that investments that are easily replicated, such as those in pure research and new plant and equipment, are unlikely by themselves to provide sustainable competitive advantage.
3. Develop a global scanning capability. Do not be blindsided by new competitors or lower-cost production techniques or locations.
4. Pick market niches where there is little competition. Be prepared to abandon markets where competitors are catching up and to apply your competitive advantages to new products or markets.

REFERENCES

Hall, W. K. "Survival Strategies in a Hostile Environment." *Harvard Business Review*, September–October 1980, pp. 75–85.

Porter, M. E. "How Competitive Forces Shape Strategy." *Harvard Business Review*, March–April 1979, pp. 137–145.

Porter, M.E. *Competitive Strategy.* -Macmillan: New York, 1980.

Shapiro, A.C. "Corporate Strategy and the Capital Budgeting Decision." *Midland Corporate Finance Journal*, Spring 1985, pp. 22–36.

Shapiro, A.C. *Multinational Financial Management.* 7th ed. John Wiley & Sons: 2003.

SAMPLE PROBLEMS

1. Historically, auto companies faced high equipment and tooling costs to develop new models. In addition, they had to shut down the production line for one to two weeks to switch over from one model to another. In order to be profitable, therefore, companies had to sell millions of copies of the same model and have long production runs, with the excess going into inventory. But consumers are no longer purchasing millions of copies of the same model; instead, they are looking for a wide — and unpredictable — variety of cars, trucks, and vans — and looking for bargains besides. In such a world, what business strategy might make sense for car companies and what investments would be consistent with this strategy?
Answer: The basic business strategy is for car companies to focus on being able to design, manufacture, and market efficiently. They must also be able to make money on short production runs. This takes investment in automated design, good market research, flexible manufacturing, and the development of teams to link these various functions together. Flexible assembly lines can switch from one vehicle to another without stopping — a truck, a car, and then another truck can follow each other down the line, with computer-directed tools adapting to the model before them. By being able to respond so quickly to shifts in demand, companies can produce the models people want when they want them. This lowers costs by reducing inventories and ending the need to discount products that are not selling but that had to be produced in large volumes because of the high production switching costs.

2. The chapter mentions that Hyundai shifted its PC business to the United States.

   a. What advantages might Hyundai realize from servicing the U.S. market locally as opposed to operating out of South Korea?
   Answer: With their low labor costs and growing mass-production skills, Hyundai and other Asian producers stamped out low-priced clones for sale in the U.S. market. But that strategy has ended its useful life because the U.S. market has been changing so fast that new products go out of date quickly, calling for on-the-spot decisions. With R&D, design, factories, and warehouses an ocean away from the U.S. market, Asian companies found it increasingly hard to meet the changing demands of U.S. consumers. In addition, individual PC buyers have grown more and more finicky, wanting their machines built with specific choices of microprocessors, disk drives, and other components. Asian factories, set up for high-volume products of a few types of machines, found it increasingly difficult to keep up with these configuration demands. They were at a further disadvantage because they must spend weeks or months shipping products to market. Hyundai concluded that it could best compete by Americanizing as much as possible.

   b. What competitive advantages is Hyundai likely to bring to the U.S. market?
   The likely answer is none. Historically, Hyundai's competitive advantage has been low-cost South Korean labor. But given that Hyundai is now cut off from its low-cost production base in South Korea and is a multifaceted conglomerate, it is doubtful that it will be able to compete effectively against U.S. firms that are devoted solely to PC research, production, marketing, and distribution.

QUESTIONS

1. One highly recommended approach to picking stocks is to select companies that have dominant market shares or, better yet, monopolies in their businesses. Do you think this approach to picking stocks is likely to be successful? Why?

2. With the advent of cable television, various new stations are entering into the broadcasting market. Many are attempting to serve a specialized segment of viewers: the all-movie channel, all-sports, or all-music. Assume that you acquired sufficient financial backing to enter this market. What segment do you feel is not yet being served? In what way could you differentiate your product to add value—value for which the customer would be willing to pay a price?

3. One of the competitive advantages mentioned in the chapter is the experience of a firm's managers. GM is trying to diversify away from producing only automobiles and has been acquiring a financial interest in firms in other product areas. To what other lines of business might GM's managerial experience be applicable? Do you think GM is likely to be successful in a diversification strategy? Why?

4. Describe the investments made by the following companies mentioned in the chapter that enabled them to pursue their business strategies: Dell Computer, Nalco Chemical, Canon, Southwest Airlines.

5. One of the more successful strategies in retailing has been the development of "designer label" lines of apparel. In what ways does a designer suit differ from its equivalent purchased from a discount chain? Is this the result of advertising, quality, or some other factors?

6. Each community has some monopoly suppliers. Common instances are the regulated monopolies: utilities, cable TV systems, local radio and TV stations. Other companies are monopolies through other means: fast-food franchises, newspapers, and car dealerships. Which monopolies in your community are profitable? Why?

7. Suppose a capital goods manufacturer brings out a new, more efficient machine.
   a. If the manufacturer holds a patent on this machine, who is likely to benefit the most from it? Explain.
   b. Who will benefit most from this machine if the technology underlying the machine is not proprietary? Explain.
   c. What are some of the things the manufacturer can do to earn higher returns from this machine even without patent protection?

8. How sustainable is a competitive advantage based on technology? On low-cost labor? On economies of scale?

9. Goodyear Tire and Rubber Company, the world's number 1 tire producer, is competing in a global tire industry. To maintain its leadership, Goodyear has invested over $1 billion to build the most automated tire-making facilities in the world and is aggressively expanding its chain of wholly owned tire stores to maintain its position as the largest retailer of tires in the United States. It has also invested heavily in research and development to produce tires that are recognized as being at the cutting edge of world-class performance. On the basis of product innovation and high advertising expenditures, Goodyear dominates the high-performance segment of the tire market; it has captured nearly 90% of the market for high-performance tires sold as original equipment on American cars and is well represented on sporty imports. Geography has given Goodyear and other American tire manufacturers a giant assist in the U.S. market. Heavy and bulky, tires are expensive to ship internationally.

   a. What barriers to entry has Goodyear created or taken advantage of?
   b. Goodyear has production facilities throughout the world. What competitive advantages might global production provide Goodyear?
   c. How do tire-manufacturing facilities in Japan fit in with Goodyear's strategy to create shareholder value?
   d. In early 1988, Japan's Bridgestone Corp. acquired Firestone Tire & Rubber Co. What possible motives might Bridgestone have had for this acquisition?

e. How will Bridgestone's acquisition of Firestone affect Goodyear? How might Goodyear respond to this move by Bridgestone?

10. Borden, already the world's largest dairy company, has made over 40 acquisitions in recent years to become the world's largest producer of pasta and the second-largest snack seller in the United States. Its basic strategy is to string together a network of regional pasta, dairy, and snack food companies to try to take advantage of various operating and marketing efficiencies.

   a. What operating and marketing efficiencies might Borden be able to take advantage of through its acquisition strategy?
   b. What valuable options does Borden's acquisition strategy create?
   c. Borden's brand of processed lemon juice, ReaLemon, was the first in the market. What advantages might Borden be able to realize by being the pioneer in this business?

11. Premier Industrial Corporation is a Cleveland-based distributor of extremely humdrum products—nuts and bolts, batteries, circuit breakers, and lubricating oil. When other distributors peddle the same products, they operate on thin margins and aspire to get rich on volume. Hence, they tend to carry only the fast-moving items. Premier, by contrast, carries just about every type of component and delivers small orders in an incredibly short time. Most of its profits come from the small maintenance and repair accounts that competitors regard as a nuisance. The average order size is $100 (competitor orders average $400), and Premier gets referrals from other distributors who do not want to be bothered by small orders. Premier's pre-tax margins run to around 18%, in contrast with competitor margins of about 1 to 2%.

   a. What is Premier's strategy for creating value?
   b. Why does Premier have such high profit margins for its industry?

12. For each of the following companies, assess the sustainability of its competitive advantage.

   a. Analog Devices, which develops specialized applications for analog semiconductors, has invested countercyclically to cash in on business upturns. The results: 80% faster growth and 50% higher profitability than the rest of the semiconductor industry.
   b. Nike's leadership in athletic shoes is built on cheap Far Eastern labor and massive investments in product development and marketing. Over the five years between 1981 and 1986, Nike averaged three times the profitability and four times the growth of the rest of the U.S. shoe industry.
   c. Lincoln Electric has been the leader in the electric welding industry ever since John Lincoln invented the portable arc welder in 1895. Since then, technological change has been incremental. Lincoln has integrated backward, customizing its production machinery and holding annual worker turnover to under 3%. It has grown more rapidly than its competitors, partly by sharing its cost reductions with customers.
   d. DuPont is a leading producer of titanium dioxide, largely thanks to a production process based on low-cost feedstock that gives it a 20% cost advantage over competitors' processes. Mastering the cheaper feedstock technology can be accomplished only by investing $50 million to $100 million and several years of testing time in an efficiently scaled plant.
   e. Tandem Computer pioneered fault-tolerant computers for processing transactions. Although the cost of adding additional processing capability once a system is up and running is relatively low, customers must first make sizable and irrecoverable system-specific up-front investments in software and training.

13. For the past two decades, Cincinnati Milacron, the largest U.S. machine tool manufacturer, has led the U.S. machine tool industry in both R&D and the size of its sales and service network,

activities that account for about a third of the value added by the industry. In the 1980s it moved into robotics in a big way. How does this move fit into its strategy for creating value?

14. Super-Valu Stores, Inc., is the nation's largest and most efficient grocery wholesaler and distributor. For example, Super-Valu has cut costs by raising storage density in its warehouses while minimizing the time and travel distance it takes workers to find and retrieve the goods. Using as many as 1,400 separate measurements, the company has been collecting data for over 10 years on how both workers and wares move throughout the system. Industrial engineers have measured the capacity of each rack layout in each warehouse down to the square inch. A computer assigns "slot positions" to the incoming merchandise and tells the workers the order in which to pick cases for delivery. The data are then fed into a simulation program that analyzes and optimizes the productivity and storage capacity of various warehouse arrangements, given the merchandise to be stored.

    a. What is Super-Valu's strategy for creating value?
    b. How sustainable is Super-Valu's competitive advantage?

15. Avis has invested a large amount of money to spread the message that "We're Number Two and trying harder." Number One in the rental car industry, of course, is Hertz. How did Avis's investment in this advertising message fit in with its strategy for creating value? (*Hint:* Against whom is Avis *really* competing for market share?)

PROBLEMS

1. Suppose the United States imposes a $10 per barrel tariff on imported refined oil products.

    a. What is the short-run profit outlook for American refineries? What is the long-term profit outlook?
    b. Suppose that eight years after imposing this tariff, the United States revokes it. What is likely to happen to the refining industry at that time?

2. Wal-Mart, the discount merchandiser, began by putting large stores in small Sunbelt towns that its competitors had neglected. The company then wrapped its stores in concentric rings around regional distribution centers.

    a. What was Wal-Mart's original strategy for creating value?
    b. How sustainable is the company's competitive advantage?
    c. How is growth in its markets likely to affect Wal-Mart's strategy?
    d. More recently, Wal-Mart has invested huge sums of money in a telecommunications system that links its stores together and accumulates information instantaneously on store-by-store sales of each item in stock. How might this investment create a competitive advantage for Wal-Mart?

3. Suppose General Motors's worldwide profit breakdown is 85% in the United States, 3% in Japan, and 12% in the rest of the world. Its principal Japanese competitors earn 40% of their profits in Japan, 25% in the United States, and 35% in the rest of the world. Suppose further, that through diligent attention to productivity and substitution of enormous quantities of capital for labor (e.g., Project Saturn), GM manages to get its automobile production costs down to the level of the Japanese.

    a. Who is likely to have the global competitive advantage? Consider, for example, GM's ability to respond to a Japanese attempt to gain U.S. market share through a sharp price cut.
    b. What are the possible competitive responses of GM to the Japanese challenge?
    c. How would you recommend that GM deal with the Japanese competition?

4. More and more Japanese companies are moving in on what once was an exclusive U.S. preserve: making and selling the complex equipment that makes semiconductors. World sales are between $3 billion and $5 billion annually. The U.S. equipment makers already have taken a beating in Japan. Their share of the Japanese market, serviced by exports, has slumped to 30% in 1988 from a dominant 70% in the late 1970s. Because sales in Japan are expanding as rapidly as 50% a year, Japanese concerns have barely begun attacking the U.S. market. But U.S. experts consider it only a matter of time.

   a. What are the possible competitive responses of U.S. firms?
   b. Which one(s) would you recommend to the head of a U.S. firm? Why?

5. Airbus Industrie, the European consortium of aircraft manufacturers, buys jet engines from U.S. companies. According to a recent story in the *Wall Street Journal*, "as a result of the weaker dollar, the cost of a major component (jet engines) is declining for Boeing's biggest competitor." The implication is that the lower price of engines for Airbus gives it a competitive advantage over Boeing. Assess the validity of this statement. Will Airbus now be more competitive relative to Boeing?

6. Nordson Co. of Amherst, Ohio, a maker of painting and glue equipment, exports nearly half its output. Customers value its reliability as a supplier. Because of an especially sharp run-up in the value of the dollar against the French franc, Nordson is reconsidering its decision to continue supplying the French market. What factors are relevant to reaching a decision?

7. Tandem Computer, a U.S. maker of fault-tolerant computers, is thinking of shifting virtually all the labor-intensive portion of its production to Mexico. What risks is Tandem likely to face if it goes ahead with this move?

8. Germany's $28 billion electronics giant, Siemens AG, sells medical and telecommunications equipment, power plants, automotive products, and computers. Siemens has been operating in the United States since 1952, but its U.S. revenues account for only about 10% of world-wide revenues. It intends to expand further in the U.S. market.

   a. According to the head of its U.S. operation, "The United States is a real testing ground. If you make it here, you establish your credentials for the rest of the world." What does this statement mean? How would you measure the benefits flowing from this rationale for investing in the United States?
   b. What other advantages might Siemens realize from a larger American presence?

9. Kao Corporation is a highly innovative and efficient Japanese company that has managed to take on and beat Proctor & Gamble in Japan. Two of Kao's revolutionary innovations include disposable diapers with greatly enhanced absorption capabilities and concentrated laundry detergent. However, Kao has had difficulty in establishing the kind of market-sensitive foreign subsidiaries that P&G has built.

   a. What competitive advantages might P&G derive from its global network of market-sensitive subsidiaries?
   b. What competitive disadvantages does Kao face if it is unable to replicate P&G's global network of subsidiaries?

10. Jim Toreson, chairman and CEO of Xebec Corporation, a Sunnyvale, California, manufacturer of disk-drive controllers, is trying to decide whether to switch to offshore production. Given Xebec's well-developed engineering and marketing capabilities, Toreson could use offshore manufacturing to ramp up production, taking full advantage of both low-wage labor and a grab bag of tax holidays, low-interest loans, and other government largess. Most of his competitors seemed to be doing it: The faster he followed suit, the better off Xebec would be, according to the conventional discounted cash flow analysis, which showed that

switching production offshore was clearly a positive NPV investment. However, Toreson is concerned that such a move would entail the loss of certain intangible strategic benefits associated with domestic production.

a. What might be some strategic benefits of domestic manufacturing for Xebec? Consider the fact that all its customers are American firms and that manufacturing technology—particularly automation skills—is the key to survival in this business.

b. What analytic framework can be used to factor these intangible strategic benefits of domestic manufacturing (which are intangible *costs* of offshore production) into the factory location decision?

c. How would the possibility of radical shifts in manufacturing technology affect the production location decision?

d. Xebec is considering producing more sophisticated drives, which require substantial customization. How does this possibility affect its production decision?

e. An alternative sourcing option is to shut down all domestic production and contract to have Xebec's products built for it by a foreign supplier in a country like Japan. What might be some potential advantages and disadvantages of foreign contracting vis-à-vis manufacturing in a wholly owned foreign subsidiary?

Glossary

Accelerated Depreciation A depreciation method that allows a firm to write off a greater percentage of an investment in the early years.

Accounting Rate of Return/Average Rate of Return/Average Return on Book Value The ratio of average after-tax profit to average book investment—the initial investment less accumulated depreciation; it is an average return on investment (ROI).

Accounts Receivable The amounts owed to a company by its customers.

Acquisition The purchase of one firm by another.

Added Investment in Working Capital The difference between the additional working capital assets and additional noninterest-bearing working capital liabilities, such as accounts payable and taxes payable (also known as spontaneously generated liabilities) associated with the investment.

Adjusted Present Value The Net Present Value (NPV) of a project if financed solely by equity plus the Present Value (PV) of any financing benefits (the additional effects of debt).

All-Equity Rate The required rate of return derived from the asset beta.

Annuity A series of equal cash payments per period for a specified number of periods.

Arbitrage Profiting from differences in price when assets are traded in two or more markets by buying in the market with the low price and selling in the market with the high price.

Asset A property that someone owns and whose economic value is determined by its ability to generate future cash flows.

Balance Sheet A financial statement that presents the firms assets, liabilities, and equity at a specific point in time.

Bankruptcy Formal legal proceedings in which a company in financial difficulty is placed under the protection of the court. The court allows a company to keep operating until a plan is developed to pay off the creditors.

Bankruptcy Costs The direct legal, accounting, and administrative costs associated with bankruptcy plus the losses associated with the sale of assets at "fire sale" prices.

Base Case Worldwide corporate cash flows without the investment, which, when subtracted from postinvestment corporate cash flows, can reveal a project's incremental cash flows.

Basis Point One-hundredth of a percentage point of interest.

Benefit-Cost Ratio A ratio attempting to identify the relationship between the cost and benefits of a proposed project.

Beta Measure of the sensitivity of an asset's return to movements in the market as a whole.

Bond Long-term debt security that promises to pay its owner periodic interest until the bond matures, at which time the bondholder will also receive a specified principal sum.

Brand-Name Capital Reputation built up through time by performance—giving customers more than they expect—or through expensive advertising that creates a quality image in the minds of customers.

Business Risk The variability of a firm's operating earnings due to the inherent risks of the markets in which it serves.

Cannibalization A new product taking sales away from the firm's existing products.

Capital Budgeting The process of determining whether projects such as building a new plant or investing in a long-term venture are worthwhile.

Capital Budgeting Decision The allocation of funds among alternative investment opportunities, crucial to corporate success.

Capital Expenditure Funds used by a company to acquire or upgrade physical assets such as property, industrial buildings, or equipment.

Capital Gain The appreciation in the value of an asset.

Capital Market The market where long-term securities are bought and sold.

Capital Rationing When the size of a firm's capital budget is constrained, either by self-imposition or external factors.

Capital Structure The combination of debt and equity used by a company to finance the purchase of its assets.

Capital Rationing A situation in which a firm's capital budget is insufficient to fund all acceptable projects.

Cash Flow Amount of money changing hands on a transaction or during a certain time period.

Certainty Equivalent That certain amount of money that the decision maker would just be willing to accept in lieu of the risky amount.

Commodity An undifferentiated product sold exclusively on the basis of price.

Common Stock A security that represents the ownership interest in a company. Holders of common stock are entitled to a pro rata share of income and assets in liquidation after creditor needs have been accommodated.

Competitive Industry An industry characterized by costless entry and exit, undifferentiated products or services, and increasing marginal costs of production.

Conglomerate Company consisting of units in unrelated businesses.

Constant Dividend Growth Model A model of common stock valuation that assumes that a firm's dividends will grow at a constant rate into the indefinite future.

Corporate Culture Set of values, norms, and beliefs held by the employees of a company.

Corporation A form of business organization which is a legal being, separate and apart from its owners.

Cost of Capital Also known as required return or the discount rate used in calculating an investment's NPV, it is the minimum acceptable rate of return on projects of similar risk.

Cost of Debt Capital The after-tax cost of raising new debt capital.

Cost of Preferred Stock The required rate of return for preferred stockholders.

Cost Reduction Project A project whose primary benefits are in the form of reducing a firm's operating costs.

Cost-of-Capital Minimum acceptable rate of return on an investment as determined by investors.

Coupon The periodic interest paid on a bond. Equals the face value of the bond times the coupon interest rate.

Covariance A measure of the degree to which returns on two risky assets move in tandem. A positive covariance means that asset returns move together. A negative covariance means returns vary inversely.

Covenants The provisions in a loan agreement that defines what the borrower must do (affirmative covenants) and the restrictions on a borrower's behavior (negative covenants).

Current Assets Assets that are expected to be converted into cash within a year.

Current Liabilities Debts that mature within one year.

DCF See Discounted Cash Flow

DDBM See Double-Declining-Balance Method

Debt Capacity The maximum amount of debt a company can add to its capital structure without incurring undue risks.

Debt Ratio Leverage ratio; total liabilities divided by total assets.

Debt-Equity Ratio Leverage ratio; total liabilities divided by equity.

Decision Trees Aid in solving problems that involve sequential decisions by diagramming the alternatives and their possible consequences.

Default Risk Chance that the debt will not be repaid.

Depreciation An annual income tax deduction that allows a business to recover the cost or any other basis of certain property over the time it uses the property.

Differentiation An attempt to build attributes into a product that distinguish it from others in the marketplace. Effective product differentiation lowers the total cost of use to the buyer.

Discount Rate The interest rate used to convert future dollars to their present value.

Discounted Cash Flow (DCF) A method used to estimate the attractiveness of an investment opportunity.

Discounted Payback The length of time it takes for the present value of a project's cash inflows to recover its investment costs.

Diversifiable Risk That portion of an asset's variability that can be eliminated by holding a well-diversified portfolio. Also referred to as unsystematic risk.

Dividend Periodic payment made to either preferred or common stockholders.

Dividend Payout Ratio The proportion of the earnings paid out as dividends.

Dividend Yield Expected annual dividend divided by the current stock price.

Double-Declining-Balance Method (DDBM) When depreciation occurs at twice the straight-line rate.

Earnings A measure of the increase in owner's wealth during a certain time period.

EBIT Earnings before interest and taxes; also referred to as the firm's operating earnings.

Economic Depreciation The decline in the economic value of an asset over some time period.

Economic Value The value of an asset (or liability) based on its ability to generate (or consume) cash over time.

Economies of Scale An economic theory stating that a plant's marginal cost of production decreases as the plant's operation increases.

Economies of Scope An economic theory stating that the average total cost of production decreases as a result of increasing the number of different goods produced.

Embedded Options Options that are an integral part of some investment project or financing choice.

Equity Risk Premium / Market Risk Premium Ordinarily assumed to equal the average historical difference between the return on the stock market and the average return on long-term Treasury bonds.

Equivalent Annual Cost An annuity that has the same life as the asset whose present value equals the cost of the asset.

Exercise Price Price at which an option can be exercised. Often referred to as the strike price.

Expansion Project A project needed to meet projected increases in demand for firm's existing products or services.

Face Value Specified principal sum a bondholder is scheduled to receive when the bond matures.

Financial Distress A situation that occurs when a company has difficulty in meeting its contractual obligations.

Financial Economics A discipline that emphasizes economic analysis to understand the basic workings of the financial markets.

Financial Risk The additional risk borne by the shareholders due to the substitution of debt for common stock.

Fisher Effect The relationship that states that the nominal interest rate is equal to the real interest rate plus the expected rate of inflation.

Float The difference between the balance shown in firm's checking account and the balance in the bank's books.

Flotation Costs The costs associated with the issuance of new securities.

Focus A corporate strategy in which management's time and energy is concentrated in its core business.

Foreign Tax Credit Home country credit against domestic income tax for foreign taxes already paid on foreign source earnings.

Forward Contract Contractual obligation to buy or sell a specific amount of a given commodity or asset on a specified future date, at a price set at the time the contract is entered into.

Free Cash Flow The cash flows available to all suppliers of long-term capital after accommodating a firm's investment needs.

Future Value The value of an asset or cash at a specified date in the future that is equivalent in value to a specified sum today.

Growth Option The opportunity that a firm may have of increasing the profitability of its existing product lines or to benefit from expanding into new products or markets.

Hurdle Rate The minimum or required return of the project's cost of capital.

Income Statement A financial statement reporting a firm's revenues, expenses, and profits (or losses) in a given year.

Incremental Cash Flow The additional revenue that will be generated or expenses that will be incurred by undertaking a particular action.

Independent Projects Projects whose acceptance or rejection is independent of the other.

Intangible Assets Assets that do not have any physical presence but may be valuable nevertheless. Intangible assets include items like patents, brand names, as well as the value of the firm's human assets.

Interest The cost of borrowing money. Typically expressed as a percent of the amount borrowed.

Interest Tax Shield The tax savings associated with debt financing.

Internal Rate of Return (IRR) The discount rate that sets the present value of the project cash flows equal to the initial investment outlay.

International Fisher Effect The theory that the interest rate differentials between two countries equals expected changes in the spot exchange rates.

Investment Banker A financing specialist who helps firms design and sell new issues of securities.

IRR See Internal Rate of Return

Lease A rental agreement.

Leverage Ratio See Debt Ratio

Liquidation Process whereby a firm's assets are sold off and the proceeds given to its creditors.

Liquidity Ability to convert an asset quickly into cash at a low transaction cost.

Long-term Debt Debt having a maturity of more than one year.

Low-Cost Provider A set of actions designed to help a company achieve the lowest possible cost for a good or service.

Marginal Cost The required return on new capital; not the past (historical) cost of raising capital from that source.

Marginal Tax Rate The tax rate at which additional income is taxed.

Market Niche A segment of the market having specific needs for products or service.

Market Portfolio Portfolio that contains all risky assets, with each asset being held in proportion to that asset's share of the total market value of all assets. In practice, a proxy portfolio that contains all shares listed on the New York Stock Exchange is often used.

Market Price of Risk The risk premium expected by investors per unit of market risk. Defined formally as the expected return on the market portfolio less the risk-free rate, divided by the standard deviation of returns on the market portfolio.

Maturity Date on which a security becomes due and payable.

Net Present Value (NPV) The present value of future cash flows, discounted at the appropriate cost of capital, minus the initial net cash outlay for the project.

Net Profit Margin Profitability Ratio: Net income divided by sales.

Net Working Capital Current assets less current liabilities. Sometimes referred to as working capital.

New Product Introduction An investment associated with the introduction of a new product or service.

Nominal Interest Rate The actual or current interest rate.

Noncash Charge One that shows up as a cost of doing business but that entails no cash outlay.

Note An unsecured bond with a short maturity.

NPV See Net Present Value

Operating Cash Flow The sum of net income plus any noncash charges to income less changes in working capital.

Opportunity Cost of Capital The return foregone on the best available investment alternative. This depends on the rate of interest at which money can be invested.

Option   The right—but not the obligation—to do something in the future.

Payback period   The length of time necessary to recoup the initial investment from net cash flows.

Perpetuity   A set of annuity payments that continue forever.

Political Risk   Uncertain government action that affects the value of a firm.

Portfolio Risk   The variability associated with the return on a portfolio of assets.

Preferred Stock   A type of equity security whose dividends take preference over the payment of dividends on common stock.

Present Value of An Annuity   The cash amount today that is the equivalent in value to a stream of annuity payments to be received in the future.

Principal   The amount invested on which interest is earned.

Product Cycle   The time it takes to bring a new or improved product to market.

Profitability Index   An index that attempts to identify the relationship between the costs and benefits of a proposed project through the use of a ratio.

Purchasing Power   The quantity of goods and services that can be bought with a given amount of money.

Purchasing Power Parity   Theory stating that the ratio between domestic and foreign price levels should equal the equilibrium exchange rate between domestic and foreign currencies.

Put Option   An option permitting its holder to sell a certain asset at an agreed price and terms within a specified time.

Real Assets   Assets whose value is tied to their physical characteristics.

Real Interest Rate   The nominal (observed) interest rate adjusted for inflation.

Refunding   Process of replacing high-interest debt with less expensive debt in the event of a decline in interest rates.

Related Diversification   A business strategy in which a firm gets involved in other businesses that are related, through either customers served or technologies utilized, to its major businesses.

Replacement Chain   Sequential replacement of an asset with an equivalent asset over some time period.

Required Rate of Return   The minimum acceptable return on an investment project.

Restructuring   A change in a firm's capital structure, incentive system, operations, ownership, or lines of business in order to increase shareholder value.

Retained Earnings   Earnings left over for reinvestment in the firm after dividends have been paid.

Return on Investment (ROI)   The profit or loss resulting from an investment transaction, usually expressed as an annual percentage return.

Revenue   The dollar amount of sales during a specific period, including discounts and returned merchandise. It is the "top line" figure from which costs are subtracted to determine net income.

Risk   The uncertainty associated with future cash flows, which is typically measured by the variance or standard deviation of these future cash flows.

ROI   See Return on Investment

Sensitivity Analysis   A procedure to study systematically the effect of changes in the values of key parameters on the project NPV.

Sovereign Risk   The risk that a foreign government will default on a loan because of a change in national policy.

Spot Rate   Price at which foreign exchange can be bought or sold today with payment made within two business days.

Spread   The price differential at which investment bankers buy a security and the price at which they can resell it to the public.

Stakeholder   One who has a share or an interest in an enterprise.

Standard Deviation   The square root of the variance of a probability distribution, which is used as a measure of risk.

Straight-Line Depreciation   With this method, a fixed asset is depreciated in equal yearly amounts over its life.

Strike Price   The cost of developing, producing, and marketing the drug.

Subsidiary   An affiliate that is a separate incorporated entity. In a global context, a foreign-based affiliate is incorporated under the laws of the host country.

Sunk Cost A cost that has been incurred and cannot be reversed.

Systematic Risk The risk inherent to the entire market or entire market segment. Also known as "un-diversifiable risk" or "market risk."

Tax Shield The value of the savings associated with a permissible tax deduction. Depreciation and interest expense are the two most important tax shields dealt with in corporate finance.

Terminal Value The value of an investment at the end of a period, taking into account a specified rate of interest.

The Cost of Equity Capital The minimum rate of return necessary to induce investors to buy or hold the firm's stock.

Time Value of Money The basic principle that money can earn interest. Also referred to as future value.

Transfer Price A price at which divisions of a company transact with each other. Transactions may include supplies or labor that are traded between departments.

Treasury Bill Short-term debt issued by the central government of many countries.

Unsystematic Risk Risk that can be eliminated through diversification. For common stock, the risk that is unrelated to movements in the market.

Variance The sum of the squared deviations between the actual and expected returns, weighted by the associated probabilities.

WACC See Weighted Average Cost of Capital

Weighted Average Cost of Capital (WACC) A calculation of a firm's cost of capital that weights each category of capital proportionately.

Working Capital A valuation metric that is calculated as current assets minus current liabilities.

Yield to Maturity The interest or discount rate that equates a bond's price with present value of its coupon interest and principal payments.

Zero-Sum Game A situation in which one participant's gains result only from another participant's equivalent losses.

Index